The Haiti Files
Decoding the Crisis

Edited by
JAMES RIDGEWAY

Essential Books/
Azul Editions
Washington, D.C.
1994

First edition.
Second printing, September 1994.

Published by Essential Books
P.O. Box 19405, Washington, D.C. 20036
and Azul Editions, Washington, D.C.

Distributed by InBook
P.O. Box 120261, East Haven, CT 06512
1-800-243-0138

ISBN: 0-96212-597-0

Library of Congress Catalog Card Number: 94-072029

Text design by Anne Galperin.
Typeset by Free Hand Press, Washington, D.C.
Printed by Balmar Printing & Graphics, Gaithersburg, MD.
Manufactured in the United States of America.

CONTENTS

PREFACE

For many Americans, Haiti must appear to be just another mixed-up Third World country which, because of its great poverty and backward political system, drives thousands of refugees to flee to U.S. shores every year—and occasionally requires the United States, with its superior civic values and skills, to go down and sort out the mess.

But there is another side to the story of U.S.-Haitian relations. The U.S. agenda in Haiti throughout the Cold War era was framed by the notion that Haiti was a strategic interest because of its close proximity to the supposed Soviet satellite of Cuba, just across the Windward Passage. Haiti was perceived as one of a long line of falling dominoes in a Soviet march through Latin America, which would eventually lead to America's southern border through the "soft underbelly" of Mexico. This ridiculous pretext led to an aggressive reassertion of the Monroe Doctrine in the hemisphere, under which the U.S. intervened in Grenada, El Salvador, Nicaragua, and Panama. It also led the United States to see any popular movement toward democracy in Haiti as a threat to U.S. national security.

In the early 1990s, with the Cold War over and the anti-Communist rationale defunct, the U.S.'s neo-colonial agenda emerged from the shadows. This agenda evolved into a broader project for the management of the political economy of the hemisphere—the New World Order in America's backyard. This project was supported first by Caribbean Basin Initiative, then by the North American Free Trade Agreement, and, on a broader landscape, by the international General Agreement on Tariffs and Trade (GATT).

The search for markets to alleviate a growing farm surplus, which has threatened to drown America's largest industry, has long been a preoccupation of the U.S. Since the turn of the century, in addition to extracting such raw materials as coffee and sugar from the Caribbean, the U.S. has sought to open up markets in these small countries where it can dump its surplus farm products. In the name of promoting economic development and political stability, one aid project after another has in fact led the populations of these countries out of subsistence farming and into a greater dependency on food imported from the U.S.

At the same time, U.S. aid programs have supported an effort to turn countries like Haiti into low-wage assembly platforms. This effort provides a cheap, easily exploitable workforce for American businesses, and simultaneously secures minimal employment for the thousands of people who have left subsistence farms in the countryside for the cities.

The provision of domestic assembly jobs is also meant to relieve some of the pressure on U.S. immigration and hence appease one of the basest and most powerful of all American political instincts—white nativist fears of alien incursions, embodied by the specter of boatloads of foreign-speaking blacks arriving on Florida's beaches.

So far from being a distant, impossibly complex, "underdeveloped" country that is beyond the understanding or civilizing influence of the United States, Haiti is another chapter in the well-read chronicle of American economic expansionism. And historically, the export of the American political and economic order has, more often than not, only contributed to the destruction of the historic civil society of the Haitian republic. At present, officials in Washington are debating the wisdom—and the potential shape—of American "intervention" in the Haitian crisis. They rarely mention the fact that the U.S. has been intervening in Haitian affairs for more than a century—seldom to the benefit of the Haitians.

The Haiti Files is an effort to set the current crisis in Haiti in context, with an emphasis on America's role in the country's political and economic processes. In that sense, it tries to get beyond the newspaper and television reportage to provide some degree of understanding of our underlying stake in the contours of Haiti's future.

Much of the material in the book has not made its way into the pages of the mainstream press or the rhetoric of U.S. policymakers—for example, the role of the big families in managing the economy, the structure of the military, and the role of American economic assistance programs, along with the U.S. efforts to inculcate "democracy" in Haiti.

The Haiti Files begins with a brief historical overview of Haiti, and then sets out the different players that shape Haitian society—the families, the military, the overseas Haitian community, and the popular democratic movement of the country. Part 3—the heart of the book—traces the history of the inept and disingenuous American policy which, following the 1991 coup, paved the way for a return of terror to Haiti, rather than a return of its democratically elected president. It also outlines the underlying aspects of the U.S.'s long-standing involvement in Haiti's political economy—especially the nature of U.S. aid programs—as well as U.S. complicity in the Haitian drug trade, and the disgrace of U.S. refugee and human rights policy toward Haiti.

At this writing, the immediate future of Haiti—and the intentions of U.S. policy—remain unclear. Whatever happens in the short run, the information and analysis provided by the many people who contributed to this book will remain relevant to an understanding of the roots and ramifications of the current crisis in Haiti.

ACKNOWLEDGEMENTS

Even more than most books, *The Haiti Files* is collaborative effort. The following people deserve special acknowledgement for their roles in creating the book:

Jane Regan—Research and Reportage
Jean Casella—Associate Editor
Susan Walsh—Editorial Assistant
Anne Galperin—Designer
Donna Colvin—Project Coordinator, Essential Books
John Richard—Publisher, Essential Books

My special thanks also go to the many others who have helped to put together this project, on extremely short notice, and to the individuals and organizations who have freely given of their advice and work: the Haitian Information Bureau for permission to use sections of *Haiti Info* and other materials; Jean Jean-Pierre; Michael Ratner; James Ferguson and the Latin America Bureau in London; Kim Ives and the staff of *Häiti Progrès*; Laurie Richardson and Marx Aristide of the Quixote Center; John Canham-Clyne; Josh DeWind and David Kinley; Noam Chomsky; Paul Farmer; Amy Wilentz—and, of course, all the others whose work is included in the book; also Rudi Stern; KK; Patrick Cockburn; Beverly Bell, Mike Levy, Steve Brescia and the staff of the International Liaison Office of Jean-Bertrand Aristide and the members of President Aristide's staff who have assisted me in my reportage; Michelle Karshan; Burton Wides; Ken Silverstein; Worth Cooley-Prost the Washington Office on Haiti; and Anne-Christine D'Adesky; Lisa McGowan of the Development Gap; staff members of *Häiti En Marche*; Laura Burstein and Ellen Braune of New Channels Communications; the National Security Archives; Human Rights Watch/Americas; Phillip Levy; and Willy Packard and Bill Covert of Free Hand Press. Thanks also to Karen Durbin, the editor of the *Village Voice*, who has supported my work on Haiti; Eamon Lynch, my colleague at the *Voice*, whose reportage has been invaluable, my editors Robert Massa, Julie Lobbia, and Doug Simmons; and former *Voice* editor Jonathan Larsen. My thanks go to the staffs of Essential Information and of the *Multinational Monitor*, including Erik Hadley, Billy Treger, Robert Weissman, and Aaron Freeman; and to Richard Schaaf of Azul Editions. Finally, thanks go out to many who must remains anonymous, especially those journalists working inside Haiti.

TO THE JOURNALISTS OF HAITI
WHO MUST REMAIN ANONYMOUS.

PART 1
THE SETTING

Kreyon Pèp pa gen gonm.
(The People's pencil has no eraser.)
—Haitian proverb

INTRODUCTION

The Republic of Haiti occupies the western third of the island of Hispaniola. The Dominican Republic comprises the other two-thirds of the island, Cuba is but 50 miles away across the Windward Passage, and the United States lies about 800 miles to the northwest.

The native population of Haiti was completely wiped out in the years following the conquest of Hispaniola by the Spanish. But over the centuries, a uniquely Haitian culture has developed, with strong roots in the heritage of the hundreds of thousands of Africans brought to the country as slaves, which has endured through years of Spanish, French, British, and American colonialism. Creole, the language spoken by all (although French also remains an official language), draws on seventeenth and eighteenth century French, on Spanish and English, and on the syntax of African languages, but is as a whole uniquely Haitian. Similarly, the saints of the Roman Catholic Church have been transferred into the uniquely Haitian figures of voudou legends, which recall the traditional religions of West Africa, and remain meaningful for many Haitians today. In Haiti it has been said that "a voudou god is more real than an astronaut." Bernard Diederich and Al Burt, in *Papa Doc: Haiti and Its Dictator*, write: "In a hemisphere where mostly Spanish or English is spoken, the uniqueness of the Haitian tongue—as with Haiti's other main cultural attributes—sets it attractively apart in some ways and in others merely isolates it. In its voudou, its blackness, its extraordinary problems brought on by the inheritance of a system of small farms, lie both a freshness and a despair."

Three-quarters of the population of Haiti gets by on subsistence farming, and half of the country's exports are based on agriculture. Most of Haiti is mountainous; rainfall is unpredictable and drought always looms as a potential disaster. The land and water of Haiti have been exploited to the point of exhaustion, and parts of the country verge on becoming environmental wastelands: The vast forests that once covered over 75 percent of Haiti were destroyed long ago, due to a century and a half of exploitative land-use policy and a growing population's desperate need for fuel. Today less than 7 percent of Haiti remains forested.

Since Haiti's tillable land is now saline, or badly eroded, the small farmers tend to push their crops onto marginal lands, often moving up the slopes of the craggy mountains, deforesting what remains of the mountain slopes, inducing more erosion, and producing lower and lower yields as they move higher. Today less than 11 percent of Haiti's land is considered "arable" (although about 43 percent remains under cultivation.) What was once called "The Pearl of the Antilles"—the richest and most fertile colony in the New World—has become a near-desert, where the vast majority of the population lives in dire poverty.

Over one million of the country's six million people cram into the slums of the capital, Port-au-Prince. Despite the fact that most of the city has virtually no sewerage, the most precarious of water supplies, and few employment opportunities, the population of Port-au-Prince is growing as people seek escape from starvation in rural areas.

While many would say that spirit of the country remains in the countryside, the money is in Port-au-Prince. This wealth is distributed in accordance with a strict class system, determined by economic power and family position and, to a lesser extent, by skin color.

This first part of *The Haiti Files* attempts to provide some context for the Haitian crisis by describing selected episodes from Haiti's often troubled history, as well as its shifting position on the world stage. It must, by necessity, give only a glimpse of "the setting" of current events in Haiti.

ㄱ

THE TRAGEDY OF HAITI
Noam Chomsky

In the world's only successful slave revolt, Haiti won its independence from France in 1804. But in Haiti, "independence" has always been a relative term. When U.S. Marines landed on Haiti's shores in 1915 (where they would remain in occupation for nearly 20 years), they represented but one chapter in a long history of often brutal domination of the country by powers from without and within. Noam Chomsky, reviewing Haiti's history in his 1993 book *Year 501: The Conquest Continues*, notes that the Haitian people have experienced "the ravages of colonialism" for 500 years "under a long line of despots from Columbus to Duvalier, and on to today's [post-coup] rulers, who have reinstated Duvalier savagery."

┐

"THE FIRST FREE NATION OF FREE MEN"

"Haiti was more than the New World's second oldest republic," anthropologist Ira Lowenthal observed, "more than even the first black republic of the modern world. Haiti was the first *free* nation of *free* men to arise within, and in resistance to, the emerging constellation of Western European empire." The interaction of the New World's two oldest republics for 200 years again illustrates the persistence of basic themes of policy, their institutional roots and cultural concomitants.

The Republic of Haiti was established on January 1, 1804, after a slave revolt expelled the French colonial rulers and their allies. The revolutionary chiefs discarded the French "Saint-Domingue" in favor of the name used by the people who had greeted Columbus in 1492, as he arrived to establish his first settlement in Europe's New World. The descendants of the original inhabitants could not celebrate the liberation. They had been reduced to a few hundred within 50 years from a pre-Colombian population estimated variously from hundreds of thousands to 8 million, with none remaining at all, according to contemporary French scholars, when France took the western third of Hispaniola, now Haiti, from Spain in 1697. The leader of the revolt, Toussaint L'Ouverture, could not celebrate the victory either. He had been captured by deceit and sent to a French prison to die a "slow death from cold and misery," in the words of a 19th century French historian. Medical anthropologist Paul Farmer observes that Haitian schoolchildren to this day know by heart his final words as he was led to prison: "In overthrowing me, you have cut down in Saint-Domingue only the tree of liberty. It will spring up again by the roots for they are numerous and deep."[1]

The tree of liberty broke through the soil again in 1985, as the population revolted against the murderous Duvalier dictatorship. After many bitter struggles, the popular revolution led to the overwhelming victory of Haiti's first freely elected president, the populist priest Jean-Bertrand Aristide. Seven months after his February 1991 inauguration he was driven from office by the military and commercial elite who had ruled for 200 years, and would not tolerate loss of their traditional rights of terror and exploitation.

"As soon as the last Duvalier had fled Haiti," Puerto Rican ethnohistorian Jalil Sued-Badillo recounts, "an angry crowd toppled the statue of Christopher Columbus in Port-au-Prince and threw it in the sea," protesting "the ravages of colonialism" under "a long line of despots" from Columbus to Duvalier, and on to today's rulers, who have reinstated Duvalier savagery. . . .

Columbus described the people he found [on the island of Hispaniola] as "lovable, tractable, peaceable, gentle, decorous," and their land as rich and bountiful. Hispaniola was "perhaps the most densely populated place in the world," Las Casas wrote, "a beehive of people," who "of all the infinite universe of humanity, . . . are the most guileless, the most devoid of wickedness and duplicity." Driven by "insatiable greed and ambition," the Spanish fell upon them "like ravening wild beasts, . . . killing, terrorizing, afflicting, torturing, and destroying the native peoples" with "the strangest and most varied new methods of cruelty, never seen or heard of before, and to such a degree that the population is barely 200 persons," he wrote in 1552, "from my own knowledge of the acts I witnessed." "It was a general rule among Spaniards to be cruel," he wrote: "not just cruel, but extraordinarily cruel so that harsh and bitter treatment would prevent Indians from daring to think of themselves as human beings." "As they saw themselves each day perishing by the cruel and inhuman treatment of the Spaniards, crushed to the earth by the horses, cut in pieces by swords, eaten and torn by dogs, many buried alive and suffering all kinds of exquisite tortures, . . . [they] decided to abandon themselves to their unhappy fate with no further struggles, placing themselves in the hands of their enemies that they might do with them as they liked."

As the propaganda mills ground away, the picture was revised to provide retrospective justification for what had been done. By 1776, the story was that Columbus found "nothing but a country quite covered with wood, uncultivated, and inhabited only by some tribes of naked and miserable savages" (Adam Smith). As noted earlier, it was not until the 1960s that the truth began to break through, eliciting scorn and protest from outraged loyalists.[2]

The Spanish efforts to plunder the island's riches by enslaving its gentle people were unsuccessful; they died too quickly, if not killed by the "wild beasts" or in mass suicide. African slaves were sent from the early 1500s, later in a flood as the plantation economy was established. "Saint Domingue was the wealthiest European colonial possession in the Americas," Hans Schmidt writes, producing three-quarters of the world's sugar by 1789, also leading the world in production of coffee, cotton, indigo, and rum. The slave masters provided France with enormous wealth from the labor of their 450,000 slaves, much as in the British West Indian colonies. The white population, including poor overseers and artisans, numbered 40,000. Some 30,000 mulattoes and free Negroes enjoyed economic privileges but not social and political equality, the origins of the class difference that led to harsh repression after independence, with renewed violence today.

Cubans may have seemed "of dubious whiteness," but the rebels who overthrew colonial rule did not approach that status. The slave revolt, which had reached serious proportions by the end of 1791, appalled Europe, as well as the European outpost that had just declared its own independence. Britain invaded in 1793; victory would offer "a monopoly of sugar, indigo, cotton and coffee" from an island which "for ages, would give such aid and force to industry as would be most happily felt in every part of the empire," a British military officer wrote to Prime Minister Pitt. The United States, which had lively commerce with the French colony, sent its French rulers $750,000 in military aid as well as some troops to help quell the revolt. France dispatched a huge army, including Polish, Dutch, German, and Swiss troops. Its commander finally wrote Napoleon that it would be necessary to wipe out virtually the entire black population to impose French rule. His campaign failed, and Haiti became the only case in history "of an enslaved people breaking its own chains and using military might to beat back a powerful colonial power" (Farmer).

The rebellion had broad consequences. It established British dominance of the Caribbean, and impelled its former colonies a long step further on their westward course as Napoleon, abandoning his hopes for an empire in the New World, sold the Louisiana territory to the United States. The rebel victory came at tremendous cost. Much of the agricultural wealth of the country was destroyed, along with perhaps a third of the population. The victory horrified Haiti's slave-holding neighbors, who backed France's claims for huge reparations, finally accepted in 1825 by Haiti's ruling elite, who recognized them to be a precondition for entry into the global market. The result was "decades of French domination of Haitian finance" with "a catastrophic effect on the new nation's delicate economy," Farmer observes. France then recognized Haiti, as did Britain in 1833. Simón Bolívar, whose struggles against Spanish rule were aided by the Haitian Republic on condition that he free slaves, refused to establish diplomatic relations with Haiti on becoming President of Greater Colombia, claiming that Haiti was "fomenting racial conflict"—a refusal "typical of Haiti's welcome in a monolithically racist world," Farmer comments. Haitian elites continued to be haunted by fear of conquest and a renewal of slavery, a factor in their costly and destructive invasions of the Dominican Republic in the 1850s.

The U.S. was the last major power to insist that Haiti be ostracized, recognizing it only in 1862. With the American Civil War underway, Haiti's liberation of slaves no longer posed a barrier to recognition; on the contrary, President Lincoln and others saw Haiti as a place that might absorb blacks induced to leave the United States. (Liberia was recognized in the same year, in part for the same reason). Haitian ports were used for Union operations against the rebels. Haiti's strategic role in control of the Caribbean became increasingly important in U.S. planning in later years, as Haiti became a plaything among the competing imperial powers. Meanwhile its ruling elite monopolized trade, while the peasant producers in the interior remained isolated from the outside world.

"UNSELFISH INTERVENTION"

Between 1849 and 1913, U.S. Navy ships entered Haitian waters 24 times to "protect American lives and property." Haiti's independence was scarcely given even "token recognition," Schmidt observes in his standard history, and there was little consideration for the rights of its people. They are "an inferior people," unable "to maintain the degree of civilization left them by the French or to develop any capacity of self government entitling them to international respect and confidence," Assistant Secretary of State William Phillips wrote, recommending the policy of invasion and U.S. military government that President Woodrow Wilson soon adopted. Few words need be wasted on the "civilization" left to 90 percent of the population by the French, who, as an ex-slave related, "hung up men with heads downward, drowned them in sacks, crucified them on planks, buried them alive, crushed them in mortars, . . . forced them to eat shit, . . . cast them alive to be devoured by worms, or onto anthills, or lashed them to stakes in the swamp to be devoured by mosquitos, . . . threw them into boiling cauldrons of cane syrup"—when not "flaying them with the lash" to extract the wealth that helped give France its entry ticket to the rich men's club.

Phillips captured prevailing attitudes with accuracy, though some, like Secretary of State William Jennings Bryan, found the Haitian elite rather amusing: "Dear me, think of it, Niggers speaking French," he remarked. The effective ruler of Haiti, Marine Colonel L.W.T. Waller, who arrived fresh from appalling atrocities in the conquest of the Philippines, was not amused: "they are real niggers and no mistake . . . real nigs beneath the surface," he said, rejecting any negotiations or other "bowing and scraping to these coons," particularly the educated Haitians for whom this bloodthirsty lout had a special hatred. Assistant Secretary of the Navy Franklin Delano Roosevelt, while never approaching the racist fanaticism and thuggery of his distant relative Theodore Roosevelt, shared the feelings of his colleagues. On a visit to occupied Haiti in 1917, he recorded in his diary a comment by his travelling companion, who later became the Occupation's leading civilian official. Fascinated by the Haitian Minister of Agriculture, he "couldn't help saying to myself," he told FDR, "that man would have brought $1,500 at auction in

New Orleans in 1860 for stud purposes." "Roosevelt appears to have relished the story," Schmidt notes, "and retold it to American Minister Norman Armour when he visited Haiti as President in 1934." The element of racism in policy formation should not be discounted, to the present day.

Such thoughts were not unusual at the time of Wilson's intervention, not only in the United States . . . Given the cultural climate of the day, the character of Wilson's 1915 invasion comes as no great surprise. It was even more savage and destructive than his invasion of the Dominican Republic in the same years. Wilson's troops murdered, destroyed, reinstituted virtual slavery, and demolished the constitutional system. After ruling for 20 years, the U.S. left "the inferior people" in the hands of the National Guard it had established and the traditional rulers. In the 1950s, the Duvalier dictatorship took over, running the show in Guatemalan style, always with firm U.S. support.

The brutality and racism of the invaders, and the dispossession of peasants as U.S. corporations took over the spoils, elicited resistance. The Marine response was savage, including the first recorded instance of coordinated air-ground combat: bombing of rebels (Cacos) who were surrounded by Marines in the bush. An in-house Marine inquiry, undertaken after atrocities were publicly revealed, found that 3,250 rebels were killed, at least 400 executed, while the Marines and their locally recruited gendarmerie suffered 98 casualties (killed and wounded). Leaked Marine orders call for an end to "indiscriminate killing of natives" that "has gone on for some time." Haitian historian Roger Gaillard estimates total deaths at 15,000, counting victims "of repression and consequences of the war," which "resembled a massacre." Major Smedley Butler recalled that his troops "hunted the Cacos like pigs." His exploits impressed FDR, who ordered that he be awarded the Congressional Medal of Honor for an engagement in which 200 Cacos were killed and no prisoners taken, while one Marine was struck by a rock and lost two teeth.

The leader of the revolt, Charlemagne Péralte, was killed by Marines who sneaked into his camp at night in disguise. In an attempt at psywar that prefigured some of Colonel Edward Lansdale's later exploits in the Philippines, the Marines circulated photos of his body in the hope of demoralizing the guerrillas. The tactic backfired, however; the photo resembled Christ on the cross, and became a nationalist symbol. Péralte took his place in the nationalist Pantheon alongside Toussaint.

The invaders "legalized" the Occupation with a unilateral declaration they called a "treaty," which the client regime was forced to accept; it was then cited as imposing on the U.S. a solemn commitment to maintain the Occupation. While supervising the takeover of Haiti and the Dominican Republic, Wilson built his reputation as a lofty idealist defending self-determination and the rights of small nations with impressive oratory. There is no contradiction. Wilsonian doctrine was restricted to people of the right sort: those "at a low stage of civilization" need not apply, though the civilized colonial powers should give them "friendly protection, guidance, and assistance," he explained. Wilson's Fourteen Points did not call for self-determination and national independence, but rather held that in questions of sovereignty, "the interests of the populations concerned must have equal weight with the equitable claims of the government whose title is to be determined," the colonial ruler. The interests of the populations "would be ascertained by the advanced nations, who best comprehended the needs and welfare of the less advanced peoples," William Stivers comments, analyzing the actual import of Wilson's language and thinking. . . .

Another achievement of Wilson's occupation was a new Constitution, imposed on the hapless country after its National Assembly was dissolved by the Marines for refusing to ratify it. The U.S.-designed Constitution overturned laws preventing foreigners from owning land, thus enabling U.S. corporations to take what they wanted. FDR later took credit for having written the Constitution, falsely it appears, though he did hope to be one of its beneficiaries, intending to use Haiti "for his own personal enrichment," Schmidt notes. Ten years later, in 1927, the State Department conceded that the U.S. had used "rather highhanded methods to get the Constitution adopted by the people of Haiti" (with 99.9 percent approval in a Marine-run plebiscite, under 5 percent of the population participating). But these methods were unavoidable: "It was obvious that if our occupation was to be beneficial to Haiti and further her progress it was necessary that foreign capital should come to Haiti . . . , [and] Americans could hardly be expected to put their money into plantations and big agricultural enterprises in Haiti if they could not themselves own the land on which their money was to be spent." It was out of a sincere desire to help the poor Haitians that the U.S. forced them to allow U.S. investors to take the country over, the State Department explained, the usual form that benevolence assumes.

Elections were not permitted because it was recognized that anti-American candidates would win, hindering the U.S. programs to help the suffering people. These programs were described as "An Experiment in Pragmatism" by one not untypical intellectual commentator, who observed that "The pragmatists insist that intelligent guidance from without may sometimes accelerate the process of national growth and save much waste."[3] . . .

The Occupation "consistently suppressed local democratic institutions and denied elementary political liberties," Schmidt writes. "Instead of building from existing democratic institutions which, on paper, were quite impressive and had long incorporated the liberal democratic philosophy and governmental machinery associated with the French Revolution, the United States blatantly overrode them and illegally forced through its own authoritarian, antidemocratic system." "The establishment of foreign-dominated plantation agriculture necessitated destruction of the existing minifundia land-tenure system with its myriad peasant freeholders," who were forced into peonage.

The U.S. supported "a minority of collaborators" from the local elite who admired European fascism but lacked the mass appeal of their fascist models. "In effect," Schmidt observes, "the Occupation embodied all the progressive attitudes of contemporary Italian fascism, but was crippled by failures in human relationships" (lack of popular support). The only local leadership it could mobilize was the traditional mulatto elite, its racist contempt for the great mass of the population now heightened by the even harsher attitudes of "ethnic and racial contempt" of the foreigner with the gun and the dollar, who brought "concepts of racial discrimination" not seen since before independence, and the "racist colonial realities" that went along with them.

The Occupation thus reinforced the internal class/race oppression that goes back to the days of French colonialism. One consequence was the rise of the ideology of *Noirisme*, in response to the racism of the occupiers and their elite collaborators. "Papa Doc" Duvalier would later exploit this backlash when, 20 years after the Marines left, he took the reins with the pretense of handing power to the black majority—in reality, to himself, his personal killers (the Tontons Macoutes), and the traditional elite, who continued to prosper under his murderous kleptocracy.

"The Occupation worsened the economic crisis by augmenting the peasantry's forced contribution to the maintenance of the State," Haitian historian Michel-Rolph Trouillot writes. "It worsened the crisis of power by centralizing the Haitian army and disarming [citizens in] the provinces," "putting in place the structures of military, fiscal, and commercial centralization" that were to yield a "bloody finale" under the Duvalier dynasty.

Through the bloodiest years of the occupation, the media were silent or supportive. The *New York Times* index has no entries for Haiti for 1917-1918. In a press survey, John Blassingame found "widespread editorial support" for the repeated interventions in Haiti and the Dominican Republic from 1904 to 1919, until major atrocity stories surfaced in 1920, setting off congressional inquiry. Haitians and Dominicans were described as "coons," "mongrels," "unwholesome," "a horde of naked niggers," the Haitians even more "retrograde" than the Dominicans. They needed "energetic Anglo-Saxon influence." "We are simply going in there . . . to help our black brother put his disorderly house in order," one journal wrote. Furthermore, the U.S. had a right to intervene to protect "our peace and safety" (*New York Times*).

Times editors lauded the "unselfish and helpful" attitude that the U.S. had always shown, now once again as it responded "in a fatherly way" as Haiti "sought help here." Our "unselfish intervention has been moved almost exclusively by a desire to give the benefits of peace to people tormented by repeated revolutions," with no thought of "preferential advantages, commercial or otherwise," for ourselves. "The people of the island should realize that [the U.S. government] is their best friend." The U.S. sought only to ensure that "the people were cured of the habit of insurrection and taught how to work and live"; they "would have to be reformed, guided and educated," and this "duty was undertaken by the United States." There is a further benefit for our "black brother": "To wean these peoples away from their shot-gun habit of government is to safeguard them against our own exasperation," which might lead to further intervention. "The good-will and unselfish purposes of our own government" are demonstrated by the consequences, the editors wrote in 1922, when they were all too apparent and the Marine atrocities had already aroused a storm of protest. . . .

With the barriers to foreign ownership of the country now overcome—admittedly, by somewhat "high handed methods"—U.S. investors quickly moved in to take large tracts of land for new plantations. Extremely cheap labor was another inducement. A New York business daily described Haiti in 1926 as "a marvelous opportunity for American investment": "The run-of-the-mill Haitian is handy, easily directed, and gives a hard day's labor for 20 cents, while in Panama the same day's work cost $3." These advantages gained prominence as the remnants of Haiti's agricultural wealth were steadily destroyed. From the 1960s, assembly operations for U.S. corporations grew rapidly in the Caribbean region; in Haiti, from 13 companies in 1966 to 154 in 1981. These enterprises furnished about 40 percent of Haitian exports (100 percent having been primary commodities in 1960), though limited employment or other benefits for Haitians, apart from new opportunities for enrichment for the traditional elite.

In the 1980s, IMF fundamentalism began to take its customary toll as the economy deteriorated under the impact of the structural adjustment programs, which caused agricultural production to decline along with investment, trade and consumption. Poverty became still more terrible. By the time "Baby Doc" Duvalier was driven out in 1986, 60 percent of the population had an annual per capita income of $60 or less according to the World Bank, child malnutrition had soared, the rate of infant mortality was shockingly high, and the country had become an ecological and human disaster, perhaps beyond hope of recovery. Through the 1970s, thousands of boat people fled the ravaged island, virtually all forced to return by U.S. officials with little notice here, the usual treatment of refugees whose suffering lacks propaganda value. In 1981, the Reagan Administration initiated a new interdiction policy. Of the more than 24,000 Haitians intercepted by the U.S. Coast Guard in the next ten years, 11 were granted asylum as victims of political persecution, in comparison with 75,000 out of 75,000 Cubans. During Aristide's brief tenure, the flow of refugees dropped dramatically as terror abated and there were hopes for a better future. The U.S. response was to approve far more asylum claims. Twenty-eight had been allowed during the ten years of Duvalier and post-Duvalier terror; 20 during Aristide's seven and a half months in office. After Aristide's overthrow, a new surge of boat people reached several thousand a month, most of them forcibly returned in callous disregard of the grim circumstances that awaited them. . . .

A U.S. AID-World Bank development strategy was initiated in 1981-1982, based on assembly plant and agro-industrial exports. The effect was to shift 30 percent of cultivated land from food for local consumption to export crops. AID forecast "a historic change toward deeper market interdependence with the United States" in this rising "Taiwan of the Caribbean." . . .

Of the array of predictions, one came to pass: the intended migration of the rural population to urban areas, and for many, to leaky boats attempting the dangerous 800-mile passage to Florida, to face forcible return if they make it (many don't). Haiti remains Haiti, not Taiwan.

Reviewing U.S. aid and development strategy for Haiti, Amy Wilentz writes that it "achieves two strategic U.S. goals—one, a restructured and dependent agriculture that exports to U.S. markets and is open to American exploitation, and the other, a displaced rural population that not only can be employed in offshore U.S. industries in the towns, but is more susceptible to army control."[4]

"POLITICS, NOT PRINCIPLE"

In June 1985, the Haitian legislature unanimously adopted a new law requiring that every political party must recognize President-for-Life Jean-Claude Duvalier as the supreme arbiter of the nation, outlawing the Christian Democrats, and granting the government the right to suspend the rights of any party without reasons. The law was ratified by a majority of 99.98 percent. Washington was impressed. It was "an encouraging step forward," the U.S. Ambassador informed his guests at a July 4 celebration. The Reagan Administration certified to Congress that "democratic development" was progressing, so that military and economic aid could continue to flow—mainly into the pockets of Baby Doc and his entourage. The Administration also informed Congress that the human rights situation was improving, as it always is when some regime requires military aid to suppress the population in a good cause. The Democrat-controlled House Foreign Affairs Committee had given its approval in advance, calling on the Administration "to maintain friendly relations with Duvalier's non-Communist government."

These gratifying developments were short-lived, however. By December, popular protests were straining the resources of state terror. What happened next was described by the *Wall Street Journal* two months later with engaging frankness:

> An administration official said that the White House concluded late last year, following huge demonstrations that hadn't been seen on such a scale before, that the regime was unraveling . . . U.S. analysts learned that Haiti's ruling

inner circle had lost faith in the 34-year-old president for life. As a result, U.S. officials, including Secretary of State George Shultz, began openly calling for a "democratic process" in Haiti.

The cynicism was underscored by the fact that the very same scenario was then being enacted in the Philipines, where the army and elite made it clear they would no longer support another gangster for whom Reagan and Bush had expressed their admiration, even "love," not long before, so that the White House "began openly calling for a `democratic process'" there as well. Both events have, accordingly, entered the canon as a demonstration of how, particularly in the 1980s, we have "served as inspiration for the triumph of democracy in our time" (*New Republic*).[5]

Duvalier was duly removed, flown out in a U.S. Air Force jet and sent to comfortable exile in France. Armed Forces chief General Henri Namphy took power. This long-time U.S. favorite and close Duvalier associate was "Haiti's best chance for democracy," Assistant Secretary of State Elliott Abrams announced, revealing once again the dedication to democracy for which he was famous. Not all were pleased. A rural priest in a small church, Father Jean-Bertrand Aristide, said that "we're glad Duvalier is gone" but "what we now have is Duvalierism without Duvalier." Few listened, but events were to prove him right in short order.

Elections were scheduled for November 1987, but Namphy and his associates, the army and the old elite, were determined that nothing would go wrong. The Tontons Macoutes were reorganized, terror continued. A particularly gruesome massacre took place in July 1987, involving the army and the Macoutes. The same groups sponsored escalating violence, leading up to an election day massacre that provided Namphy with a pretext to cancel the elections. Throughout, U.S. military aid continued on grounds that it helped the army keep order—which was disputed by army-Macoute violence and atrocities. Military aid was finally suspended after the election day terror, with over 95 percent of the 1987 funds already disbursed.

A fraudulent military-run election followed, then a coup restoring Namphy to power and a rash of Duvalierism-without-Duvalier atrocities by the army and Macoutes, including repeated attacks on union offices and peasant groups. Asked about these events by U.S. human-rights organizations, Ambassador Brunson McKinley said, "I don't see any evidence of a policy against human rights." True, there is violence, but it is just "part of the culture." Whose, one might wonder.[6]

A month later, a gang of killers attacked Aristide's church as he was saying mass, leaving at least 13 dead and 77 wounded. Aristide fled underground. In yet another coup, Duvalierist General Prosper Avril arrested Namphy and expelled him. The Haitian head of Aristide's Salesian order authorized him to return to his church, but not for long. To the dismay of the conservative Church hierarchy, Aristide continued to call for freedom and an end to terror. He was duly ordered by his superiors in Rome to leave the country. Popular protests blocked his departure, and he went into hiding. At the last minute, Aristide decided to take part in the December 1990 elections. In a stunning upset, he won 67 percent of the vote, defeating the U.S. candidate, former World Bank official Marc Bazin, who came in second with 14 percent. The courageous liberation theologist, committed to "the preferential option for the poor" of the Latin American bishops, took office in February as the first democratically elected President in Haiti's history—briefly; he was overthrown by a military coup on September 30. . . .

NOTES

1. Lowenthal, *Reviews in Anthropology*, 1976, cited in Paul Farmer, *AIDS and Accusation: Haiti and the Geography of Blame* (University of California Press, 1992), the source for much of what follows along with Hans Schmidt, *The United States Occupation of Haiti, 1915-1934* (Rutgers University Press, 1971). The classic account of the revolution is C.L.R. James, *The Black Jacobins*. The high population estimates are from Sherburne Cook and Woodrow Borah, *Essays in Population History: Mexico and the Caribbean* (University of California Press, 1971).

2. Farmer, *AIDS*, p. 153; Las Casas, passages in Chicago Religious Task Force on Central America, *Dangerous Memories: Invasion and Resistance Since 1492* (Chicago, 1991); David Stannard, *American Holocaust* (Oxford, 1992); Kirkpatrick Sale, *The Conquest of Paradise* (Knopf, 1990).

3. Chomsky, *Turning the Tide*, (South End Press, 1985) p. 46. William Stivers, *Supremacy and Oil*, (Cornell University Press), pp. 66-73.

4. Ulysses B. Weatherly, "Haiti: An Experiment in Pragmatism," 1926, cited by Schmidt.

5. Carmen Diana Deere, et al., *In the Shadows of the Sun*, (Westview, 1990), pp. 144, 35, 174-5 (excerpt from Josh DeWind and David Kinley III, *Aiding Migration* [Westview, 1988]). Kathy McAfee, *Storm Signals* (South End Press, 1991), p. 17; Chomsky, *On Power and Ideology* (South End Press, 1986), p. 68; Wilentz, *The Rainy Season* (Simon & Schuster, 1989), pp. 272 ff. Refugees, Chomsky and Edward Herman, *Political Economy of Human Rights* (South End Press, 1979), II, pp. 50, 56; Wilentz, *New Republic*, March 9, 1992; Bill Frelick, NACLA *Report on the Americas*, July 1992; Pamela Constable, *Boston Globe*, August 21, 1992.

6. Chomsky, *On Power and Ideology*, pp. 69 ff., *Wall Street Journal*, February 10, 1986. *New Republic*, p. 194, above.

7. Wilentz, *Rainy Season*, 341, 55, 326, 358.

PRESIDENT FOR LIFE
Bernard Diederich and Al Burt

In 1957, a "mild-mannered, soft-spoken country doctor" was elected president of Haiti. François (Papa Doc) Duvalier had the support of the army, but he also had the support of the Haitian peasants, whose plight he had empathetically championed in his reformist-sounding campaign rhetoric. Duvalier, a black candidate in a country where mulattoes held much of the economic power, also gained popularity by promoting *Noirisme*—a sense of pride in the Haitian's African heritage—and by his knowledge and understanding of voodoo. But as journalists Bernard Diederich and Al Burt note, within a few years, "Haitians knew that Papa Doc was only different from his predecessors in the volume of his brutality and greed. Under him Haiti became the horror of the hemisphere." In their definitive book *Papa Doc: Haiti and Its Dictator*, Diederich and Burt describe events surrounding the 1964 "election" that named Papa Doc "president for life"—a title that would pass, at his death in 1971, to his son Jean-Claude (Baby Doc).

┐

A new campaign of adulation for Duvalier began in the newspapers and it soon became clear that Haiti was in for another ritual of reverence. He was preparing the public for an "election" whose purpose it was to name him President for Life. [Minister of Information] Paul Blanchet organized the campaign, bringing a variety of delegations to the palace to pay homage to Duvalier.

The *Haiti Journal* on 4 March [1964] declared without the hint of a smile:

> Duvalier is the professor of energy. Like Napoleon Bonaparte, Duvalier is an electrifier of souls, a powerful multiplier of energy. . . . Duvalier is one of the greatest leaders of contemporary times . . . because the Renovator of the Haitian Fatherland synthesizes all there is of courage, bravery, genius, diplomacy, patriotism, and tact in the titans of ancient and modern times.

Blanchet's propaganda campaign reached full proportions as the annual Mardi Gras drew to a close. Street bands included among their carnival songs and dancing some new numbers based on the theme *Papa Doc pour la vie*. The National Security Volunteers, a label Duvalier put on the militia for the sake of respectability, paraded to the palace. Blanchet issued special gasoline rations to the Tourist Guides Association (taxis) so they could provide horn-honking accompaniment as the militia marched through the rutted streets. . . .

The next day, 1 April, the army played its role. A delegation of officers visited the palace and General Constant read a declaration in which the army swore allegiance to Duvalier for life:

...with all the ardour of our patriotic convictions . . . thanks to you, Excellency, and under your prestigious command, the armed forces of Haiti have many times fulfilled with honour and competence the sacrosanct mission of maintaining territorial integrity, victoriously holding battle against occult forces which had organized with the aim of compromising national sovereignty and independence. . . .

While the rest of the world may have been startled to hear of Duvalier's declared intentions there was precedent for it inside Haiti. Since 1804 seven Haitians, three as monarchs, had decided to rule for life. In fact, few Haitian presidents ever left office voluntarily. Dessalines, Christophe, and Soulouque had proclaimed themselves respectively emperors and king. Sylvain Salnave, Pétion, Jean-Pierre Boyer, and Fabre N. Geffrard has assumed life terms. Salnave, elected in 1867 for four years, two years later decided to hold the office for life, which he did until shot by a firing squad. . . .

Deputy Ulrick Saint-Louis, head of the constitutional revision committee, drafted a nineteen-page report explaining why the Constitution had to be changed and presenting the new one. He said the new constitution, Haiti's twenty-first, provided a "revolution through law," which he called the ultimate aim of a democracy. It had 201 articles, the most significant of which gave Duvalier the Presidency for Life and absolute powers. Throughout the constitution Duvalier was referred to as "Le Souverain," a title so liked by Emperor Faustin Soulouque. The rubber-stamp assembly on 25 May approved it with what was called "respectable speed." And Duvalier announced that a Presidential referendum for approval would be held on 14 June.

To justify the Constitution, Deputy Saint-Louis quoted Robespierre: "The greater one's power, the freer and more rapid his action." Saint-Louis was rewarded by being named president of the Assembly. . . .

Between the April declaration to the army and the election of 14 June Blanchet continued forming delegations to go to the palace and praise Duvalier. . . .

All the palace worshippers were frisked for weapons as they entered the Duvalier presence, and watched carefully during their performances. They came to praise Duvalier, and the Tonton Macoutes and Presidential Guard were on hand to insure that no Brutus slipped in to bury him. . . .

[Shortly before the referendum, one] delegation heard Duvalier declare:

> After this political act [referendum] there will never again be an election to elect a chief of state on the soil of Haiti. . . . I shall be lord and master. . . . I have always talked with the wild energy that characterizes me; with all the savagery which characterizes me . . .
>
> The revolution is the revolution. If you must be a deputy at the chamber, you will be because the revolution is like a river. If one puts himself across the river he will be carried away.

Everyone is turning his ass the way he can. . . . Why can't the Haitian people turn their ass the way they want? Why not? They are starting to recognize that Duvalier is not the Lucifer of the Caribbean. . . .

Well, each one turns his ass the way he wants. We have what is called a democracy. It is one of the most beautiful ones. De Gaulle has a democracy; it is one of the most beautiful ones. Mao Tse-tung has a democracy; it is one of the most beautiful ones. Well, let every country develop its functions, customs, and traditions, because it is an ethnologist talking to you. . . .

You know that Dr. François Duvalier even under cannon fire will not back down. I have already said it. If my militia is afraid, it just has to look at my face. If the Duvalierist cohorts feel a tinge of fear, they will have to look at my face. My face stays just like you have known it in 1956. The man will remain equal to himself.

This speech, later run in a newspaper under the title *Un Dialogue Passionnant*, seemed an effort by Duvalier to match up his personalities. The little doctor was striding hard to keep pace with the "sun-eclipsing giant" of his other self.

Voting, if it could be called that, began at 6 A.M. Sunday, 14 June. Blue, pink, red, and yellow ballots were handed out by the fistful. Kids made gliders of them, even pasted some together for kites. To vote was embarrasingly easy, for all the ballots said the same thing.

Oui was the only answer, and if anyone had the temerity to try a write-in *non*, he faced charges of defacing a ballot. Government employees hurried to the polls early so that they could be seen. The radio blared out "Duvalier for Life" *méringues*. Little red-and-black flags flew. Peasants, trucked into the city, danced to rara bands and drank clarin. Everyone, including foreigners, was invited to step right up and vote. Militiamen thoroughly enjoyed themselves. By 11:15 A.M. Duvalier appeared on a palace balcony with his acceptance speech:

Today the people have already manifested their desire. I mean that at this time that I am speaking to you I already am President for Life of the Republic. . . .

What the government wants is that you must fight, look, and watch so as the traitors of always, those who betrayed Jean-Jacques Dessalines the great, those who betrayed General Salomon, those who betrayed General Soulouque, so as these same traitors may know that now things have changed and that Dr. Duvalier is neither Dessalines, nor Soulouque, nor General Salomon, of whom he is, however, the pupil. But he is a very distrustful man. He wants to lead as a master. He wants to lead as a true autocrat. That is to say, I repeat, he does not accept anybody else before him but his own person.

A great man on the other side of the Atlantic knows what he is doing. He is called General De Gaulle. He is a great Frenchman. Another one who may be compared to Duvalier is President Sukarno of Indonesia. He is a great man. He knows what he is doing. Other great citizens who lead their countries with firmness and with all the necessary savagery know what they are doing. Duvalier also, ever since he was practising the profession of doctor, knew what he was doing.

Following this remarkable speech, Duvalier went to the polls and cast a *oui* ballot for himself. Newspapers reported 2,800,000 *ouis* as against 3,234 *nons*, although it was never clear how even this handful managed to vote against Le Souverain.

That night some 3,000 supporters sang and danced before a twenty-four-foot-high monument "to perpetuate the memory of the Duvalierist revolution." The "flame" was a flashing sign of revolving red, blue, green, yellow, and violet neon tubes. On 22 June 1964, Inauguration Day, the flame officially was lighted. One observer remarked: "It is a true monstrosity; a fitting end to the day."

The three days of celebrations for the inauguration were marred, in Duvalier's eyes, because a priest at the Te Deum in the cathedral inserted a clemency plea for political prisoners in his sermon. Duvalier made the priest, Monsignor Claudius Angenor, resign and placed him under house arrest.

The new Constitution gave the new *Président à Vie* a host of new titles: Supreme Chief of the Haitian Nation; Uncontestable Leader of the Revolution; Apostle of National Unity; Renovator of the Fatherland; Chief of the National Community; Worthy Heir of the Founders of the Haitian Nation . . .

Article 106 credits Duvalier with provoking a national *prise de conscience* (decision) for the first time since 1804 "through radical political, social, economic, cultural, and religious challenges in Haiti. . . .[Thus] he is elected President for Life so as to ensure the conquests and permanence of the Duvalierist revolution . . . "

The Consitution also praises him for ensuring peace and order through a reorganization of the armed forces, laying the bases of national prosperity through "works of infrastructure" for the promotion of agriculture and industrailization; organizing the protection of the working masses and giving justice to the peasant; creating organizations for the protection of mothers, children, women and family—creating a strong nation, the pride of its sons!

But the most staggering bit of self-flattery of them all was a government-printed booklet, *Le Catéchisme de la révolution*. It contained litanies, hymns, pryers, doctrine. It substituted the Roman Catholic explanation of the Holy Trinity with a Papa Doc version.

(Q) Who are Dessalines, Toussaint, Christophe, Pétion and Estimé?
(A) Dessalines, Toussaint, Christophe, Pétion and Estimé are five founders of the nation who are found within François Duvalier.
(Q) Is Dessalines for life?

(A) Yes, Dessalines is for life in François Duvalier.

[This same question and answer were listed for the other four historical figures.]

(Q) Do we conclude then that there are six presidents for life?

(A) No, Dessalines, Toussaint, Christophe, Pétion, and Estimé are five distinct chiefs of state but who form only one and the same President in François Duvalier.

There were pictures of the flag, of the President, and his First Lady, and then the "Lord's Prayer" followed:

Our Doc who art in the National Palace for life, hallowed be Thy name by present and future generations. Thy will be done at Port-au-Prince and in the provinces. Give us this day our new Haiti and never forgive the trespasses of the anti-patriots who spit every day on our country; let them succumb to temptation, and under the weight of their venom, deliver them not from any evil . . .

HAITI IN THE
EYES OF THE WORLD
Rod Prince

Haiti, the poorest country in the Western Hemisphere, has had an uneasy and often exploitive relationship with its neighbors—particularly the Dominican Republic, with which it shares the island of Hispaniola, and the United States. In his 1985 book *Haiti: Family Business*, Rod Prince observes that much of Haiti's turmoil is attributable to historical and external forces. Yet the nation's problems—from dictatorships to AIDS—have often been "seen as in some way the fault of the Haitians . . . a mystery only to be explained by some deficiency in organization, energy or consciousness on the part of the Haitian people."

┐

THE DOMINICAN REPUBLIC

Haiti's most problematic relations have been with the Dominican Republic next door. The two countries have rarely been on normal business-like terms, let alone amicable ones. At the peak of their revolutionary zeal, the Haitian slave armies occupied Santo Domingo. It did not return to Spanish sovereignty until 1809 and was occupied by Haiti again between 1822 and 1844. Echoing Toussaint L'Ouverture's words a generation before, President Jean-Pierre Boyer in 1822 declared the island to be "one and indivisible."

The presence of Haitian troops, the imposition of Napoleonic law (particularly its effects on property ownership), and the post-1825 decision to increase taxes in the former Spanish colony to help pay Haiti's indemnity to France, all helped create an independence movement which eventually saw the birth of the Dominican Republic in 1844. Further attempts at reconquest by President Faustin Soulouque (later Emperor Faustin I) in 1849 and 1855-56 reinforced the legacy of hostility.

Subsequent key events in the relationship between the two republics were the 1937 massacre of Haitians, by which Trujillo established himself as the effective power in the whole island, and the brief conflict in 1963, when in the heady post-Trujillo days, President Juan Bosch concocted a plan to invade Haiti and overthrow Duvalier. Bosch had himself received information that Duvalier was planning his assassination, and was also provoked by a Haitian army incursion into the grounds of the Dominican embassy in Port-au-Prince, in search of a group of anti-Duvalier conspirators. He was unable to persuade his military commanders to take his plan seriously, however, and was overthrown shortly afterwards by General Elías Wessin y Wessin, the armoured corps commander.

For the rest of the 1960s and most of the 1970s, relations between the two countries remained frozen. President Joaquín Balaguer, who ruled the Dominican Republic from 1966 to 1978, observed a studiously correct policy towards Haiti. The border was closed in 1967, although [it was] subsequently reopened for the movement of contracted cane-cutters, and Balaguer sent a number of anti-Duvalier refugees back to Haiti. President Antonio Guzmán, the social democrat who succeeded Balaguer in 1978, broke new ground with a frontier meeting with Jean-Claude Duvalier in June 1979. The two met again at the end of the year to inaugurate a jointly-built dam on the Pedernales river. These meetings led to the reopening of the border for trade and helped to encourage economic cooperation. Bilateral trade nevertheless remained at a very low level, although smuggling swelled the total. With the Dominican Republic currently in a severe economic crisis (exemplified by the collapse of its currency), the frontier [was again closed in] November 1983 in an attempt to reduce the volume of cheap Dominican goods being smuggled into Haiti due to the fall in the Dominican Republic's currency.

Despite their economic problems, many Dominicans still feel a mixture of superiority, contempt and fear where the Haitians are concerned. The more developed Dominican Republic not only has a higher standard of living than Haiti, but has succeeded in maintaining a democratic system of government since the overthrow of Trujillo and the subsequent civil war and U.S. invasion. For the largely white or mulatto Dominican middle and upper classes, there is also a strong element of anti-black racism against the Haitians. The able and ambitious Secretary-General of the governing Partido Revolucionario Dominicano, José Francisco Peña Gómez, for example, is the subject of a whispering campaign which seeks to denigrate him because he is black and of Haitian origin. These differences in culture, language, politics and economic development will continue to present serious obstacles to the normalization of relationships. The present unequal relationship is symbolized by the lot of thousands of itinerant Haitian cane-cutters simultaneously valued by the state sugar corporation as virtual slave labour, and regarded by prosperous Dominicans with anxiety; the advance guard of a horde of hungry Haitians allegedly poised to pour over the border and plunder the Republic. [True to this assessment, President Balaguer announced, in June 1991, that all Haitians "over the age of 60 and under the age of 16" would be expelled from the Dominican Republic. About 20,000 were forced to leave over the next three months. The age parameters exempted the most able-bodied Haitians at work in the sugar cane fields and elsewhere. At the same time, the Dominican border has reportedly been the main entry point to Haiti for gasoline and other supplies during the post-coup embargo.]

HAITI IN THE EYES OF THE WORLD

It is not only in the Dominican Republic that Haiti is seen this way. Outside observers have, ever since Haitian independence, held a series of contradictory notions about the country's people. They are dignified and unspoiled, poor but happy, primitive and ignorant, oppressed and terrorized, kindly and gentle, lazy and incapable of running their own country, or brutal and depraved. Travellers like Hesketh Prichard sought to show that the Haitian example proved the impossibility of successful black government, just as property owners immediately after the slave revolt had argued that the Haitian experience showed the necessity for slavery. James Franklin, a British resident in independent Haiti, wrote in 1828:

> The system of labour so pursued in Hayti, instead of affording us a proof of what may be accomplished by it, is illustrative of the fact that it is by coercion, and coercion only, that any return can be expected from the employment of capital in the cultivation of the soil in our West India islands. I shall be able to shew that Hayti presents no instance in which the cultivation of the soil is successfully carried on without the application of force to constrain labour.

In modern times, the plight of Haiti under the Duvaliers is often, albeit unconsciously, seen as in some way the fault of the Haitians. Even sympathetic observers have been known to ask why there is no effective opposition to the regime, or when a change can be expected; as if the survival of the Duvaliers is a mystery only to be explained by some deficiency in organization, energy or consciousness on the part of the Haitian people. The number of Haitians who have died, or who have been jailed, tortured or exiled for their opposition to the regime is one answer to that line of thinking. Another is to seek to understand the conditions in which Haiti came into existence and survived: its history and culture, the limits imposed on every Haitian's freedom to determine his or her own future by the country's position in the world system of power, and the crippling effects of its extreme poverty—much of which derives from historical and externally conditioned factors.

An interesting barometer of prevailing attitudes to a country is its tourist trade. In the mid-1960s, when Duvalier meant terror and the United States government felt he was a liability rather than an asset, Haiti's hotels were empty. As the Jean-Claudist "development decade" got under way, the image changed; Haiti was being modernized and liberalized, and a tourist boom duly developed. The brochures described a country of "incomparable splendour . . . unspoiled beaches . . . French and Creole haute cuisine, vibrant open-air bazaars . . . a fascinating blend of industrious and hospitable people." The regime's success in internal pacification meant there was no street crime, and tourists managed not to see the squalor. At the premium end of the market, you could dine at the Oloffson, where in one evening you could spend the equivalent of a year's income for a Haitian peasant for the privilege of stepping into Graham Greeneland—as if Papa Doc had just been a character in fiction.

The current tourist slump, in which Haiti has fared worse than other Caribbean countries, reflects Haiti's image of the 1980s: the boat people, human rights violations and AIDS. Refugees had been sailing across to the Bahamas and Florida for more than a decade before the term "boat people" was used in 1980. As early as 1968, the numbers arriving were sufficient to cause concern to the Bahamian and U.S. governments. But it was the nightly televised scenes as the Haitians scrambled ashore which established the idea in the public mind. Likewise, it was the U.S. administration's keenness to get value for their aid money that led it to highlight the human rights issue in Haiti, forcing the Haitian government to respond. Against this background, Haiti was in no position to counter the panic which broke out when Haitian immigrants were made responsible for the outbreak of AIDS in the United States.

Ironically, the high rate of disease and infant mortality in Haiti has meant that surviving Haitians are uncommonly rich in anti-bodies; hence the demand for Haitian blood, which once supported a thriving trade in blood to the United States. The trade was organized by the then interior minister, Luckner Cambronne. At different times an estimated 6,000 donors sold their blood at U.S. $3.00 a litre, and five tons of blood a month were shipped to U.S. laboratories run by companies such as Armour Pharmaceutical, Cutter Laboratories and Dow Chemical.

When allegations were made that AIDS, thought to have originated in Central Africa, was endemic in Haiti, the government reacted by ordering the closure of gay bars in Port-au-Prince and the expulsion of members of the U.S. gay community. In August 1983 Health Minister Ary Bordes went to Washington for talks on the issue. But the image of AIDS as a "Haitian disease" is hard to shake off, despite the statement in April 1985 by the U.S. Centre for Disease Control in Atlanta that Haitian immigrants would no longer be classified as high AIDS risks because there was no medical justification for doing so. . . .

The way that Haiti and Haitians are seen from abroad is affected not just by what happens in Haiti itself but also by changing perceptions outside the country. These are frequently influenced by developments in Haiti which are themselves the result of external factors. In short, to understand Haiti, look to the United States. . .

PART 2
THE PLAYERS

Se chat kay k'ap manje poul kay.
(Your own house cat is the one who is
eating your chickens.)
—Haitian proverb

INTRODUCTION

In accounts from abroad, Haiti has often been depicted as a kind of "heart of darkness"—a desperate, black-ruled country where bizarre and brutal dictators wield sole power. In fact, political and economic power in Haiti depends to a great extent on subtle distinctions in color, reinforcing a long-standing economic class system of whom the dictators are only the most visible manifestation.

Ensconced at the top of Haitian society is a mostly mulatto oligarchy, composed of a few thousand families who continue to embrace a sort of feudal life that it is hard to believe exists at the end of the 20th century. The less than one percent of the population represented by these "ruling families" controls over 44 percent of the wealth in Haiti.

The members of Haiti's oligarchy live in Port-au-Prince and other major towns, and typically arrived in the country about a hundred years ago to become merchants. Today they are also involved in production—the fabrication of iron and steel products, and the manufacture of plastics, cement, shoes, pharmaceuticals, and sometimes illegal drugs. These families have used the army, the Tonton Macoute, and the overall power of the state to maintain themselves in a sort of decadent splendor, and have long been a reactionary force in Haitian politics, often aligned with the Duvalierists. They are not nationalist in any sense, but inextricably tied to the vicissitudes of foreign commerce, and over time, their businesses have come to depend on a growing consumer class. That makes their ingrained resistence to any sort of change even harder to fathom, because it cuts against their own self-interest. Finally, certain of these families functioned as surrogates for U.S. business interests in the earlier part of the century, and currently look to and expect protection from the United States.

Organized beneath this increasingly isolated and defensive *haute* bourgeoisie an urban *petite* bourgeoisie of sorts—doctors, professionals, intellectuals, shopkeepers—black and mulatto, many of them with their roots abroad. They tend to look enthusiastically towards change and to be strongly nationalist. Many supported the Lavalas alliance that propelled Aristide to power, though they eschewed its more revolutionary currents. Their future well-being depends on the growth of the Haitian middle class, which will utilize their services and buy their products. Many members of this sector were driven out of Haiti during the rule of the Duvaliers, and now live in the diaspora—especially in the U.S.—from which they send considerable sums of money home to support relatives. One of the terrible ironies of Haitian society is that the very people who held out such great hope for building a civil society in Haiti were driven from their homeland by Duvalierism, and now in effect finance the decadence of the oligarchy by sending money home to help keep their relatives alive.

Next comes a black, urban, wage-earning middle class, which is frightened of change for fear it will mean the loss of jobs that are at best precarious. These people, whose existence is always tenuous, are manipulated and terrorized by the army and its appendage, the Tonton Macoute. Beneath this middle class is the mass populace, which looks to change as a way of gaining ground amidst their desperate poverty. Their concern is daily survival—yet they provided the groundswell of popular support that helped to oust Jean-Claude Duvalier in 1986 and elect Aristide in 1990.

This class system has its replica in the rural countryside, where the big landowners maintain their position through the appendages of the state, especially the army and the Church, and like their counterparts in the city, see no reason to change. Thirty percent of the landowners hold two-thirds of all the arable land in Haiti. The rural middle class is more open to new ideas, as is the peasantry, though much of the peasantry is suspicious of culture and politics from the city. Ninety-five percent of this rural population lives below the poverty level.

Cutting across this class system is the army, which has been able to achieve a certain degree of internal cohesion. Like the oligarchy, it maintains authority through a patronage system—rewarding an officer with purchases through the civilian shop he runs on the side through his family, or with the right to take some of the graft from smuggling goods through port installations, or by dragooning peasants to work on an officer's farm. But even within the army there is some possibility of change, since its members are themselves treated as servants by the oligarchy, and looked down upon by their own compatriots.

In all, because of its steadily declining production of basic commodities and the oligarchy's ties abroad, the political economy of Haiti is increasingly determined by circumstances and powers outside the country.

The entries in the following section set forth the outlines of Haiti's social structure, describing first the activities of the big families, then the structure of the army, the Tonton Macoute, and their new manifestation in FRAPH. The section goes on to discuss the Haitian overseas community, which some say totals well over a million (close in number to the population of Haiti itself). Finally, it introduces the many popular currents in Haiti's democratic movement, which came together to briefly bring to power the nation's first democratically elected president, Jean-Bertrand Aristide.

┐

1

THE RULING FAMILIES

HAITI'S FAMILY AFFAIRS
James Ridgeway

The Duvaliers are the most famous members of Haiti's ruling oligarchy—but not the only members. For two centuries, a small group of wealthy, mostly mulatto families have wielded enormous power in Haiti, working in cooperation with dictators and juntas and controlling much of the economic life of the nation. These families continue to be major players in the current Haitian crisis—not only in Haiti, but also in Washington, D.C.

¬

Democracy is not going to be restored in Haiti by foreign service officers in the State Department or by a can-do admiral in the Pentagon. What happens in Haiti—whether the terror continues, whether American soldiers die there—is being decided in the homes of a handful of wealthy Haitian families. Traditionally, the Haitian military answers to them, not the other way around. And currently they are frightened of losing everything if Jean-Bertrand Aristide regains his presidency. The families' growing desperation, transmitted to Washington by their American lawyer-lobbyists, is at the heart of U.S. policy.

Who are the Haitian elite Clinton finds such a tempting alternative to Aristide? There are several dozen major families, most of them mulatto. Two of them are powers to be reckoned with.

There are the Brandts, originally from Jamaica, where they still maintain businesses. In Haiti they have interests in edible oil, poultry, and banking. They have been key participants in a World Bank-financed tomato-paste project, and historically have had holdings in coffee, textiles, and autos. The Brandts have long been regarded as the richest family in Haiti, richer even than former president-for-life Jean-Claude (Baby Doc) Duvalier.

As one Haitian diplomat put it, speaking about the family scion O.J. Brandt, "he is the king maker." When François (Papa Doc) Duvalier wanted to build a paved road in downtown Port-au-Prince, O.J. Brandt put up the money to pay for it. If Duvalier needed money, he would stop Brandt at the border, on one occasion allowing him to reenter only after he bought $2 million in government bonds.

Today, the Brandts are believed not only to have funded the coup but to be currently underwriting its activities by providing part-time jobs to its leading members. In Washington, Gregory Brandt helped pay for the services of lawyer Robert McCandless, who at one time also represented the interim coup government. Unfazed by the embargo, the Brandts have close ties to FRAPH, the army's civilian front, and recently have discussed buying a bank in Paris.

Second only to the Brandts are their enemies the Mevs, dominant in sugar, in the manufacture of shoes, plastics, and detergents, and in assembly work, including the production of baseballs. Accused of supporting the coup, they angrily insist the family has opposed the military rule and embraced Aristide. In Haiti, according to a former minister who asked to be anonymous, the Mevs provided cover for members of the rightist governments so they could secretly run businesses that they were forbidden to engage in. The Mevs' attorney in Washington is Greg Craig.

Beneath the Brandts and the Mevs are several lesser-known members of the Haitian oligarchy—the Accras, flush from textiles; the Bigios (one of the country's few Jewish families; Gilbert Bigio is Haiti's honorary Israeli consul), with a monopoly on iron and steel fabrication; the Behrmanns, with concessions to import automobiles and trucks; the Apaids, with electronics factories; and the Madsens, with coffee holdings and beer production. Lillian Madsen (who married into the family and then split in a divorce) is the great and good friend of Ron Brown, Clinton's secretary of commerce and former representative of Baby Doc Duvalier.

These mulatto families, some of whose forerunners came from Syria and Lebanon years ago, have been employed from the early part of the century as puppets for the U.S. During the American occupation of Haiti (1915-34), U.S. officers, many of them Southerners, preferred dealing with light-skinned mulattoes. Today the descendants of the early traders from France, Poland, Germany, and the Middle East control Haiti's economy, rooted mostly in farming.

The mulatto elite shares power with the military, an easier career ladder for the Haitian blacks who dominate the institution. Yet even in calmer times, there have been tensions between the elite and the army; for example, the oligarchs might have been forced to pay off the army for a license to do business. But the uneasy alliance has been sorely strained in recent months. Perhaps the most telling event was the brazen attack on Antoine Izmery, the businessman and Aristide supporter who was dragged from church last year and slain.

The Haitian oligarchs also have branches in the neighboring Dominican Republic. They are reported to have teamed up with the Dominican military in ripping off gigantic profits from gasoline sales. A diplomat recalls, for instance, that one family paid off its debt to a businessman by directing him across the border to a private house, where he was allowed to fill up his truck from a swimming pool filled with gas.

These Haitian families run their businesses in an old-fashioned way. "They are traditional people who are used to running the country without doing any great amount of work," another Haitian diplomat explained. "They could invest more, but why? Then they'd have to work harder and ruin their lives." Even the younger family members, educated at Harvard and Yale, resist the lures of the free market on grounds that they then would have to compete with other newly educated Haitians and risk the loss of their way of life.

Unlike other prominent Haitian families, the Mevs, realizing things have to change in Haiti, have put their money into politics. Through lawyer Greg Craig in Washington, they have established a back channel for handling matters in Haiti—indeed, since 1992, the only serious channel. As a result, what Haitian policy there is has been concocted in the Mevs' Port-au-Prince living room.

Craig, a partner at the prestigious Williams & Connolly law firm, also heads a Washington-based group of lawyers who practice human rights law. He went to Yale law school with the Clintons, though he says he has never spoken to the president about Haiti. Craig defended John Hinckley, the young man who shot President Reagan, and has worked for Senator Edward Kennedy. (Craig was on hand to help Senator Kennedy during the rape trial of his nephew William Kennedy Smith.) In addition to the Mevs, Craig has represented Haiti's embattled prime minister Robert Malval.

As a representative of the Mevs, Craig has been involved in behind-the-scenes maneuvering on Haiti at least since early in the summer of 1993. "I went down there in July with the embargo imminent. The Mevs put together meetings with the military, trying to persuade them to agree to go to New York. And I left thinking we had failed." Two days later, the military leaders changed their minds and went to New York to cut the Governor's Island deal.

He says the Mevs were trying to put together a coalition of "the great impoverished masses" of Haitians and the business elite, and that the real division in Haiti is between these two and those who ran the country under Duvalier. "Both the economic elite and the masses have been denied access to the instruments of power," he argues. "[Prime Minister] Robert Malval has persuaded the left down there that this is the only way the country can go without having a sort of French Revolution magnitude of violence."

Craig's work began when he submitted a statement of principles to the Bush administration on behalf of the Mevs. Later he arranged for family members to visit Bush's point men on Haiti, Bernard Aronson and Robert Gelbard, who stayed on during the early months of the Clinton administration. These back-channel meetings opened the way for the Governor's Island accords. "I don't think without him we could have gotten an agreement," one State Department official told the *Miami Herald* earlier this year.

Not everyone shares Craig's enthusiasm for the Mevs. Charles Kernaghan and his associates at the National Labor Committee, a labor education group that represents 23 national unions, published a stinging indictment of Haiti's elites and their American business partners. It singled out the Mevs, claiming they made money smuggling cement during the embargo, and quotes an unnamed religious figure that "it is public knowledge that Mevs was one of the chief organizers of the coup."

Craig denies Kernaghan's charge that the family was involved in the coup. Not only was that untrue, Craig said in a letter threatening legal action and demanding that publication of the report be halted, but, "The Mevs family has been actively engaged—sometimes at the request of and working with the U.S. government—in a process aimed at restoring the democratically elected government in Haiti."

For the coup government, the most vociferous advocate has been Robert McCandless, a solo practioner who has represented both the existing military government and a group of businessmen headed by Gregory Brandt. In 1968 he was Hubert Humphrey's campaign director. He has also been a member of Clinton's Business Leadership Council, which raised money for Clinton-Gore.

Liberals have often thought of McCandless as a sort of prince of darkness, who masterminded a campaign against Aristide picturing the exiled Haitian leader as a dangerous wacko. And indeed, as McCandless says in his filings as a foreign agent with the Justice Department, he has assiduously warned of the danger of Aristide's return, arguing that he should be brought back to his native country to face a parliamentarian tribunal orchestrated by some well-known personage such as Barbara Jordan or Vernon Jordan and broadcast by CNN so that everyone can see just how dangerous the president really is.

After the coup, McCandless represented the military-installed president, Joseph Nerette, and subcontracted public-relations work for the coup government to Craig Shirley Associates, the conservative PR outfit in the Virginia suburbs.

In the spring of 1992, the Treasury Department ordered McCandless, as he puts it, "to cease and desist" representing the Haitian military government on the grounds he was breaking the embargo. According to recent statements filed at the Justice Department, McCandless no longer receives funds for representing Haitian public officials or businessmen, including the Brandts. His filings show a continuing "pro bono" advocacy through last winter.

From Clinton's nomination onward, McCandless wrote his "friend" Sandy Berger—now Clinton's deputy assistant for national security affairs, then on the transition team—arguing against Aristide's return, pleading with him to hold up any commitment until a delegation of Haitians arrived to talk directly to the White House. He wrote president-elect Clinton himself, and put together another letter to Clinton for President Nerette to sign. When Berger moved on to the National Security Council, McCandless sent him a lengthy detailed memo with advice on what to do in Haiti.

Throughout, McCandless has claimed that Aristide is responsible for a reign of terror, inciting mob violence, and embezzling funds. "Aristide's election raised the hopes of a whole nation," he wrote in August 1992, "but Aristide cruelly dashed these hopes when it became clear that he was just another tyrant and that Haitians suffered as much at the hands of his Lavalas as they had under Duvaliers' Ton Ton Macoute."

In an interview in late 1993, McCandless said bitterly, "Our government took their American lawyer [meaning himself] away from them. They had to go to that Governor's Island thing without effective American counsel. They had to see that ship coming in and make all these decisions without someone who is in Washington and knows about the political system. . . . The Haitian mind, you know, is just different. I mean they don't understand why we react to things that they don't and why we don't react to things that they do.

"When the Treasury ordered me to cease and desist from representing them, it was a terrible unconstitutional violation of the first and fourth articles. . . . If you're a noncombatant, nonterrorist country, why in hell can't you have a lawyer in Washington? I mean, whether you are right or wrong, whether your country is a dictatorship or whatever, I mean, if Washington is formulating policies that can literally starve your people to death . . . what are we afraid of?

"Clearly the military distrusts [UN envoy Dante] Caputo, the UN, and the OAS," he continued. "The one thing is, they love America. They can't resign as far as I can tell, those two guys [Cedras and Michel François, the police chief] because they are protectors of the peace. Whether we laugh at that or not, they see themselves as protectors of the people against foreigners and domestic violence and if they left, they would be violating their constitution. . . ."

Once more he suggested that Aristide step aside for the good of the Haitian people: "Aristide has never thought of anybody but himself. `Me, me, me,'" he said. "[But now] somebody's leaked the whole story on him," he added, referring to the recent rash of broadcasts and articles reviving speculation, which McCandless says comes from the CIA, that Aristide is a nut case. "He put us through an awful lot. Clearly we've got to have new elections. . . ."

In early May, McCandless updated his assessment of the situation: "If they cut off the escape route for the generals, they will stay until there is an invasion. You can't Harlan County this deal any more," he said, referring to the U.S. Navy ship that abruptly departed Port-au-Prince harbor when confronted by a screaming mob. He continued: "You're not going to get in there this time without guns. There will be no white flag raised. . . . [Haiti's military ruler Lieutenant General Raoul] Cedras did say in March in my hearing that he was ready when the Harlan County came, that he was ready to work out a deal for them to come ashore. But it was [Port-au-Prince police chief] Michel François who said, also in my hearing, that his men were ready to fire if they had unloaded that ship.

"I think the attitude today is probably basically the same. . . . Michel François is sworn to not let Aristide come back. You're not going to work a deal with him. . . . They're going to have to kill François." In McCandless's view, an invasion would also allow the United States to "put the military along the coastline and keep out the refugees. You cannot win Florida if you over-run 'em with a bunch of Haitians," he said.

As for the future of the Brandts and the other big families, McCandless says that for the first time since he's known them, the families are thinking about getting out.

Although the Mevs could not be reached and their attorneys declined comment, an individual knowledgeable in Haitian political and legal affairs over the last few years said he thought the family had lost patience with the United States. They believe that the U.S. should either knock off the moral rhetoric and act—even if that means invasion—or shut up and get out. . . .

HAITI'S "ECONOMIC BARONS"

Memo from
Congressman Walter E. Fauntroy

The clout of the ruling families in Haitian affairs has long been known to political insiders, if not to the mainstream media and readers who rely on it. In 1989, while Haiti was still under the post-Duvalier dictatorship of General Prosper Avril, Congressman Walter Fauntroy wrote a letter to President Bush denouncing the powerful families and their "allies within the U.S. apparatus." Fauntroy, a Democrat from the District of Columbia who had chaired a special task force on Haiti, warned: "It is imperative that the U.S. and other nations face up to the fact that these economic barons constitute the brains and wealth behind the unrest and anti-democratic agitation carried out by thugs at their service."

¬

To: President George Bush
From: Congressman Walter E. Fauntroy
         Chairman, Congressional Task Force on Haiti
Date: March 3, 1989
Subject: Haiti: What Must Be Done

I. The most important action that the U.S. and other nations with influence in Haiti must take, if they are serious in their belief that democratization and economic reform are in their interest, is to send a clear and unambiguous, indeed, aggressive message to those blocking democracy that their actions will not be countenanced.

A. Identification has been made of a number of powerful businessmen who control the commanding heights of the Haitian economy. These powerful forces have benefited from monopolies, corruption, and in at least one case, it is alleged, from the traffic in illicit drugs. These personalities and their associates have been identified as being in the forefront of those financing thuggery and terror to intimidate the Haitian people and the democratic sector. These economic barons have made it clear that they wish at all costs to maintain a strangled economy based on government concessions, franchises, and monopoly. They fear that a freely elected government accountable to the Haitian people would intrude on their privileges and force them to compete in a world economy. Such a change would threaten their short-term interests and for this they have and continue to finance an apparatus of terror to block change. One major fear is that Haitians from the diaspora would provide both capital and technology to a developing Haiti and that such an intrusion would put an end to this elite group's domination in a closed economy.

B. It is imperative that the U.S. and other nations face up to the fact that these economic barons constitute the brains and wealth behind the unrest and anti-democratic agitation carried out by thugs at their service, elements within the Army and the Ton Ton Macoute apparatus. Therefore, an effective strategy to safeguard democratization and economic reform must include actions to convince these interests to cease and desist. Without such actions the attempt, the second time around will result in another bloodbath which will eliminate the core of Haiti's democrats in the foreseeable future. This would leave Haiti as an open field for instability and destabilization in the Caribbean.

C. Specifically, there are five key families which have been identified as major players in blocking change in Haiti. In the recent past these families have thrown their financial support to Namphy and Clovis Desinor. The five families are as follows:

— The Brandts with interests in edible oil, poultry financed with a $15 million loan from the World Bank's International Finance Corporation (IFC), banking through the Bank L'Union Haitienne, agricultural plantations in the south of Haiti, and, it is alleged by some, connections with drug traffickers.

— The Mevs family with monopoly sugar production, the manufacture of shoes, plastics, import of sugar giving it almost total control over the sugar industry of Haiti.

— The Accra family with the monopoly on the production of internally sold textile products for the 500,000 plus uniforms for school children, large contracts for the supply of uniforms and food for the army and various agribusiness activities.

— The Bigios with the monopoly on steel and construction materials, a share in the edible oil market and jewelry. The steel plant controlled by this family when operated at full capacity would consume 50% of all the electrical power available in Port-au-Prince.

— The Behrmann family with concessions to import automobiles and trucks.

It should be noted that many of these same families and/or lesser economic actors associated with them dominate the assembly industry subsector. Representative of this group is Jean Edouard Baker and the D'Adesky family. With a few exceptions this sector on which the U.S. government relied for modernization deserted that very process in the last eighteen months working hard at apologizing for the Namphy dictator.

It should also be noted that there are a number of courageous members of the private sector who have stood up for democracy and free markets and who have in varying degrees suffered for that patriotism. Among these are to be found: Andre Apaid, Ralph Perry, the Duvall family, Raymond Lafontant of ADIH, Josseline Fethiere and Marie Michele Ray of the National Bank of Paris, and FHAF funded by the InterAmerican Foundation. These people deserve the full support of the United States.

D. The five families that have been identified above and are working to block democracy are a formidable force in Haiti. Not only do they control sizable shares of the Haitian economy, but they have also used this control to establish a network throughout the country. Their reach extends to voodoo priests, the secret societies, and military commanders in the countryside where over 80% of the Haitian people live. One illustrative example of this is the network of coffee speculators (middlemen who purchase coffee from the small growers) and military personnel in the rural areas. The estimated interest rate is 18% per month or 216% annually. This form of financial control easily translates into political power and an army of terror. Most importantly, this financial network gives access to the Chief of Section, a body of 555 appointed officials who are the arbiters of life in the rural sections of Haiti. The rural section is the most immediate element of governance in Haiti.

It should be noted that under the March 1987 Constitution, these officials will be elected, offering the possibility that they will be held accountable to the population they are supposed to serve. This comparative strategic advantage in the countryside forms the basis for the current Duvalierist strategy of fomenting unrest and terror in the countryside. For example, just last week, Macoute elements wearing the red armbands denoting Ogun, the voodoo God of War, attacked a school house in Labadie in the Artibonite Valley. This repeat of an attack made in the Namphy summer of 1988 is a clear message of terror. It also signals that other incidents are coming that will replicate the intimidations designed to reduce participation in the electoral process envisaged in the electoral decree issued on February 24, 1989 by the Avril government. This decree which complied with the recommendation of the recently held electoral forum and the March 1987 Constitution calls for the designation of members to form the independent electoral council from constituent groups as mandated by Article 289 of the Constitution. A translation of this decree is attached. Such a positive development is anathema to the five families and their allies, as it could reduce their influence on the process and outcome of the elections at both the local and the national levels.

E. It should be mentioned that there are two other sources of threat to the implementation of a democratic process in Haiti. One of these auxiliary threats emanates from the Dominican Republic and that government's toleration of Macoute elements residing there. It is suspected based upon past patterns and practices of the Dominican authorities that policy makers are likely to continue with initiatives that would relegate Haiti to its present state of underdeveloped on the short-sighted thesis that Haiti's misfortune accrues to the benefit of the Dominican Republic.

The second threat, which is complementary to the danger posed by the activities of the five families cited above and their allies issues from the

Macoutes at their service. At the time of the removal of Jean Claude Duvalier a list was compiled of Macoute personalities that required attention. That same list is for the most part operative and the people named should be monitored.

F. There are clear indications that these five families and their allies are considering a number of political options to keep the Duvalierist political economy intact, one of which is to create the conditions in which the Presidency can be handed over to former Duvalierist Minister of Foreign Affairs and Cults, Jean Robert Estime. Another option is that of former Ambassador Fritz Cineas, who presently resides in the Washington Metropolitan area.

G. Clearly this present time period is crucial. If democracy is to have a chance in Haiti, the U.S. and other nations must act to prevent a repeat of the tragic and vicious terror which culminated in the disgrace of the November 29, 1987 massacre of Hatian voters.

II. It is, therefore, recommended that the U.S. immediately take the following steps:

A. Signal the five families that we are aware of their activities antithetical to U.S. interests and advise them to cease and desist. This signal should be given through appropriate and credible channels. It is estimated that it would take a period of ten days to see a reduction in terrorist incidents and fifteen days for an almost total shutdown of the terrorist apparatus.

B. If the signal is not complied within this period, steps should be taken to seize the assets of these families in the U.S. It should be noted that language contained in the 1987 authorization, the Democracy for Haiti Act passed in the Fall of 1986 could be read as giving the President the authority to do this under the International Emergency Economic Powers Act.

Specifically, in the authorization, "the President shall exercise the authorities granted by Section 203 of the International Emergency Economic Powers Act (50 U.S.C. app. 1702) to assist the government of Haiti in its efforts to recover through legal proceedings, assets which the Government of Haiti alleges were stolen by former President for Life Jean Claude Duvalier and other individuals associated with the Duvalier regime."

Additionally, if the families are resistant all U.S. visas of family members should be canceled and their names should be put on the watch list.

C. Clifford Brandt should be targeted regarding credible allegations of narcotics trafficking.

D. It must be taken into account that these families have allies within the U.S. apparatus and it can be expected that they will seek to mobilize these assets to dilute and defeat any measures that might be considered.

E. Affirmatively, the U.S. and other nations must move to provide the democratic sector, those organizations and personalities, who are seeking fair and open elections under the Constitution financial support and security. It must be recognized that the anti-democratic forces are well-financed and enjoy the protection of thugs. In a war, and democrats in Haiti are the object of a war against them, one cannot and should not be left naked by those who profess to encourage them. . . .

AS BROWN FIDDLED, HAITI BURNED

Juan Gonzalez

Among the Haitian families' powerful friends in Washington in the early 1980s was the law firm of Patton, Boggs & Blow, and its then-little-known member, Ron Brown. Brown, of course, went on to become chair of the Democratic National Committee and, under President Clinton, Secretary of Commerce. But a decade ago, Brown had another job: lobbyist for Baby Doc Duvalier. Brown's connection to the Haitian dictator was uncovered in February 1994 by the newsletter *Counterpunch*, and discussed by *New York Daily News* columnist Juan Gonzalez.

┐

The nine-page private memo is written in French and addressed to Jean-Claude (Baby Doc) Duvalier, the Haitian dictator ousted in a popular uprising in 1986.

Though written in November 1983, it was just unearthed by *Counterpunch*, a muckraking newsletter of the liberal Institute for Policy Studies.

The memo's author is a one-time Washington lobbyist whose firm represented Duvalier government interests in the early 1980s. But he was no run-of-the-mill lobbyist.

He was not only a partner at a powerful Washington law firm, but also Vice Chairman of the Democratic National Committee. He went on to become the party chairman and a major force in Bill Clinton's presidential victory.

He is Commerce Secretary Ronald Brown, just cleared by the Justice Department of charges that he solicited a bribe from a Vietnamese businessman to lobby for lifting the U.S. trade embargo against Vietnam.

While a partner in Patton, Boggs & Blow, Brown represented Haiti from 1982 until just before Baby Doc's overthrow.

What's so important about a 10-year-old memo?

Yesterday, four more dead Haitian boat people washed up on a South Florida beach. Two weeks ago, Haitian peasant leader Luckner Elle was grabbed by 17 armed men, shot to death and hanged. Last Wednesday, 12 pro-democracy activists were massacred by soldiers who attacked their secret meeting north of Port-au-Prince, Haiti.

This week, on the third anniversary of the inauguration of Jean-Bertrand Aristide, Haiti's only democratically elected president, who was overthrown in a 1991 coup, the terror continues while the world community fiddles.

The Brown memo reveals why it's been so difficult to get the U.S. government to squarely oppose Haiti's thugs—the thugs know how to play the Washington game of having friends in high places.

When Brown wrote his memo, Amnesty International had accused the Duvalier regime of torture, detentions without trial and "disappearances."

Here is some of what Brown reported to Baby Doc:

• "Despite the unfair image of Haiti by the American media, and despite the opposition expressed by some members of Congress, it is certain that today. . . a growing number of people—both members of Congress and government officials—stand ready to defend the interests of Haiti. This . . . is essentially due to the work of our Washington team. . . ."

• "We continue to pay a great deal of attention to the Black Caucus and to other "liberal" members of Congress . . . [who] are now, thanks to our efforts, ready to help. Although some of them continue to make negative comments about Haiti, all, without exception, have proved to be cooperative on the issue of aid."

Brown was reporting on his success in getting Congress to *say one thing but do another*. On foreign aid, he proved more than worth his firm's $150,000 annual retainer. While he represented Haiti, annual U.S. assistance increased from $35 million to $55 million.

Not a word in the memo about human rights.

Yesterday, Brown's press secretary, Carol Hamilton, explained: "That doesn't mean other issues weren't raised in other memos over the course of time."

Brown also used his position as a Democratic Party honcho to get things done for his clients.

In the memo he reminds Duvalier, with the 1984 presidential campaign about to begin, that "while we've always maintained excellent relations with the government of President Reagan, we've set out to establish personal contacts with virtually all of the Democratic candidates, thereby ensuring access to the White House regardless of who wins in 1984.

"My current role as deputy chairman of the Democratic National Committee has served us well."

Ten years later, you have to wonder what behind-the-scenes role cabinet member Brown has had in the two-headed Clinton administration policy, which condemns the military dictatorship publicly but refuses to impose a full boycott to topple it.

Brown "has not been consulted nor has he weighed in on any of the decisions that have impacted on Haiti," Hamilton said.

Meanwhile, time is running out for Aristide and Haiti. Even if he returns to power soon, only two years remain in his term and he can't succeed himself.

The insiders have already won.

2

THE MILITARY

PAPER LAWS, STEEL BAYONETS
Lawyers Committee for Human Rights

As the Lawyers Committee for Human Rights outlines in a 1990 report, the Haitian military maintains its power and dispenses its own brand of justice not only through the top generals who have frequently occupied the presidential palace, but also through a complex and omnipresent system of low-level, semi-official armed operatives—the "section chiefs" and their assistants— who rule the rural areas through fear and bribery. According to the report, "for the 75% of Haitians who live in the countryside, the section chief *is* the government."

⌐

THE ORGANIZATION OF THE HAITIAN MILITARY

The U.S. Marines helped create the modern Haitian military during the American military occupation of the country from 1915 to 1934. Today, however, no foreign power threatens the national security of Haiti and no armed insurgency seeks to overthrow the government. Nevertheless, Haiti's commitment to its armed forces rivals that of many of its Latin American neighbors engaged in expensive civil wars. Haiti is the poorest country in the western hemisphere but devotes approximately 35% of its national budget—$42 million annually—to the military.[1] Estimates of the FADH's [Haitian Armed Forces] size range from 7,000 to 14,000, depending on whether or not unauthorized rural assistants are counted.

OFFICIAL MILITARY

The military hierarchy put in place by the Marines has remained largely untouched for more than 50 years. The General Headquarters, directed by the Commander in Chief, holds ultimate authority over all officers and soldiers in the FADH. It oversees the 14 military corps, one for each of the nine geographic Departments, Port-au-Prince police, the Navy, the Air Force, the Presidential Guard, and the Armed Infantry.

Each of the geographic departments, supervised by a colonel, is divided into districts which are overseen by FADH captains. The districts are further divided into sub-districts which are under the command of a lieutenant or sub-lieutenant. Finally, the section chief lies at the lowest level of the military hierarchy. Each of Haiti's 515 communal sections, the smallest administrative unit in the country, is under the command of a section chief appointed by the military commander of the sub-district with jurisdiction over the section.[2]

SECTION CHIEFS AND RURAL AREAS

Understanding the role of the section chiefs is crucial to understanding the power of the FADH in rural Haiti. For the approximately 75% of Haitians who live in the countryside, the section chief *is* the government. In theory, section chiefs have limited authority. FADH regulations identify the section chief's principal duties as (i) protecting people and property in his communal section, (ii) guarding the fields and the farm animals in the section, and (iii) maintaining order and public peace. The regulations specify that every person arrested by a section chief or an assistant must be taken within 24 hours to the nearest army post and the section chief must prepare a detailed report. Section chiefs must also have an arrest warrant from the proper judicial authorities except in cases of *flagrant délit*.

The regulations also explicitly prohibit section chiefs from certain activities, including:

— acting as a judge or imposing or receiving fines;
— imposing entry or exit taxes on peasants taking farm animals through their jurisdiction;
— forcing residents to pay for their freedom or rights;
— accepting bribes; and
— mistreating residents of the section.[3]

In fact, a section chief has life and death power over the residents of his section. He often serves as *de facto* executive, legislature and judiciary for the areas under his command. Section chiefs do not refer cases to the judicial system; rather, they make arrests, detain prisoners, conduct trials and settle disputes. According to one U.S. embassy official, "section chiefs are at the heart of the human rights violations in Haiti."[4]

A former rural justice of the peace succinctly summarized the justice system's dilemma:

> The section chief and his assistants establish their own administration; they arrest and try people themselves and don't involve the justice of the peace or the civil court system at all . . . The justice of the peace does not know what is going on in the hills; the people arrested who can't pay the $50 or whatever the section chief charges to be freed just stay in prison until the section chief feels like releasing them. Milo Joséf, the section chief for my area, commits all kinds of abuses and he charges for everything.

ABSENCE OF TRAINING FOR POLICE WORK

Nothing in a soldier's background prepares him to respect the rule of law or protect human rights. Basic training does not distinguish between military activity and police work. Nor does it teach respect for the rights of civilians while performing police duties. Like the vast majority of Haitians, soldiers are poor and largely illiterate. The average educational level is low and recruits receive no formal schooling after joining the army.

The army provides weapons to new soldiers with little training about when the use of armed force is—or is not—appropriate. Neither officers nor enlisted men learn how to control public demonstrations, make arrests legally, interrogate prisoners constitutionally, conduct criminal investigations that yield evidence admissible at trial, or respect the rights of prisoners. Record-keeping, fingerprinting, and forensic techniques are rudimentary at best. The army simply does not provide soldiers adequate training or equipment necessary to investigate crimes. This problem is compounded by the frequent transfer of the few officers who receive some training to positions where their training is not relevant.[5]

A recruit's sensitivity to human rights remains dependent on the initiative and personal resources of his commanding officer.[6] The military hierarchy has never placed great emphasis on respect for the rule of law or protection of civil liberties. The FADH expressed reluctance even to educate its soldiers about human rights or the Haitian Constitution. In December 1988, the Haitian Center for Human Rights (CHADEL) offered to teach a course on human rights and penal administration to military officials. The FADH responded favorably and an organizational meeting was held in January 1989. The initiative lapsed when the FADH failed to respond to CHADEL's proposed curriculum. More than a year later, CHADEL finally received permission and a class for army officers was scheduled in May 1990; a similar course for section chiefs took place in August. The section chiefs received four days of instruction on human rights provisions in the 1987 Constitution, the Universal Declaration of Human Rights and various provisions of the Rural Code.[7] Yet violations continue.

Without an independent police force, cooperation between law enforcement and justice officials is minimal. Without a police force free from military domination, civilians cannot control the administration of justice. When soldiers perform a police function for which they have not been trained, violations of human rights are inevitable. They become pervasive when the judiciary is too weak to hold violators accountable for their actions.

CORRUPTION OF MILITARY PERSONNEL

For many members of the security forces in Haiti, enforcing the law is a money-making enterprise. Poorly paid by the state, housed in cramped and often unsanitary conditions, soldiers regularly use the power of their official positions—including the force of their weapons—to improve their circumstances.[8] Corruption is rampant. One rural parish priest emphasized that "you have to pay someone to have anything done: to be released, not to be beaten, to get food or even to win a case." Former Justice Minister Fritz Antoine wryly observed that the overcrowded prison in Port-de-Paix always maintained a level inmate population because of "escapes" by "the most financially solvent" prisoners.[9]

SELECTION OF RURAL MILITARY PERSONNEL

In rural areas, corruption is often institutionalized by the local section chiefs. The selection of section chiefs is driven by greed. In St. Louis de Nord, a small town in northern Haiti, a peasant who wants to be named section chief must pay the FADH officer in charge of the sub-district anywhere from $400 to $8,000.[10] This practice is repeated in other rural communities, though the prices vary depending on the wealth of the region.[11]

Since a section chief can be dismissed at any moment, he has a strong incentive to accumulate money as quickly as possible. He can recoup some of his investment by hiring assistants (generally called *attachés*) who must pay for their jobs. Though the law restricts each section chief to two such assistants, the limitation is regularly ignored. In fact, each section chief in rural Haiti contains a private militia under the control of the local chief.

These rural militia have no legally recognized status, but their hierarchy rivals the FADH. Each section chief generally appoints at least one, and up to five, *secretary-maréchals* who serve as his first deputies.[12] They supervise the approximately 30 "*adjoints*" who in turn direct an average of 50 "*police.*"[13] The "*Souket-Larouze*"[14] serve at the bottom rank of the rural militia. Up to one hundred *Souket-Larouzé* serve in each section. Each position in the militia hierarchy can be bought for the right price:

Secretary-Maréchal	$150
Assistant/Adjoint	$50-$150
Police	$50
Souket-Larouzé	$20

Not surprisingly, those appointed to the section militia have neither interest in rural policing nor training for such service. The successful applicants frequently seek to recoup their investment immediately. They do so by extorting, fining, and stealing money or goods from the people they are supposed to be protecting. According to Renaud Bernadin of the Catholic Commission for Justice and Peace, "The [attaches] get a little badge and then terrorize the local population to extort money to avoid arrests or beatings."[15]

The militarization of the Haitian countryside caused by these rural forces cannot be overstated. The number of rural police has greatly increased since

1986.[16] Reports of section chiefs with as many as 200-300 assistants are now common. For example, the section chief in Platona, near St. Michel de l'Attalaye, reportedly appointed 574 assistants; the section in a nearby community reportedly named 200.[17] The unrestrained power of section chiefs and their assistants combine with their need to make money to create a system that runs on oppression and corruption. . .

NOTES

1. *Washington Post*, November 30, 1981 (for the 1989-90 fiscal year). The figure represents an increase of 30% over the 1988-89 fiscal year.

2. FADH regulations, published July 13, 1987. A decree dated December 16, 1988 proposed certain revisions to FADH rules regulating section chiefs, including popular election of section chiefs. The FADH commander of the district, however, would retain complete control over the section chief and his assistants. The decree also requires that rural police agents be "subject to evaluation reports every three months by the FADH commander of the district." Like other announcements of reform promised by the military, this decree has never been implemented.

3. General Rules of the Armed Forces of Haiti, *Le Moniteur*, July 13, 1987.

4. Lawyers Committee interview with Steven Kashkett, Human Rights Officer, U.S. Embassy, Port-au-Prince, December 12, 1989.

5. Lawyers Committee interview with U.S. official, Port-au-Prince, July 1989 (name withheld on request).

6. Lawyers Committee interview with Lt. Col. Himmler Rébu, New York, April 10, 1989.

7. CHADEL, "Human Rights Situation," August 1990.

8. A U.S. official noted that living conditions for soldiers were not much better than the horrendous conditions prevailing in the prisons. Lawyers Committee interview with Major Robert Goyette, Defense Attaché to the U.S. Embassy, Port-au-Prince, July 19, 1989.

9. Radio Nationale, September 5, 1988, as reported in FBIS, September 8, 1988.

10. This information, excerpts from a study prepared by a peasant group from the region, appears in *Haiti Information Libre*, no. 40, March 1989.

11. *Ibid.* Much of the following description of the rural military hierarchy was provided by Fr. Giles Danroc, a French priest who has lived in rural Haiti for seven years. Lawyers Committee interview, Verrettes, June 30, 1990.

12. *Ibid.*

13. Josama Joslen, a human rights monitor based in Petite Rivière d l'Artibonite, provided the following figures for assistants/adjoints in the six rural sections of Petite Rivière that he monitors: 1st rural section, 52; 2nd rural section, 35; 3rd rural section, 40; 4th rural section, 40; 5th rural section, 50; 6th rural section, 45. Lawyers Committee interview with Josama Joslen, Port-au-Prince, July 2, 1990.

14. They are called *Souket-Larouzé*, the creole word for "those who collect the dew," because they perform the most basic police work.

15. *Ibid.*; Lawyers Committee interview with Renaud Bernadin, Catholic Commission for Justice and Peace, Port-au-Prince, July 19, 1989.

16. Danroc interview.

17. Lawyers Committee interview with Michelle Montas, Executive Director, Radio Häiti-Inter, Port-au-Prince, July 19, 1989.

THE TONTONS MACOUTES
Michel S. Laguerre

Among the quasi-military groups that have wielded power in Haiti was the infamous Tonton Macoute, created as a private force by Papa Doc Duvalier, following his election to the presidency in 1957, as a counterpoise to the army. The Macoutes were a network of paramilitary activists, loyal to the president, who served as a secret police to terrorize the populace. During Papa Doc's 14-year rule, 50,000 Haitians were estimated to have been killed by state-sponsored terror. Recruited among the poor Haitians and black middle class, the Macoutes were allowed to prosper through corruption, extortion, and patronage, as described by Michel S. Laguerre in his 1993 book *The Military and Society in Haiti*. The name Tonton Macoute is derived from the name of a boogeyman thought to carry off children at night in a bag.

┐

The creation of the Tonton Macoute force was an attempt at redefining the center of civil society, given that the relations between the army or the government and the civilian population are of center to center in nature. The Tonton Macoute force became the center of civil society in as much as they were called to harass, exploit and repress the civilian population.

The establishment of the Tontons Macoutes as a repressive force was a slow process. It evolved in three steps. They began as *cagoulards*, intimidating and doing physical harm to members of the opposition, especially to the followers of the other presidential candidates in 1957 and 1958. At this stage, their identity and activities were kept secret. That period of harassment was designed to secure the tenure of the regime. However, their activity was not exclusively aimed at the opposition. Individual Duvalierists were also targeted, mostly to neutralize or eliminate dissenting voices among the inner circle of Duvalierists. At the time, there was a struggle for power as one clique was intent on eliminating another competitive group.

Basically, the *cagoulards* began as an organization of spies for François Duvalier. Slowly, they started to carry out arrests and to proceed with their own judicial interrogations. Whereas the government denunciation was used as a preventive against dissent, for the *cagoulards* it was a way of scoring for themselves and for the regime. It was a way of protecting their jobs.

After the invasion of July 1959 and the control of the Casernes Dessalines by the invading commando (composed of American mercenaries and former Haitian army officers living in exile in Florida), Duvalier conceived the formation of a civilian militia to serve as an auxiliary to the army, supposedly to help the army in case of a national emergency such as an invasion. In practice, the formation of this militia took a couple of years of experimentation since the idea of an auxiliary force was not a practical one. It required the cooperation of the army, the acceptance by militia members of their inferior position vis-à-vis the army, and the ability of the army to maintain them as a disciplined unit. After a short period of collaboration as an auxiliary unit, they eventually evolved into a parallel force.

The establishment of the Tontons Macoutes as a paramilitary force was the result of their legal recognition as volunteers of national security. External factors such as the invasions in the 1960s staged by Haitian expatriates in the United States, the Bahamas and the Dominican Republic contributed to the prominence of the Tontons Macoutes as they were called to fight the invaders. They became more assertive and formed permanent units. As the *cagoulards* were being transformed into Tontons Macoutes, they continued to receive elementary military training from the army. With the regular contacts between their national leaders and the executive branch and with the government relying more and more on them for internal security, their power and activities exceeded eventually the control of the army, and sometimes resulted in direct conflict with the army.

Once the government changed the name *cagoulards* to Tontons Macoutes, it redefined the primary role of their existence from that of serving as a reserve force in case of an invasion or any other emergency to that of a permanent, repressive militia. Instead of a reactive role, they took a proactive role. This proactive role allowed the leadership to be in close contact with the president and his subordinates; by excess of zeal, they continued to denounce whomever they wanted, whatever their reasons. Personal animosity, jealousy and competition were the main motivations for their political denunciations.

The denunciation of army officers and soldiers by Tontons Macoutes led to the dismissal or retirement of many in the military. As the Duvalier clique gave more credence and encouragement to what the Macoutes said against the words of the military officers and soldiers, the morale of the army increasingly declined and the Macoutes increasingly strengthened their positions.

The organizational structure of the Tontons Macoutes has never been highly regimented. At the local level, the structure varied from one locale to another. This lack of uniformity created a number of problems. Among them was a lack of discipline resulting in part from poor training. The line of command from top to bottom was never made clear. Also, the number and identity of the Tontons Macoutes were not always known by the central government. It was in view of solving this organizational problem that Jean-Claude Duvalier finally wrote to Mrs. Max Adolphe, the head of the Macoutes, requesting her to give every Tonton Macoute an identification number and to register their names in the central bureau of Port-au-Prince (*Le Moniteur*, 12 April 1984). There was basically an administrative incoherence in the national structure of the Tonton Macoute force. This was encouraged by the government in order to preclude paying all of them a monthly salary and also to weaken the ability of any regional Macoute headquarters to mount an attack against the government.

The Macoutes had some form of monetary compensation for their services. Occasionally, some received cash or a monthly salary from their bosses; others had jobs in the public sector; some used their authority to get monies from whatever sources possible; still others were able to get parcels of land from the government for farming. . . .

The Macoutes were organized according to the military division of the territory, and each military district had its Macoute headquarters. Some were more active than others. . . .

There was no formal chain of command within the geographical department itself. For example, an influential Duvalierist could have his own group of Macoutes (people he had recruited and who depended on him monetarily), forming a distinct unit within the department that served as his own private army. Essentially, each headquarters was composed of aggregates of Macoute cells who served the location because it was near their places of residence (koté io mangé sé la io sèvi). Although the head of each headquarters was known, between him and the lower-ranking Macoutes there was a loose power structure composed of the most important civil servants of the town (mayor, judge, city council members). Each head had his own followers for personal protection against the ambitions of any other cliques of Macoutes within the same zone. The Macoutes were as afraid of members of other cliques as the civilian population was afraid of them all. . . .

Although in the rural areas the Macoutes formed groups distinct from units of the regular army, in Port-au-Prince that was not always the case. Although they had their own organization, they tended to mingle more with the regular army. This was the case for both the upper- and lower-ranking Macoutes. Some of them served as both Macoutes and soldiers.

The leadership structure of the Tonton Macoute forces has always been a mixed operation, comprising both civilian and military Tontons Macoutes. The latter were regular members of the army who wore either the blue denims of the Tontons Macoutes or the khaki uniforms of the military at will. For example, a few years before the collapse of Jean-Claude Duvalier's regime, the leadership structure of the Tontons Macoutes was composed of five individuals: three civilian Macoutes, including the head of the organization, Mrs. Max Adolphe, and two military Macoutes, one of whom was Colonel Jean-Claude Paul, assistant commandant of the Casernes Dessalines.

Just below that structure, there were three Macoute headquarters in the Port-au-Prince metropolitan area: the National Palace, Fort Dimanche, and Pétionville. The Macoutes attached to the prefecture and the mayor's office in Port-au-Prince were useful mostly for intelligence matters. The local stations in the crowded neighborhoods of the capital city depended on these larger Macoute stations for leadership.

The National Palace Macoutes were trained by the army and were better organized hierarchically than the other two headquarters. They formed a structure parallel to the presidential guards and were composed of three hundred individuals in active service whose numbers could be enlarged with reservist Macoutes. The majority of these were not stationed in the palace but instead were in neighborhood Macoute stations. However, the most influential Macoutes were often seen in the corridors of the palace, especially during the reign of François Duvalier. Whenever there were national holidays they could be seen parading in front of the palace along with the soldiers of the regular army.

The Fort Dimanche headquarters of the Macoutes housed an infamous jail and was a company of the police department of Port-au-Prince. This structure served as an extension of the Commission d'Enquête (Palace Intelligence Agency), housed in the yard of the Casernes Dessalines. After being interrogated and tortured by National Palace Macoutes to force confessions of their sins, the accused were sent from the Casernes Dessalines to Fort Dimanche, where they were inflicted with more torture and from which some detainees did not return alive. At Fort Dimanche, the Macoutes were for the most part executioners who received their orders directly from the Commission d'Enquete.

The Macoutes of Pétionville (an upper-class suburb) had their own building, separate from the army barracks of Pétionville. The territorial criterion cannot be used here to understand the extension of the power of the metropolitan Macoutes, since a Macoute could live in Port-au-Prince and serve in Pétionville, and vice versa. He could also exert his authority outside his territorial area. For example, a Pétionville Macoute who lived in Port-au-Prince could arrest someone in Port-au-Prince. There was no territorial boundary to the power of the Macoutes.

The Macoutes did not form an homogeneous group because of their diverse social backgrounds. Some were Duvalierists who were eager to keep the regime in place; others joined the organization as a means of self-protection, especially those who belonged to political groups other than the Duvalierists during the electoral campaigns. The latter were known as the Sans Rancunes. The terror that the Macoutes maintained in Haiti was partly due to orders received from their superiors, mostly politicians who wanted either to humiliate or eliminate competitors. However, Tonton Macoute terror was exerted not only on members of the opposition but also on Duvalier's followers who fell victim to competitors' drives for power or who were simply out of step with the official line.

Among the military Macoutes, there were two kinds. The true believers were those who were with the pro-Duvalier camp during the electoral campaigns. These were individuals who were ready to risk their jobs for the candidate because either they knew him or agreed with his political platform.

The other type of military Macoutes was composed simply of opportunists interested in advancing their careers. In the local parlance, they were referred to as chameleons because of their ability to adapt to new circumstances.

The substantial number of Macoutes entering the army led to the deprofessionalization and continued politicization of this military institution. The Duvalierization of the army continued unabated with massive transfer, dismissal and imprisonment of professional officers and with their replacement by Duvalierist partisans and Macoute soldiers. As this changeover in personnel was being pursued, the heads of military units and departments were losing their power to effect changes. Indeed, owing to their political leanings and connections, subordinates sometimes had more power than their bosses. One officer recalled how a lieutenant under him refused to follow orders because of his direct access to the palace. Another recalled how he lost his job because he was wrongly denounced by a subordinate. Coupled with the fact that officers were dismissed before their cases could be heard by a martial court, morale plummeted in the army. Overall, it was a climate where officers spied on or denounced each other in order to get career promotions or to inherit lucrative posts. . . .

The Macoutes were engaged in harassing, curtailing and eliminating opposition forces. The Catholic church was disempowered with the expulsion of the archbishop and bishop of Port-au-Prince, the jesuit order influential among the educated elite, and the Holy Ghost Fathers who ran a high school attended mainly by the sons of upper-middle-class and bourgeoisie families. Trade union, university and high school student leaders were jailed. Heads of political parties and their most visible and active partisans were taken at night to jail unless they managed to leave the country ahead of time. The harassment and persecution was done on a massive scale. As resistance voices arose, they were eliminated. The Macoutes were able to establish a reign of terror during the administration of François Duvalier through illegal break-ins, arrests, denunciations, assassinations, infiltration of dissenting groups and espionage directed at the underground political activities of potential political leaders.

By silencing the democratic voices and by occupying the people's political space, the Macoutes became, in the government's eyes, the effective force needed to eliminate dissent among the civilian population. The tension between civil society and the government thus became institutionalized as the opposition attempted timidly to voice its discontent, bringing a new equation into the mathematics of civil-military relations. For the relations at issue now involved the government, the military (i.e., the Duvalierist military men engaged in silencing the opposition within the military), and the Tontons Macoutes (engaged in silencing the opposition within the civilian population, including members of Parliament). All of the novelty of the Duvalier regime resides in these structural and hierarchical shifts in the relations between these three units.

However, it must be emphasized that the Macoute forces were never a purely civilian organization. At their inception, there were both civilians and military men involved in the collaboration among the Duvalier secret service, the *cagoulards* and police intelligence in the early years of the Duvalier regime.

So, too, there were always pockets of institutional collaboration between the army and the Macoutes. These relations were more functional at the command level than at the level of low-ranking Macoutes and soldiers. At the command level, the military trained the Macoutes. These military exercises were performed in various parts of the country used in the military barracks conjointly with the regular army.

My data reveals an organic integration between the military and the Macoutes. Many army men willingly served as Tontons Macoutes and had no second thoughts about wearing the Macoute uniform (which created much confusion in the minds of the civilian population). This intermixing of duties occurred because of the trend of sending Macoutes for training to the *camp d'application,* basically a training ground for soldiers. As the Macoutes completed their training at the *camp d'application*, some of them were assigned to army duties and others to Macoute duties. . . .

THE BIRTH OF FRAPH
Haitian Information Bureau

In the Fall of 1993, Haiti saw the widespread institution of a new political apparatus, strongly rooted in the army, and in certain aspects a direct descendant of Papa Doc Duvalier's Tonton Macoute. Following the signing of the Governor's Island accords in July, Aristide's then-prime minister, Robert Malval, welcomed back all Haitians to the country, saying, in the spirit of reconciliation, that he wouldn't even stop Baby Doc himself from returning. (In fact, the Haitian constitution of 1987 forbids the Macoutes of the Duvalier era from taking part in politics for 10 years.) Soon after these welcoming gestures, many former Duvalierists reentered the country to join their colleagues who had remained behind, and a new right-wing political grouping emerged, called the Front pour l'Avancement et le Progrès Haitien, better known as FRAPH.

FRAPH would have its moment on the world stage when, standing on the wharf and brandishing their guns, its supporters successfully frightened the U.S. into abandoning its plans to land a detachment of Canadian and American military instructors sent to begin the process of reestablishing civil order. Instead, the USS *Harlan County* sailed back out to sea, leaving the FRAPH thugs victorious on the docks. In a pair of dispatches published in its news bulletin, *Haiti Info*, in the weeks immediately preceding the *Harlan County* incident, the Haitian Information Bureau in Port-Au-Prince describes FRAPH's rising reign of terror.

┐

PORT-AU-PRINCE, October 1, 1993—Several hundred people held an anti-democracy march on the anniversary of the coup d'état. Chanting slogans like "Aristide eats people" and "Ariside is a communist" and carrying a U.S. flag, the demonstrators wound their way through downtown, handing out leaflets with a photo of Jean-Claude Duvalier and slogans like "Make Aristide president of Venezuela."

Although police and paramilitary attaches have viciously attacked any pro-democracy gatherings, yesterday's rowdy marchers were escorted by police.

The march was organized by the recently formed FRAPH (*Front pour l'Avancement et le Progrès Haitien*) a supposed "popular organization" which announced its founding a few weeks ago by threatening U.N./O.A.S. negotiator Dante Caputo with a 72-hour ultimatum. Gun-toting FRAPH members also burst into the foreign affairs minister's installation on September 17.

In another offensive, former Duvalierists, well-known supporters of the coup d'état, and the city's deputy mayor last week founded a political party, *Rassemblement des Démocrates pour la Republique* (RDR) on September 22, the anniversary of the beginning of François Duvalier's reign of terror.

Surrounded by black and red Haitian flags (Duvalier had replaced the traditional blue with black), pro-coup politicians Hubert Deronceray and Reynold Georges, former Deputy Gabriel Agustin and Deputy Mayor Gerald

Salomon led the ceremonies—a march and speeches—attended by hundreds of attaches, police, former Tonton Macoutes and others. The party "headquarters" is a city hall annex occupied by Salomon supporters.

"Long live François Duvalier, the emancipator, the civilizer, the protector of the urban and rural masses!" said the aging Agustin, himself a Duvalier victim who spent over a year in Fort Dimanche in the seventies.

"There is a vacuum of power!" shouted Salomon into the microphone. "We are demanding power! We are acting!"

In a related ceremony in a downtown park, FRAPH members released white doves as a sign of "reconciliation" and leader Louis Jodel Chamblain burned a red flag.

"We don't like this flag, we don't like communists," he said, and displaying a U.S. flag, added, "Here is the flag that we like."

FRAPH "supporters" were later spotted picking up their pay at the Celeste restaurant, a well-known "Macoute" hangout. The same day, the National Museum opened an exhibit of Duvalier artifacts.

While many have remained quietly horrified at the brash reappearance of Duvalierists, this week Prime Minister Robert Malval was quoted as having said in *Newsweek* magazine, "It could be a good thing for the Duvalierists to found a party . . . I encourage them."

In stark contrast, Jean-Claude Bajeux, head of the Ecumenical Center for Human Rights, was outraged. "The 'Macoutes' are there. They celebrate. They take to the streets," he said in a television interview. "This is the only country in the West Indies that is going backwards."

Bajeux, who lost his father and three siblings to Duvalierist repression, said Duvalierism symbolizes "totalitarianism and dictatorship" and asked the Malval government to "take all measures to make this provocation cease."

┐

PORT-AU-PRINCE, October 12—Last week's attacks and actions by the ultra right-wing *Front pour l'Avancement et le Progrès Haitien* (FRAPH) provoked harsh criticism from the prime minister and others and exposed more clearly the relationships between those forces opposed to democracy here.

FRAPH thugs attacked journalists on October 5, shut down the capital and other cities in an enforced "strike" on October 7, and held a rowdy demonstration here on October 8.

The stated goals of the actions—which included an attempt on [Port-au-Prince] Mayor Evans Paul's life—were to replace U.N./O.A.S. negotiator Dante Caputo with a U.S. "negotiator" and also to force Prime Minister Robert Malval to include Duvalierists and others who supported the coup d'état in his cabinet.

"We will open the door to democrats . . . but these people are not democrats," said Malval on October 7 after the "strike" during which perhaps a dozen people, mostly market ladies, were shot at and wounded.

"These people are terrorists," he continued. "Their place is not in the government, it's in prison."

Lt. General Raoul Cédras later rejected those allegations, saying the FRAPH "demonstrators" are merely protesting "a violation of their national sovereignty."

Two days earlier, at least 30 machine-gun-toting FRAPH thugs, many of them recognizable paramilitary policemen or attaches, amassed outside a hotel where Paul was meeting some teachers. He was able to escape, but the men threatened journalists, shooting numerous rounds into the air.

FRAPH then called a "strike" for Thursday, threatening that anyone who ventured out would face grave consequences.

On October 7, armed thugs circulated in pick-ups and other vehicles, many of them from state institutions like the telephone, water and electric companies. Police, requested by the constitutional government to "provide security," did not attempt to protect people as the thugs searched, threatened and shot at cars and drivers, including Senator Fignole Jean-Louis (FNCD).

The "strike" was also enforced in Jacmel, Leogane, and other towns. Soldiers assisted by blocking traffic from some provincial towns into the capital.

That night, the O.A.S./U.N. International Civilian Mission denounced FRAPH and "the participation of army and police in the acts of terror and intimidation."

As in the Duvalier era, FRAPH then sent government trucks to the countryside to pick up peasants for Friday's demonstration. The next day, about 400 people, many armed, marched with U.S. and Haitian flags from the headquarters of the new *Rassemblement des Démocrates pour la Republique* (RDR), a usurped city hall building, to the U.S. consulate, where they stopped and gave speeches. Again, police and soldiers escorted the march and chatted with FRAPH leaders.

Despite their repeated threats to Caputo and usage of the U.S. flag, the U.S. embassy did not react or condemn FRAPH for four weeks, allowing the group to build up steam. Finally, last Friday, a spokesman said the U.S. supported Caputo and "energetically condemn[ed] the FRAPH demonstration and the abusive use of the U.S. flag."

The week's actions clearly illustrate FRAPH's relationship to the army and paramilitary forces, according to many in the democratic movement here.

"FRAPH is basically a political front for the army, is supported and protected by the army, and its 'members' are mostly soldiers, paramilitary attaches and former Tonton Macoutes and others who benefited from the Duvalier regime," explained a human rights observer who asked not to be identified.

3

THE DIASPORA

THE TENTH DEPARTMENT
Jean Jean-Pierre

Haiti is divided into nine regions, known in French as *départementes*. In a 1990 campaign planning session, Aristide referred to Haitian's living abroad as "the Tenth Department." An estimated 1.5 million Haitians—about one-fourth of all Haitians—now live outside of Haiti, in such cities as New York, Boston, Miami, Chicago, Montreal, and Paris as well as in Africa, the Dominican Republic, and other parts of the Caribbean. In 1993 Jean Jean-Pierre, a New York-based radio journalist who hosts the shortwave English and Creole program "Radyo Neg Mawon," noted that the Haitian diaspora's "size and strong ties with the homeland have made [it] a political and economic force that every Haitian government must reckon with."

⌐

It is a commonplace in the Haitian community that most discussions among more than two Haitians will inevitably revolve around politics. Haitians in the diaspora are no exception to the rule. Politics in the homeland has always captured their attention. Prior to 1971, the single purpose of most Haitian political groups in the diaspora was the overthrow of the Duvalier regime. Most Haitians of this generation believed that they would return to their country once this temporary obstacle disappeared.

The politically ambitious took advantage of this deep-seated desire to return that so many Haitians harbored. Some of these "candidates" raised—and many pocketed for themselves—large sums of money to plot the overthrow of Papa Doc. One such candidate, Bernard Sansaricq, a Senator in the current Haitian parliament, organized annual invasions of Haiti over the course of almost two decades. With two exceptions—when he sent a few subordinates to their deaths—his groups never reached Haitian shores. (A recently published document alleged that the Senator was a CIA operative.) Other would-be invaders only succeeded in dropping a few gas explosives on the Haitian capital. These attempts consistently failed because the opposition movement never had a strong and well-organized base in Haiti. In addition, unlike its support for the Miami Cubans, the United States consistently applied the Neutrality Act to prevent these Haitian exile groups from reaching Haiti.

The Haitian "boat people," although not admitted to the United States in great numbers, became the impetus for the rise of new Haitian-American political organizations while their treatment became a rallying cry for existing ones. This new influx, says Lionel Legros of the Haitian Information Center in Brooklyn, represented "a turning point in Haitian immigration to the United States." In contrast to the secretiveness of traditional political activity in the diaspora, the new groups began to stage public demonstrations to denounce the U.S. role in Haitian politics. Until then, Haitians had protested with their faces hidden for fear of being recognized by the hundreds of spies working for Papa Doc Duvalier.

Divisions between the old and new generations of Haitian immigrants made unity within the diaspora almost impossible to achieve. A multitude of political organizations—80 at last count—have sprung up in the last couple of years. "Ninety percent of these groups are composed of 20 people or fewer," says Jocelyn McCalla, executive director for the National Coalition for Haitian Refugees. This fragmentation, he adds, makes it "hard to politically influence their representatives, whether local or national." In a "permanent ad hoc" approach, these groups come and go depending on the nature and duration of the crisis at hand.

These differences were momentarily put in abeyance in April 1990 when over 85,000 Haitians and Haitian-Americans shook the Brooklyn Bridge in one of the largest marches ever organized in New York. They came out to protest against the U.S. Federal Drug Administration (FDA), which had included Haitian-born immigrants among the high-risk groups prohibited from donating blood because of the HIV-virus. The specter of ostracism, job losses, and stigma forced Haitians of all walks of life—doctors, lawyers, and factory workers—to come together in protest. The FDA lifted the ban a few weeks later. Many saw this important victory as the seed that would grow into a more organized, unified diaspora. But the "Tenth Department" remains riven by divisions among the different Haitian groups.

The common thread weaving all the different political groups into a single fabric has always been opposition to the Duvalier regimes and their military successors. But marring even this basis of unity is the knot of conflicting political and social interests. These conflicts are reflected in the fractious relations among the three major competing Haitian weeklies. Published mostly in French, these newspapers were—before the advent of daily radio programs—the way that the "Tenth Department" kept abreast of events in Haiti. A mirror of the rips and tears in Haitian society, the rivalry among these weeklies often borders on ideological war.

Häiti Observateur, the voice of the conservative sector, is the oldest of the three. It was founded in 1971 in Manhattan. Raymond Joseph, its owner and editor, staunchly opposes Aristide. His virulent attacks against the exiled president have earned him the ire of most of the "Tenth Department." Indeed, many consider *Häiti Observateur* the voice of the putschists. Joseph's acidic editorials are often directed at *Häiti Progrès*, the second oldest newspaper. Founded in Brooklyn in 1983, the paper has a Marxist-Leninist political slant. An early supporter of Aristide, *Häiti Progrès* became one of his most outspoken critics, even though its co-director, Ben Dupuy, was the Haitian president's ambassador-at-large until last July. The paper accuses Aristide of selling out to the international community.

Completing this three-way literary scrimmage is *Häiti en Marche*. Following a more moderate line, this Miami weekly, founded in 1986, is perhaps the most recognized among the three by the international community. Its editors, Marcus Garcia and Elsie Etheart, won the 1990 Maria Moors Cabot Prize awarded annually by Columbia University for excellence in journalism. The unyielding support of *Häiti en Marche* for Aristide has landed it the sobriquet "mouthpiece of the bourgeoisie" by *Häiti Progrès*.

With circulations ranging from ten to fifty thousand each, these three weeklies are filled with political analyses and commentaries, and are considered the Haitian "think tanks." Even though *Häiti Progrès* and *Häiti en Marche* are opponents of the military regime, all three newspapers are allowed to be distributed in Haiti. Of course, because the majority of Haitians do not read French, the papers' influence is somewhat muted.

Radio, by contrast, seems to be the optimum medium of communication among the diaspora, as it has always been in Haiti. Wherever Haitians reside, a radio program in Haitian Creole on AM/FM or short-wave can be found. The oldest, *L'Heure Haitienne*, is a political weekly program on Columbia University's WKCR FM. It was founded in 1972. The latest additions in the tri-state area are sub-stations Radio Tropicale and Radyo Soléy. Transmitting on special AM frequencies, these two stations do not fall under the direct control of Federal Communications Commission (FCC) regulations, and listeners must have special receivers to pick up their programs.

Because of the Haitian passion for politics, the sum of all the programs on these stations amounts to a 24-hour-a-day-long talk show in New York. The frustration and anger at the political situation back home among radio listeners who call in sometimes translate into high-decibel shouting matches. Radio is also the foremost vehicle for political activism. Through radio announcements, thousands of Haitians can be assembled for a demonstration with only a day's notice. In the "Tenth Department," radio gives a voice to the voiceless. Even the Haitian military and their supporters have managed to use this medium in the diaspora—some say for large sums of money—to spread their propaganda.

When Aristide took office in February 1991, he suggested to a visiting group of Haitian émigrés that they form a "Tenth Department" organization. He understood that the "Tenth Department" had tremendous financial and political clout. Haitians living abroad annually send over $100 million back home to families and relatives, estimates Fritz Martial, a prominent Haitian economist in New York. The U.S. State Department last year publicly denounced such transfers for spoiling the already porous OAS embargo against the military regime. In addition to remittances, Haitians also dig deep to contribute to political causes. According to Cesar Dismay, Aristide's campaign treasurer, two thirds of the $300,000 spent on the priest's 1990 presidential bid came from the disapora. . . .

The September 29, 1991 coup caught the "Tenth Department" organization in the middle of consolidating and defining the roles of the many groups working under its umbrella. . . . Yet the organization managed to spearhead several successful political actions. On October 11, 1991, over 60,000 people blocked downtown Manhattan for hours to protest against apparent tacit U.S. support of the military coup. The "Tenth Department" organization also deserves credit for the turnout of between 260,000 and 300,000 Haitian-Americans who voted overwhelmingly for Bill Clinton in the last U.S. presidential election.

The coup had, ironically, the salutary effect of bringing together the different factions of the "Tenth Department." Haitians not previously involved in politics became active. They discovered that the decision-making center affecting Haiti's future is not Port-au-Prince, but Washington, D.C. . . . While the international community led by the United States waffles, the "Tenth Department" has kept the issue of President Aristide's return alive for over two years. . . .

HAITI IS HERE

James Ridgeway

Along with hundreds of thousands of ordinary Haitians, most of them supporters of Aristide, the Haitian diaspora in New York and other cities includes members of FRAPH, the civilian arm of the coup government. FRAPH has sought to put a mild-mannered and "friendly" face on the military regime, but by the spring of 1994, many believed that it had begun importing terror onto U.S. soil.

¬

One recent Saturday night, Haitian-born Jocelyne Mayas was driving down the Long Island Expressway when she suddenly realized the car in the next lane was veering into her. The men in it were shouting angrily.

"I have a bumper sticker on the back of my car which reads 'Haiti plus Aristide equals democracy," recalls Mayas, an advocate for Haitian immigrants. "They told me the next time they see this car, or any other car with this bumper sticker, they are going to make sure they break it apart." Alarmed, Mayas sped up and swerved, barely avoiding a crash.

Still trembling, Mayas drove to her Queens precinct and filed a complaint. "I told the police," she says, "these are the people from FRAPH." The cops had no idea who she was talking about.

Who in America would know what she was talking about? But the Front Pour l'Avancement et le Progrès Haitien, or FRAPH, terrifies most Haitians. In the six months since it first appeared in Haiti, FRAPH—which rhymes with "wrap" and puns on the French word for "punch" or "blow"—has become a death squad, the latest edition of the Duvaliers' Tonton Macoute. And it has evolved into the political front for the Haitian military. Yet FRAPH is now portraying itself as an upstanding group of conservatives, and is trying to become the image-maker for the military rulers.

This is especially true in the U.S., where FRAPH is hard at work putting on a friendly face, to take advantage of the already pliant and confused Clinton administration. The administration has made every effort to seal off Haiti, refusing to deal with its terror—a terror Jocelyne Màyas and other Haitians are nonetheless beginning to feel within the U.S. itself.

The ruling Haitian military knows well that the lifeblood of President Jean-Bertrand Aristide's movement—indeed, the country's cash flow—lies not only with the democratic movement in Haiti itself, but with the 1.5 million Haitians living in the U.S. and Canada, especially in New York, Miami, and Boston. The money that emigré Haitians send home to their families exceeds what the country makes in foreign exchange. To maintain power and get rid of Aristide, the Haitian military must neutralize the Haitian communities in North America.

Having scared off the American navy last October, when a handful of armed anti-Aristide protesters forced a U.S. ship to flee the Port-au-Prince harbor, FRAPH understandably might think it can get away with exporting the same strong-arm tactics into the U.S. It has allegedly threatened politicians here and has even been accused of killing two journalists in Miami. (Miami police claim those homicides were not politically motivated.) FRAPH denies any wrongdoing.

Blitzing the media with faxes and phone calls at every mention of Aristide, FRAPH is trying hard to portray itself as a group of misunderstood conservatives falsely accused of being a terrorist mob.

"Every time we see an article in the newspaper that is wrong, we write a letter," says Lyonel Sterling Jr., the FRAPH coordinator in New York. "We send out hundreds of faxes."

Over the last month people saying they are from FRAPH have made repeated phone calls late at night to Jacqueline Thomas, whose generally pro-Aristide cable TV appearances have inspired FRAPH organizers to new tactics of media manipulation. "They threatened to cut me off the air," Thomas says. Indeed, FRAPH sent a letter to the Federal Communications Commission accusing Thomas of falsely labeling them as members of death squads and murderers.

By using respectable channels of protest and media-savvy countercampaigns, FRAPH has already created the appearance of legitimate conservative opposition to Aristide in the American Haitian community. Splintered as they are, Haitians here are linked through their own media. The newspapers, mostly in French, tend to divide along the lines of two Brooklyn-based tabloids, the proconservative *Häiti Observateur,* which runs FRAPH stories, and *Häiti Progrès*, which doesn't. In Miami, *Häiti En Marche* is pro-Aristide.

But the most passionate political debate plays out on the radio, particularly the Creole signals concentrated around two sub-band stations, Radio Soleil (pro-Aristide) and Radio Tropicale (anti-Aristide). "It's scary," says Patrick Jean Pierre of Radio Soleil. "Sometimes we have telephone calls on this station telling us if we keep doing the thing we're doing now, they'll do this, they'll do that. I'm not saying FRAPH are doing it. But having an organization like FRAPH right now in New York is really scary for progressive journalists and for the Haitian community."

The Brooklyn FRAPH founders insist they are not menacing. But recently their friendly facade crumbled with a fax to a man they really don't like, UN Secretary General Boutros Boutros-Ghali:

> You are, sir, killing a country who would rather die standing up than grovel.
> Mr. Secretary General, you and the so-called four friends of Haiti will have to murder more than the majority of my country men before you are

able to bring Jean-Bertrand Aristide back to Haiti. Even then you will have to stay with him to help him murder the rest of us for the time he stays in power, and finally you will have to take him back with you—HE IS YOURS.

WE FROM FRAPH HAVE NOTHING BUT CONTEMPT AND HATRED FOR THE TRAITORS OF OUR ANCESTORS . . . Mr. Boutros Boutros-Ghali, your name will be part of our Folklore as the evil man from the twentieth century apocalypse, THE HITLER OF OUR TIME. May the blood and the misery of our people haunt you and yours for eternity.

Scrunched together on a couch in an East Flatbush apartment, a trio of FRAPH New York organizers were eager to set the record straight—if only they could find an unbiased newspaper. They have serious Haitian credentials. Lyonel Sterling Jr.'s father was a member of Papa Doc Duvalier's personal bodyguard. He is the spokesman.

"Until now, I was never involved in politics," Sterling said, "but I have heard so many lies! I got a phone call last December and the person said, 'Why don't you help us and tell the truth because they are only pro-Aristide?' One of the first things he said when he became president was, 'I am the president of the poor.'"

Sterling paused, then continued, "What happened to the middle class? What happened to the rich? You are president of a whole country, not just part of a country."

Also on the couch was Rigaud Noel, who came to America in the 1980s and is known in the Haitian community as a longtime supporter of the late pastor Sylvio Claude, who was burned to death after the coup overthrowing Aristide. (FRAPH blames Aristide followers for the murder, and the Aristide camp blames the military.) Noel, an accountant, says he has long been a member of the Haitian Christian Democratic party. Then, finally, there is the soft-spoken Sylvestre Jean-Leger, who identifies himself as a FRAPH political adviser, a community organizer, and formerly involved in the pharmaceutical industry.

All three insist they don't want a return of Duvalier or Duvalierism; they're only looking for a president of Haiti who can represent everyone. They claim that Aristide is a phony Catholic, and above all they want a government that reflects power sharing, the euphemism throughout Latin America and the Caribbean for letting the army run things. They say they are opposed to violence.

"Do we look like terrorists to you?" asked Sterling. He readily agreed to a request to put in a call to the FRAPH command in Port-au-Prince. In a minute or so, he had Lionel Castana, the organization's secretary, on the line. "The main thing is to have a government," the secretary said in a quiet, reasonable voice. That, he added, is what FRAPH is trying to make happen. "We now have groups in Miami, Boston, Chicago, Montreal, and in two weeks we will open one in California.

"I'm a product of the United States," Castana explained. "So are [FRAPH leader] Mr. Immanuel Constant and most of us. I went to Annapolis and was a member of the marines.

"Aristide knows very well that he will never set foot in Haiti again," Castana said. "Everybody's suffering just for one man. We have people who are dying because of lack of medication. Even in the morgue, people start to smell very bad. All of that because of Aristide."

What about the reports that people are being shot and tortured every night in Cité Soleil and elsewhere throughout Port-au-Prince?

"It's the United Nations observers," Castana argued. "These people keep saying that every morning there are cadavers all over the place. The funny thing is these things started happening when the observers came back here. Before that, everybody was really living in peace until they come back. There is no such news in Haiti."

4

THE POPULAR MOVEMENT

HAITI'S POPULAR RESISTANCE
Marx V. Aristide and Laurie Richardson

Despite the historic stranglehold of the military and the ruling families, popular movements for democracy and reform have sprung up throughout Haiti's history. In the years following the fall of Jean-Claude Duvalier, the popular mobilization that helped drive him from power gained momentum. And although their visions for Haiti's future often differ, progressive currents in Haiti forged a "tactical unity" to mobilize "Operation Lavalas," which voted Jean-Bertrand Aristide into office in 1990. The evolution of Lavalas (which means "flood," and evokes biblical images of a force that will sweep the nation clean of terror and corruption) is traced by Marx V. Aristide and Laurie Richardson, coordinators of the Quixote Center's "Haiti Reborn" campaign.

┐

As the oft-invoked Haitian adage says, "*dèyè mòn, gen mòn*"—beyond these mountains lie more mountains. This adage reflects the saga of Haiti's popular movement. Having emerged from Duvalier's 30-year reign of terror with little organizing experience, the movement is still struggling to overcome a seemingly inescapable legacy of marginalization. Made up of a wealth of base ecclesiastical communities, peasant groups, labor unions, student organizations and neighborhood associations, the popular movement espouses mass mobilization as the means to institute revolutionary changes in the country's traditional order and to establish a truly participatory democracy. Through demonstrations, strikes, land takeovers, written and audio publications, and the occasional use of "popular justice," popular organizations have advanced demands ranging from agrarian reform to university autonomy.

The movement's effectiveness has been mitigated by brutal repression, a chronic lack of resources, and political opportunism. Add to these a U.S. offensive aimed at coopting grassroots cadres and the absence of a political party or a united front capable of concretizing popular demands, and the challenges facing the movement are revealed. . . . Despite these challenges, Haiti's popular movement has grown bigger and stronger over the past decade.

After months of sustained popular mobilization, Jean-Claude "Baby Doc" Duvalier was finally whisked away to France on a U.S. jet on February 7, 1986. As the Haitians say, *"baboukèt-la tonbe"*—the horse was unbridled. The masses once again took to the streets, this time to celebrate. The makeup of this collective victory party reflected the broad tactical unity which had formed in opposition to the dictator. Landless peasants danced alongside large land-owners, and slum-dwellers celebrated beside industrialists.

With the bit of brutal Duvalier dictatorship out of the people's mouth, everything seemed possible. This newfound taste of liberty whetted an appe-tite for justice and a desire to organize collectively for fundamental change. For the first time in nearly three decades, the voices of Haiti's poor majority found expression in a myriad of grassroots organizations, some newly formed and others emerging from clandestiny. These groups began to articulate a range of concrete demands—from land reform to Creole-language literacy programs. Uniting virtually all sectors across ideological and class divides, however, was the clarion call to banish the hated Duvalierists from the politi-cal scene.

Clearly, there was more to Duvalierism than the Duvaliers themselves. Despite Baby Doc's departure, the pillars of Duvalierism remained intact. Baby Doc had passed the baton to the Duvalierist National Governing Council (CNG), a six-member junta headed by Gen. Henri Namphy. Brutal section chiefs still ruled the countryside with impunity, the public administration remained bloated with corrupt civil servants, and the Tontons Macoute still held powerful government posts. Explained "Fritz," a well-known militant who has spent over 20 years in the struggle, "we all witnessed Duvalier's de-parture. Theoretically, there was no more dictatorship, and the era of repres-sion was over. Then, we began to realize that Duvalier was just the tip of the iceberg, and that we had to start mobilizing on all fronts."[1]

One of the strategies employed in this mobilization was *Dechoukaj*. Trans-lated literally as "uprooting" and often equated singularly with "necklacing"— execution by means of a burning tire—the concept of *Dechoukaj* embraced much more than popular street justice. In fact, its most potent dimension was political. Peasants organized to eliminate the brutal section-chief structure, students fought to end state control of the university, and the masses were galvanized to dismantle not just the Tontons Macoute themselves, but the political machine that created and sustained them for 30 years.

Popular militants were convinced that *Dechoukaj*, left to gain momen-tum, could successfully transfer real power from the Duvalierists and the elites to the poor majority. Indeed, it was this potential that most unnerved the reformist camp, many of whose adherents benefited at least indirectly from the status quo and would—if political *Dechoukaj* were allowed to run its course—ultimately be held accountable to the more militant bases.

Echoing the Duvalier-appointed Catholic Bishops, the reformists launched a propaganda offensive highlighting the street-justice aspect of *Dechoukaj* and calling for national reconciliation. By virtue of greater resources and control of major media outlets, they were able to bring *Dechoukaj* to a halt by mid-1986. . . .

Haitian wisdom warns that *"kay koule twonpe solèy; men li pa twonpe lapli"*— the leaky house may fool the sun, but not the rain. In early 1987, merely one year after Duvalier's downfall, tensions between the revolutionary ideals of the militant camp and the petit-bourgeois tendencies of the reformists flared. While a general consensus had emerged around the need to eventually replace Haiti's Constitution and hold new elections, there was debate about whether or not such steps could be taken in the repressive climate under CNG rule. . . .

In January, 1987, a broad spectrum of democratic groups was invited to participate in the Congress of Haiti's Democratic Movements (KONAKOM). The Congress produced a platform endorsing the constitutional referendum and laying the groundwork for a center-left political party. The more militant sector of the popular movement was skeptical. It saw the focus on the referendum and elections as a maneuver designed to stave off more radical change. "We were in the streets yelling, 'Namphy is going to fall!'" said "Fritz," "so [Namphy] sent everybody back home to study the Constitution."[2] In March, the newly formed National Popular Assembly (APN) called for a boycott of both the referendum and the elections. Others, such as the Peasant Movement of Papaye (MPP), took a more nuanced position, endorsing the Constitution despite certain misgivings.

After the Constitution was approved in March, debate shifted to the November elections. Even many who endorsed the elections doubted the will of the CNG to play fair. *"Rache manyòk"*—literally "pull out your roots"—became the order of the day as the junta was urged to exit the political scene. The July massacre in Jean Rabel of over 300 peasants advocating land reform reinforced this mistrust of the electoral process and fueled calls by militants for a total boycott. Port-au-Prince's Ti Legliz Coordinating Committee urged the people to "remain mobilized against these elections, whose results—no matter what—will not resolve the fundamental problems of the people."[3] As election day neared, however, *"rache manyòk"* was modified to encourage the masses to shift their energies from street mobilization to an "electoral clean-up"—voting Duvalierists out of office.

The army responded with a "clean-up" of its own, massacring voters as they turned out to cast their ballots. While temporarily forcing the movement to retreat, the aborted elections paradoxically advanced the popular movement's long-term struggle by highlighting the limitations of the reformist strategy in confronting the Duvalierists. The reformists "need the popular mobilization when they are under fire," said "Fritz," "but once they get the Macoutes off their backs, they make an alliance with the bourgeoisie to block any deeper change. They always say it's not to block you. They say you are unrealistic, you are extremist, you are a purist. They have all kinds of names for you. But when the Macoutes come back to haunt them, they are quick to cry for help."[4]

Two coups and one bogus election later, the popular movement emerged to reclaim the streets in March, 1990 to force dictator-of-the-hour Gen. Prosper Avril from power. Yet, once again, their victory was cut short. In a familiar scenario, the newly opened political space was monopolized by traditional reformists who made an unholy alliance with interim President Ertha Pacal-Trouillot, a Duvalierist.

"After we braved the army's bullets and riot gear to force Avril out, the suit-and-tie types took over," explained Calixte, a leader of the Coordination of Popular Organizations. "They essentially informed us that our involvement in the process was over and that the affair had moved to air-conditioned suites where we, the masses, were not welcome."[5] A 12-member interim State Council, co-governing with Trouillot, was created to prepare elections. Popularly denigrated as being "two-headed," the government was quickly discredited for its complete inability to respond to the demands of the masses. . . .

Aristide's last-minute entry into the presidential contest instantly changed this equation. Only seven months earlier, reformists had ignored calls by the APN and the National Front Against Repression to install the populist priest as interim national leader.[6] Faced with the return from exile of hard-line Duvalierist Roger Lafontant and the slick, U.S.-funded campaign of Marc Bazin, it was now the reformists who asked Aristide to join with them to stave off these threats. The strategy worked brilliantly. Within a week, electoral rolls doubled as over a million new voters flocked to register.

This marked the birth of "Operation Lavalas." Since its inception, Lavalas was an arranged marriage between the popular movement from which Aristide sprang and anti-Macoute elites characterized by the National Front for Change and Democracy (FNCD), whose legal status Aristide used in his run for the presidency. "What is important," said Aristide announcing his candidacy, "is to know the moment when history calls upon us to forge a tactical unity . . . in order to stop the Macoutes."[7]

Not surprisingly, the Lavalas alliance was marred by internal friction from the outset. The previous favorite for the FNCD presidential nomination, KONAKOM's Victor Benoit, quickly dubbed Aristide's bid "political adventurism," and called upon party members to suspend all electoral activities.[8]

This time, however, the militant camp had the upper hand. With a legitimate representative of the masses shaping the political debate, the reformists could not control the outcome. And, while FNCD sought to usher candidates into other offices on Aristide's coat-tails, the popular movement saw the elections only as a vehicle for mobilization, and reiterated its readiness to boycott them if necessary. "We will either take it all the way," warned Aristide, "or reject it categorically."[9]

On February 4, 1991—three days before his inauguration—Aristide announced the replacement of the "Lavalas Operation" with the "Lavalas Organization." His motive was clear: to build an independent political structure around the mass mobilization of the people. This signified a divorce from the FNCD, which became threatened by the prospect of a rival party that would inherit Lavalas' glory. Because FNCD reformists could not control the alliance, they became Aristide's most bitter enemies, and many actively participated in destabilizing his government.[10]

Shortly after his inauguration, President Aristide welcomed the MPP to the National Palace. After an arduous six-hour drive from the Central Plateau, the 100-member delegation from Haiti's oldest peasant group presented their demands, [and] talked with the President about their future. . . .

With a democratically elected popular government in power for the first time in Haiti's history, the climate was ripe for grassroots organizations to solidify their structures, empower and expand their bases, and advance their demands. "During Aristide's presidency," explained Ben Dupuy, co-director of the weekly *Häiti Progrès* and a founder of the APN, "APN's concern was to . . . make people aware that even though they were formally in power . . . the forces against progress were still very strong and there was no guarantee the present situation would last. So, the people had to take advantage of this space and period to consolidate themselves instead of looking for quick solutions or individual benefits."[11] . . .

The September 1991 coup came mercilessly. One of its primary objectives was to destroy the popular movement and drive the masses away from the political arena. To withstand the repression, the Haitian people revived the concept of *mawonaj* (marronage), a form of clandestine resistance deeply rooted in their historical rebellion against slavery. Haiti's contemporary maroons have replaced the conch shell that revolutionary maroon leader Boukman used to call the slaves to action with underground bulletins, leaflets and cassette tapes. They disguise meetings as games of dominoes or *konbit*, the traditional cooperative work teams used in rural areas. They use the vehicle of the popular church to spread the message of hope.[12]

Yet, with President Aristide in exile and isolated from his popular bases, reformist elements within Lavalas came to dominate its policy-making structure. They chose to rely almost exclusively on internationally sponsored negotiations to resolve the crisis. Many within the popular movement were leery of this strategy, warning, in the words of MPP spokesperson Chavannes Jean Baptiste, that "only the heat of mobilization will make the pot of negotiations boil." . . .

The failure of the [Governor's Island] accord has reinforced the popular movement's conviction that they can no longer wait for deliverance and must mobilize their own forces to topple the coup regime. Discussions of "a new formula of struggle" and a more activist resistance are multiplying as militants strategize about how to turn disillusionment into defiance and how to rejuvenate international solidarity. . . .

The dialectical debate between these two camps continues. It is the popular movement, however, which is gaining in strength, insight and stamina for the long journey up this mountain range and on to the next. In the words of one peasant organizer: "with the increased repression, the struggle just takes different forms depending on the circumstance. If the road has thorns, we know what shoes to wear; if there's a river in our path, we are prepared to swim. But above all, we keep struggling because that's our only chance for a brighter tomorrow."[13]

┐

PROFILES OF THE POPULAR CURRENTS

TI LEGLIZ – THE LITTLE CHURCH

Many of Haiti's popular organizations trace their roots back to the Ti Kominote Legliz (TKL), for it was in these ecclesiastical base communities that activists found cover during the repressive Duvalier era. Springing from the current of liberation theology, the Ti Legliz movement took off in the mid-1970s, providing a common thread to link catechists, peaseants, students and workers. The use of church-based training programs and the emergence of the church-funded popular radio station Radyo Solèy further politicized and fortified the Ti Legliz sector.

After Baby Doc's downfall, the movement sought to formally structure itself. A National Coordinating Committee was established with representatives from diocesan TKLs throughout the country. Other religiously-based groups cropped up, including Solidarite Ant Jén and Veye Yo. The political opening allowed activists to spin off and build peasant, student, and other popular organizations.

PEASANT GROUPS

The seeds of Haiti's peasant movement were planted in the late 1960s in the form of farming cooperatives, or *gwoupman*. Consisting of ten to 15 members, *gwoupman* gave peasants a collective base of resistance against the rural structures of exploitation and repression.

By 1986, *gwoupman* had become widespread and extremely politicized. After Duvalier's fall, they developed into a myriad of local and regional peasant organizations. Relying on tactics such as marches and land takeovers, peasant groups demanded agrarian reform, elimination of the repressive section chiefs, repopulation of Creole pigs eradicated by U.S. AID between 1981 and 1983, tax reform, and promotion of Haitian Creole.

Founded in the early 1970s and operating in semiclandestinity until 1986, the Peasant Movement of Papaye (MPP) is Haiti's oldest peasant organization. In March, 1987, the MPP formed the National Peasant Movement of the Papay Congress (MPNKP), which reported 100,000 members before the 1991 coup d'état. Another national movement is Tèt Koile Ti Peyizan (Heads Together Little Peasants), which has its roots in meetings held by peasant delegates starting in September, 1986. Tèt Kole has *gwoupman* in each of Haiti's nine departments, and is strongest in the northwest town of Jean Rabel.

STUDENT MOVEMENT

Although Haitian students have been active since the U.S. occupation in 1915, François "Papa Doc" Duvalier dealt a serious blow to the movement by elminating the leadership of the National Union of Haitian Students (UNEH) in the late 1960s. Although student participation in the ouster of Jean-Claude "Baby Doc" Duvalier was massive, it was largely unorganized. Not until late 1986 did the movement begin to restructure itself.

UNEH's successor is the National Federation of Haitian Students (FENEH), formed in March, 1987, and based in Port-au-Prince. Calling for university autonomy and the removal of Duvalierists from the educational system, FENEH's methods of organizing include boycotts, demonstrations and building takeovers. A variety of high school and youth organizations have also emerged, key among them Zafè Elèv Lekòl (ZEL). Founded in November, 1986, ZEL has campaigned to demand free basic education for all.

LABOR UNIONS

Haiti has a rich tradition of cooperative and union organizing. Yet, until Duvalier's downfall, virtually all unions—with the exception of the U.S.-backed Federation of Workers Union (FOS)—operated underground. The Autonomous Central of Haitian Workers (CATH) emerged out of clandestinity in 1986 to become the most powerful federation of unions in the country. However, a series of internal crises, compounded by a stepped-up U.S. destabilization campaign, split CATH into various factions.

Today, the Central Workers Union (CGT), founded in October, 1986, is the most militant of Haiti's three federations of unions. The other two—FOS and OGITH—both receive funding from the National Endowment for Democracy (NED), and toe a more moderate line.

NEIGHBORHOOD COMMITTEES

Primarily organized in poor urban areas, neighborhood committees emerged as marginalized residents sought to improve the lot of their communities. Committees organize to demand potable water and electricity, to protest the high cost of living, and to defend themselves against crime and extortion.

Committees often formed "vigilance brigades" which erected barricades, and interrogated and searched suspicious individuals in an effort to provide security to residents. The brigades also served as dynamic networks of information sharing and political organizing.

Today various neighborhood committees are loosely linked under the umbrella of the Federation of Neighborhood Committees (FEDKKA).

OTHER

Not all of Haiti's popular organizations can be easily classified into categories. Many have broad-based constituencies which include workers, peasants, students and others. One such example is the National Popular Assembly (APN). Founded in March, 1987 as a popular alternative to KONAKOM, the APN is represented throughout the country in the form of local popular assemblies. One of the more militant organizations within the popular movement, the APN was the first to propose Aristide as a national leader. More recently, the organization has been a vocal critic of the reformist sector within the Lavalas camp.

NOTES

1. Phone interview with authors, November 4, 1993. Because "Fritz" is underground, his real name cannot be used in this article.
2. Phone interview, November 4, 1993.
3. *Häiti Progrès*, November 25 to December 1, 1987.
4. Phone interview, November 4, 1993.
5. Interview, September 14, 1993, Port-au-Prince.
6. *Häiti Progrès*, March 7-15, 1990.
7. *Häiti Progrès*, October 24-30, 1990.
8. Radio Mètropole, October 18, 1990.
9. *Häiti Progrès*, October 24-30, 1990.
10. Many FNCD parliamentarians aligned with other blocs to create gridlock by blocking key initiatives of the executive branch. They also joined the call to take a vote of no confidence against Artistide's Prime Minister René Preval in the summer of 1991, just before the coup. After the coup, FNCD parliamentarians Eddy Dupiton and Bernard Sansaricq became prominent negotiators for the coup regime.
11. Phone interview with authors, October 28, 1993.
12. Boukman, a maroon of Jamaican origin, led the 1791 slave revolt that culminated in Haiti's independence.
14. Interview conducted by the Haitian Information Bureau on September 8, 1993, Port-au-Prince.

PROVERBS OF THE PEOPLE
Haitian Information Bureau

The strength and perserverence of Haiti's popular movement is in evidence all over the country: It is seen in the slogans written on walls, especially in the poor neighborhoods of Port-au-Prince. And it is found in popular proverbs, many of them bearing powerful political meaning. The following list of Creole slogans and proverbs, with their English translations, was compiled over several years by the Haitian Information Bureau in Port-au-Prince.

┐

SLOGANS FOUND ON WALLS DURING THE 1990 CAMPAIGN AND AFTER THE ELECTION OF ARISTIDE

LAVALAS SE LAMOU
(Lavalas is love)

TITID AK NOU SE LAVALAS
(Titid with us is Lavalas[1])

TITID POU SENK AN
(Titid for five years)

VIV 7 FEVRIYE 1991
(Long live February 7, 1991[2])

AK TITID KÈ'M PA SOTE
(With Titid my heart is not pounding)

MAKOUT PA LADANN
(No Macoutes allowed[3])

ABA MAKOUT NAN LACHANM
(Down with Macoutes in parliament)

VIV DEMOKRASI POPILÈ
(Long live popular democracy)

SE PA LAJAN, NON, SE VOLONTE
(It's not money, no, it's our will)

PÈP VANYAN SE PÈP KI OGANIZE
(A strong people is an organized people)

LIT PÈP-LA FEK KÒMANSE
(The people's struggle has just begun)

MEN NAN LA MEN, ANNOU SOVE PEYI NOU-AN
(Hand in hand, let's save our country)

MEN AMPIL CHAY PA LOU
(With many hands, the burden is not heavy[4])

ANSANM N'AP REBATI AYITI
(Together we will rebuild Haiti)

YON SÈL, NOU FÈB
ANSANM, NOU FÒ
ANSANM, ANSANM, NOU SE LAVALAS
(Alone, we are weak;
Together, we are strong;
Together, together we are the flood)

WORDS OFTEN FOUND PAINTED ON WALLS

AYITI	(Haiti)
LIBÈTE	(Liberty)
JISTIS	(Justice)
CHANGMAN	(Change)
LANMOU	(Love)
LINYON	(Union)
KÈPOZE	(Calm Heart)
DIYITE	(Dignity)

PROVERBS

Bat chen-an, men tann met li.
(Beat the dog, but wait for its master.)

Rayi chen, di dan'l blanch.
(You hate the dog, but you have to admit its teeth are white.)

Chen gen kat pat, men se yon sel wout li fe.
(The dog has four paws, but it can only go in one direction.)

Lè yo vle touye yon chen, yo di'l fou.
(When they want to kill a dog, they say its crazy.)

Lè vant chat plen, bounda rat anmè.
(When the cat's stomach is full, the rat's behind is bitter.)

Chat chode nan dlo cho—li wè dlo frèt, li pè.
(The cat scalded by hot water is afraid when it sees cold water.)

Se chat kay k'ap manje poul kay.
(Your own house cat is the one who is eating your chickens.)

Pa janm mete chat veye mantèg.
(Never leave the cat to guard the butter.)

Bourik chaje pa kanpe.
(A loaded donkey does not stop.[5])

Ou pa rele "Fèmen baryè" lè chwal finn pase.
(You can't yell "Close the gate" when the horse has already escaped.)

Manjè'd ze pa konn doulè manman poul.
(The egg-eater does not know the pain of the mother hen.)

Kote y'ap plimen kodenn, poul pa ri.
(In the place where they pluck the turkey's feathers, the chicken does not laugh.)

Plimen poul-la, men pa kite'l rele.
(Pluck the chicken, but don't let it squawk.)

Avantaj kòk se nan zepron'l li ye.
(The advantage of a cock is its claws.)

Mennen koulèv lekòl pa anyen. Se fè'l chita ki rèd.
(It's nothing to lead the snake to school. Making it sit down is the hard part.)

Se lè koulèv mouri, ou wè longè'l.
(It's when the snake dies that you see its real length.)

Petit tig se tig.
(The child of a tiger is a tiger.[6])

Makak karese piti li jouk li touye'l.
(The monkey caresses its child until it kills it.)

Malfini manke ou, li pa bliye ou.
(The hawk missed you, but it didn't forget about you.)

Tout bèt jennen mòde.
(All cornered animals bite.)

Kay koule twompe solèy, men li pa twompe lapli.
(The leaky house can fool the sun, but it can't fool the rain.)

Nanpwen cho ki pa vinn frèt.
(There is nothing that is hot that doesn't eventually become cold.)

Dan pouri gen fos sou bannan mi.
(Rotten teeth are strong against ripe bananas.)

Lè dlo ap desann, ou pa foure pye ou.
(When the river is rising, you don't put your foot in it.)

M'pat manje pwa, m'pap ka poupou pwa.
(I didn't eat beans, I cannot shit beans.)

Moun sòt se levenman.
(A stupid person is a real event.)

Nan mitan avèg, boyn se wa.
(In the midst of blind people, a one-eyed person is king.)

Kapab pa soufri.
(He who has means does not suffer.)

Milat pov se nèg, nèg rich se milat.
(A poor mulatto is a black man, a rich black man is a mulatto.)

Lè ou malere, tout bagay samble ou.
(When you are poor, everything can be blamed on you.)

Malere volè, gran nèg pèdi lajan.
(A poor man is blamed for stealing, but a rich man merely "loses" money.)

Bel dan pa di zanmi.
(Beautiful teeth doesn't mean he's your friend.)

Se lè ou pase maladi, ou konn remed.
(When you are finished being sick, you know the remedy.)

Se apre batay ou konte blese.
(It's after the battle that you count the wounded.)

Bay kou, bliye. Pote mak, sonje.
(The one who gives the blow forgets. The one who gets hurt remembers.)

Kreyon Pèp (Bondye) pa gen gonm.
The people's (or God's) pencil has no eraser.

Wè jodi, men sonje demen.
(See today, but remember tomorrow's coming.)

M'fin mouri, m'pa pè santi.
(I'm already dead, so I'm not afraid of smelling.)

Dèyè mòn gen mòn.
(Beyond mountains, more mountains.)

Wè pa wè, lantèman pou katrè.
(No matter what, the funeral is at four o'clock.)

NOTES

1. Titid—from *petit*—is an affectionate name for Aristide.
2. February 7, 1991 is the date of Aristide's inauguration.
3. This slogan, and the one that follows it, refer to an article in the 1987 Constitution barring former Tonton Macoutes or anyone associated with the Duvalier dictatorship from holding public office.
4. This was reportedly Aristide's response to then-U.S. Ambassador to Haiti Alvin P. Adams, who said, when Aristide announced his candidacy, "*Apre bal, tanbou lou*" (After the dance, the drums are heavy), which some interpreted as a warning.
5. The same Ambassador Adams had earlier quoted this proverb in reference to the electoral process. Thereafter, Adams was popularly referred to in Haiti as "the loaded donkey."
6. This proverb appeared, in the spring of 1994, in a Port-au-Prince newspaper beneath a picture of Raoul Cedras's father, a well-known Tonton Macoute.

5

JEAN-BERTRAND ARISTIDE

WORDS OF DELIVERANCE
Amy Wilentz

Amy Wilentz travelled to Haiti days before the fall of Jean-Claude Duvalier, and documented the subsequent waves of popular uprising and brutal backlash in *The Rainy Season: Haiti After Duvalier*. She also met Father Jean-Bertrand Aristide, then priest of St.-Jean-Bosco Church in Port-au-Prince.

┐

Aristide's face was not a face to forget: hollow-cheeked, goggle-eyed, wide-mouthed. The foreign journalists called him diminutive, bespectacled. "His Holiness" was the nickname Harry and others used, though not in print. It was hard to believe that this small person, who took up virtually no room at all, could bring thousands of people to their feet and lead Port-au-Prince's slums with a wave of his hand.

As one of the few prominent people in Port-au-Prince who had stuck their necks out in Jean-Claude's waning days, publicly expressing the growing discontent and disgust with Duvalierism, Aristide had helped to create in the capital the same climate of unrest and protest that already existed in the countryside, and that made the dictator's departure necessary. By the end of Jean-Claude's days, Aristide was the most visible of the many young progressive priests and nuns—together called Ti Legliz, the Little Church—who had been organizing peasants and slum-dwellers since the late 1970's. . . .

Aristide preached a brand of liberation theology that pleased no one except his extended congregation: the poor in the slums, the peasants who heard him on Radio Hāiti-Inter and Radio Soleil, a scattering of young jobless lower-middle class youths with no future in the country, and a few liberals among the Haitian bourgeoisie and the exile community. He had all the right enemies. The Army hated him, because he mentioned colonels and sergeants and lieutenants by name in his sermons, and excoriated them for the abuses they committed against the people in their regions. "Namphy," and a flick of the wrist: onto the garbage heap goes the president. "Régala." Another flick. The American Embassy hated him because he held the United States and its economic system responsible for much of Haiti's economic woe, and thus for the misery of her people, his congregation. The Church hierarchy feared him because he did not often miss a chance to include them in his list of enemies of the people, and they were jealous of him, too, for the loyal following he had attracted, and for the attention he received from foreign journalists. The very wealthy few in Haiti despised him also, because he accused them of betraying their countrymen and stated baldly that the system by which they enriched themselves was corrupt and criminal, and an offense against their fellow Haitians. He frightened them all with the violent honesty of his sermons. And the worst part was that he had a reputation for being Haiti's foremost biblical scholar, and was always ready with a quote from the gospels to support his message. His targets did not like to hear Christ quoted against them.

Aristide's message was doubly frightening, because, try as they might, his enemies could not properly accuse him of preaching Communism. He gave sermons in which he lauded the sanctity of private property. "The peasant's land," he said, "the land that he and his family have worked for generations, that is his private property; no one else has the right to take it. The shopkeeper's little store, that he bought fair and square with his little savings, and from which he makes a decent income, that is his private property. But the class of landowners and the bourgeoisie who live off the corrupt system we have in Haiti, who do nothing, who give nothing back to the country, who steal what little wealth we have and put it into banks in foreign countries, their private property is the property of the peasants. Their private property is Haitian property, it does not belong to them. It should be taken from them."

Like other liberation theologians in Latin America, who use Jesus' teachings to raise the political consciousness of the poor, Aristide tried to make connections between the struggle of the Haitian people for freedom and what liberation theologians see as the struggle of Jesus for the liberation of Jerusalem.

"What weds the movement within the church to the movement within Haitian society as a whole," he said," is liberation theology, which has filtered into the youth of our country, which invigorates them, which purifies their blood, which teaches these youths that either you are a Christian or you are not. And if you are a Christian, you cannot allow what you are seeing to happen without saying something, because if you say nothing, you will be sinning by your silence. You will be sinning by your complicity. So in order to avoid that sin, which is a mortal sin, we refuse to accept what is happening. We cast off corruption."

"If you're a Christian, you cannot accept to continue the Macoute corruption in this country. Well, then, you are obliged to take historic risks. You are obliged to participate in this historic movement of liberation theology. In other words, the resurrection of an entire people is occurring right now. It is liberation theology that is lifting our children up against a corrupt generation, against a mentality of the Church and the society which sees corruption as the comfortable norm, and which one cannot stomach if one is truly a Christian. It is the history of the Jews and Jesus Christ that we ourselves as Christians are living through now. We have become the subjects of our own history. We refuse from now on to be the objects of that history."

When Aristide begins to talk, he no longer seems small. He leans forward and fixes you with a look from behind those glasses that makes you squirm and wish you could escape it. Unlike many Haitian politicians, and unlike many Haitian men when they talk about politics, he doesn't shout in conversation. He seems to give thought to your questions. But the timbre of his voice is intense, and his imagery is arresting. "Port-au-Prince," he said to me, the day after Jean-Claude Duvalier left, "face it, for years, forever, it has been the headquarters of corruption. It was the regime's central nervous system: Port-au-Prince speaks, and the order goes out, and the provinces react. The extremities tremble, they twitch, and people, the Duvaliers' enemies, die. That's how Duvalier organized it, Papa Doc, I mean.

"But then, in the months before Jean-Claude left, you had a situation where, suddenly, Port-au-Prince isn't giving any orders. Where Jean-Claude and his people don't know what to do, and can't get anyone to follow orders. Where they don't even know what order to give. Where the extremities, the provinces, are suddenly not responding. Instead, they're turning against the cerebral cortex, eating away at the nerve tissue, exploding. First the provinces revolted, then, finally, after far too long, Port-au-Prince. When Port-au-Prince started to move against Jean-Claude, that's when the Americans realized he had to go."

I always liked Aristide. Almost everyone did, if they had the chance to meet him. He would say brutal things, and yet the most decent Haitian matrons turned around and kissed him afterward. His colleagues in the Ti Legliz ranted about his irresponsibility behind his back, but then when they were with him their anger dissolved into a kind of mushy affection, as though he were an incredibly cute kid who had just broken a precious heirloom. . . .

In the sacristy one Sunday after mass, a year after Duvalier's downfall, Antoine, the blind beggar who comes by every week, puts out a hand in front of him and leans on his cane, a golf club, for support. A woman guides his searching hand toward Aristide's slight shoulder. The little girl whom Aristide is holding in his arms looks at Antoine over the priest's shoulder. "Five years old," Aristide is saying to her. It's her birthday, and already she is almost half his size. He kisses her lightly, and she pulls back her head to look into his eyes. The beggar's hand on Aristide's shoulder is becoming more insistent; without turning, the priest reaches back and takes Antoine's wrist in his hand, encircles it with his fingers. He puts the girl down and goes on talking to her mother. A knot of people is closing in on him. The small room is full, with people's heads sticking in at the two doors and others looking in through the windows.

Watching the circle of people from a few yards away, you wouldn't know that the priest is at its center; you have to push through to see him. A young man saunters forward and through the crowd, nudging the girl and her mother away. He puts a heavy arm around Aristide's shoulders and another over the priest's head, holding Aristide in a lock grip and cupping his ear. He starts whispering into it, and Aristide nods, and nods, smiles, shakes his head, says, "No, no, no," a small staccato sound full of disapproval, puts his free arm around the young man's neck and whispers something back to him that makes the young man tremble with laughter for a moment and give the priest an affectionate shove on the back of the head.

A young, smiling woman is waiting at the edge of the circle to talk to Aristide, watching this performance with her arms folded. He notices her suddenly and lifts his chin toward the young man, half in acknowledgment, half dismissal. He moves toward the girl, she takes him by the lapels of his shirt, he puts an arm around her waist, and they start whispering. A French reporter tries to interrupt, but Aristide, without looking up, puts out his palm to ward off the interruption. "In a moment," the young man, who is still standing by, says to the French reporter. The room is hot with bodies. Three Ti-Legliz priests are waiting in the doorway for the ritual to end; there is a meeting scheduled for noon.

A commotion begins, it seems to erupt right beneath the feet of the three priests in the doorway. Half naked, Waldeck and four more urchins burst into the room, tumbling through the door in a comic fistfight. They scramble through the circle and then around and through Aristide's legs, looking for protection. The girl moves away, laughing. Antoine the beggar leans into the priest, unsure of what is happening. The boy keeps dodging in among the crowd, and Aristide swats at them absently while he talks to Antoine. The boys use Aristide's legs as a shield. Waldeck holds on to a thigh and peers out from between the priest's legs, daring his enemies to attack him in that well-defended position.

In the midst of the tumult, Aristide reaches into his pocket and takes out a few bills that he always has ready for Antoine each Sunday. He says a few more words to the beggar as he hands him the money—"Do you have enough to eat?" "How is your health?" "Is someone taking care of you?"—and then grasps Antoine's shoulders with both hands, making a final connection and at the same time redirecting him toward the door. Aristide turns away to find a small boy hurtling toward him, the edge of a razor blade flashing in a little angry fist. He grabs the boy's arm as the razor is about to come down across Waldeck's face, takes the blade out of his fist, breaks it in two throws it out the window.

"I didn't realize you were armed," he says. The boy laughs, all the boys laugh, the whole room repeats the phrase over and over, until the priests in the doorway seem to be saying it, too, and laughing in spite of their increasing impatience. The story of the razor blade will become an anecdote. But Aristide has already forgotten it. He puts his hand on Waldeck's head and starts up a conversation in Spanish with two nuns, liberation theologians on a visit from somewhere in Central America. Waldeck stands there, silent for once and smiling, the priest patting his head. He puts an arm around Aristide's leg and listens to the conversation. The other boys stop hitting each other for a few minutes. They want to hear Aristide speaking the funny language. He goes on and on, the nuns listen and reply and listen, the three Haitian priests linger in the doorway, shifting from foot to foot.

Waldeck, bored, gets out from under Aristide's hand, scoots around the feet of the French reporter and taps at his legs, punches his thighs. "*Fè foto m*," he says, punching. Take my picture. The French reporter looks at the priest for help, but Aristide responds by raising both his hands in a gesture of humorous helplessness. Behind him, his white robe, hanging now from a rack in front of the slatted-glass window, shakes slightly in the infrequent breeze. A simple white cassock, swaying in the background, with "*Parol Delivrans*" embroidered down one side of the chasuble, meaning Words of Deliverance, and down the other, "Haiti.". . .

PART 3
THE CRISIS

Bel dan pa di zanmi.
(Beautiful teeth doesn't mean he's your friend.)
—Haitian proverb

INTRODUCTION

Haiti is, by far, the Western Hemisphere's poorest country. With a per capita gross domestic product of $218, it stands at the level of poor African and Asian nations, not poor Caribbean and Latin American ones. Similarly, on the United Nations' Human Development Index, a device designed to measure standards of living rather than just income, Haiti ranks at the bottom of the hemisphere, resting firmly in the misery levels of the world's worst-off countries.

The roots of Haiti's poverty run deep, to its colonial history, its 200-year dependence on the major Western industrial powers and its narrowly-based oligarchy. In the latter half of the twentieth century, the oligarchy has maintained its tight control of the economy with the sometimes implicit, sometimes explicit—but always crucial—support of the United States.

One of the most important manifestations of that support has been aid from the United States, especially that allocated through the U.S. Agency for International Development (U.S. AID). Allocated for the overt purpose of eradicating Haiti's awful poverty (which it has dismally failed to do), the aid has in fact provided support for Haiti's elites—but it also has played a critical role in directing the Haitian economy in line with U.S. multinational corporate interests.

With the Cold War over and communism gone as a rationale for U.S. foreign policy in the Caribbean and in Latin America, these economic interests were more clearly exposed than ever. The economic dictates of the New World Order essentially envisioned transforming the economies of nations like Haiti from dependence on bare subsistence agriculture to dependence on modern-day, export-oriented assembly industries, which would provide a cheap and docile workforce for American corporations.

After the departure of Jean-Claude Duvalier, the U.S. had hoped to promote in Haiti, as elsewhere in the hemisphere, some measure of "power sharing" between civilian leaders and the military. A new government set up along these lines would, presumably, deliver some small measure of democracy—at least on paper—while continuing to cooperate with the United States' economic agenda. Washington had invested millions of dollars over several decades in reforming and cleaning up the army so it could help rule civil society. But instead of a reformed, civic minded army, the U.S. found a corrupt, reactionary military suddenly confronted by a mass popular movement, which would coalesce around Father Jean-Bertrand Aristide. The popular "flood" that brought Aristide to power in the 1990 elections was in part a reaction against foreign intervention, and especially against the American-conceived economic programs that were attempting to reorganize Haitian society away from its traditional rural, peasant life. This popular democractic movement and its leader—the first democratically elected president in the history of Haiti—threatened the underlying order on which the U.S. had so long depended.

So from their appearance on the political scene, the U.S. had no great affection for Aristide or the Lavalas movement, which lay outside U.S. control. Even Aristide's modest economic reforms—for instance, his move to raise the minimum wage from 25 cents to 37 cents an hour—were opposed by U.S. AID.

While the coup that drove Aristide into exile was an embarassement to the United States, both the Bush administration and later the Clinton administration seemed less than anxious to see him restored to full power. Following the coup, the U.S. therefore set about paying lip service to the democratic process which had elected Aristide, while at the same time engaging in a broad behind-the-scenes effort to discredit him. American-led diplomatic efforts, including the much-touted Governor's Island Accords, appeared geared toward arranging the long-desired power-sharing arrangement with the military, with a weakened Aristide as a temporary transitional president to some far more agreeable regime (say, a government run by the former World Bank technocrat Marc Bazin, whom the Americans had supported in the 1990 election). When Aristide resisted such compromises, he was widely accused of "intransigence."

But the American srategy fell apart when the Haitian military grew ever more brutal and audacious, refusing to cooperate with the dictates of Governor's Island. And as time goes on, the disingenuousness of U.S. policy has become harder and harder to disguise.

This part of The Haiti Files begins with a series of articles and documents that seek to "decode" American diplomatic strategy toward Haiti following the coup. It goes on to examine U.S. AID programs in Haiti, and their long-standing efforts to reorganize the Haitian political economy. Finally, it documents the seldom-addressed involvement of the Haitian military—including high-ranking members of the coup regime—in international drug trafficking, and describes the effects of American dissemblance and betrayal with regard to human rights and refugee policy.

┐

1

THE COUP AND
U.S. FOREIGN POLICY

THE UNMAKING OF A PRESIDENT
Kim Ives

Kim Ives of *Häiti Progrès*, the Brooklyn-based Haitian weekly, sets out the details of the United States' dealings with Aristide following the October 1991 coup. Writing in the North American Congress on Latin America's journal, *Report on the Americas* (January/February 1994), Ives argues that the essence of U.S. strategy has been to drive Aristide to strike a deal with the coup leaders and invite military intervention.

¬

On the afternoon of October 2, 1991, two days after the September 30th coup d'état against Haitian President Jean-Bertrand Aristide, the Organization of American States (OAS) held an extraordinary emergency session at its headquarters in Washington, D.C. The immense marble "Hall of the Americas," normally serene with its dignified flags and soaring pillars, was crammed with dignitaries, diplomats and journalists straining to see the podium where the ousted president and a long succession of Latin American ministers spoke. The air was electric with TV lights, camera flashes, and official outrage. The distinct strains of bull-horns and choruses from the hundreds of Haitians demonstrating their support for President Aristide outside the building added to the excitement within.

A hush fell over the hall when it was addressed by U.S. Secretary of State James Baker. The slightest nuance in the U.S. position would be more weighty than the combined bombast of the OAS's other 33 member nations. "This junta is illegal," Baker solemnly declared. Until President Aristide's government is restored, this junta will be treated as a pariah, without friends, without support, and without a future. This coup must not and will not succeed." The hall gave up thunderous applause. "It is imperative," he went on, "that we agree for the sake of Haitian democracy and the cause of democracy throughout the hemisphere, to act collectively to defend the legitimate government of President Aristide."

"We want to see President Aristide returned to power," President Bush echoed two days later after a 20-minute discussion and a photo-op with Aristide at the White House. In those early hours of the coup, to the surprise of many, the U.S. government seemed to unequivocally champion the return to power of the anti-imperialist liberation theologian priest. The coup's days seemed numbered.

But, over the weekend of October 5 and 6, the focus of U.S. government reproach shifted 180 degrees from the coup d'état to President Aristide's human rights record. The slow strangulation of Haiti's first democratically elected president and his nationalist program had begun.

Most likely, Baker and Bush forcefully supported Aristide's return in that first week after the coup so as not to challenge the shock and indignation of Haitians and other Latin Americans against so brazen and illegal an ouster. But, in concert with the press, the U.S. government soon began tempering its call. "It is the rule of democracy that we support," White House press secretary Marlin Fitzwater announced on October 7. "We don't know [if Aristide will return to power] in the sense that the government in his country is changing and considering any number of different possibilities." Fitzwater stressed that during President Aristide's near eight months in office—from a triumphant inauguration on February 7, 1991 to the start of the coup on September 29—he had relied on "mob rule," a theme which was bleated in dutiful unison throughout the mainstream media. "Returning President Aristide to Haiti is going to be difficult for reasons to which he himself has greatly contributed," asserted an October 6 *Washington Post* editorial. "The president is a hero to the desperate people who live in the slums of Port-au-Prince . . . He has organized them into an instrument of real terror . . . He has left the country deeply polarized between his followers and the substantial numbers of people who have reason to fear them."[1]

The October 7 *New York Times* explained the dumbfounding rash of nationwide press reports attacking the beleaguered Haitian president: "American officials are beginning to quietly disclose a thick notebook detailing accounts of human rights abuses that took place during Father Aristide's rule" which "jeopardized his moral authority and popularity." This "thick notebook" of abuses was compiled by Jean-Jacques Honorat, whose human rights outfit, CHADEL, was a recipient of National Endowment for Democracy (NED) funding to the tune of about $40,000 a year.[2] Within a week, Honorat was appointed by the military-controlled parliament to be the first post-coup prime minister.

Despite the State Department-driven media campaign targeting Aristide's human rights record—which, Aristide correctly asserted, contained not a single case of government-endorsed or government-encouraged vigilante violence—international support and Haitian community mobilization remained very strong. On October 2, OAS ministers met late into the night drafting and adopting a resolution to embargo and diplomatically isolate the renegade regime. On October 11, over 100,000 Haitians marched six miles from central Brooklyn to a rally in downtown Manhattan, all but shutting down the Wall

Street area. The multitude then marched through rain another four miles up-town to the United Nations, where the 166 members of the General Assembly were unanimously voting a resolution which bolstered the OAS embargo and branded as "illegal" the junta of coup leader Lt. Gen. Raoul Cédras and his confederates. The document also dismissed as illegal any puppet governments that the military might set up.

Not until November 5, almost a month later, did President Bush decree U.S. compliance with the trade and oil embargo recommended by the UN and OAS resolutions. The embargo, however, was tough only on paper. The U.S. government never enforced it against the coup-makers. The restrictions were jauntily breached by exporters and importers not only from Europe, but from the United States and Latin America too. In Port-au-Prince, rich families who had helped finance the coup made fortunes selling goods at inflated prices in the pseudo-black market. Oil tankers from Europe soon replaced those from Venezuela and Mexico. The rocky dirt route from Jimani on the Dominican border to Port-au-Prince became so travelled by trucks carrying fuel, arms, and other merchandise from the Dominican Republic that the coup-makers resurfaced it in smooth blacktop, making it far and away Haiti's best road.

As the months passed, the completely porous embargo became a symbol of the U.S. government's contempt for Aristide's return. But Aristide clung to the embargo, mainly because he was unprepared or unwilling to choose either of his other two alternatives: U.S. military intervention or popular revolution. Over the two years since the coup, the mass movement behind President Aristide has gradually split into two distinct currents adhering to Aristide's diametrically opposed choices. Aristide, perhaps unwillingly, has chosen the path of calling for military intervention.

By forging a coalition between the popular movement and the traditional bourgeoisie, Aristide soundly defeated the U.S.-baptized candidate in the 1990 presidential elections. But rather than judging his electoral victory as a fluke, Aristide has tried to universalize the tactic into a political strategy of trying to beat the system at its own game. The question: Has the U.S. government lured Aristide into a new, hopelessly rigged game by letting him think he can win again? In the high-stakes match, Aristide has seen his strength and resources whittled down by time and compromise. Throughout, the essence of the U.S. strategy has been to drive Aristide to surrender to Duvalierism and imperialism by striking a deal with the coup leaders and inviting foreign military intervention.

Aristide's circle of advisors and diplomats, particularly since the coup, are almost all drawn from the democratic sector of the traditional bourgeoisie. With time, Aristide has even turned toward the more conservative and "pragmatic" of this group, which better understand and conform to the U.S. optique. The traditional bourgeoisie, rather than calling on the Haitian masses to defend their nascent revolution after the coup, sought to compromise with the ruling powers in Haiti and the United States.

The democratic sector ridiculed the popular sector's revolutionary goals as utopian and unrealistic. They said a non-violent settlement could be negotiated using the influence of North American and European powers. Even though the United States had been wary of, if not obsessed with Aristide the liberation theologian, the Lavalas bourgeoisie thought they could sell Aristide the states-man to the United States as the man who could make Haiti safe for investment. "The United States is best served by a democratic and stable Haiti which is able to pursue economic and social development for its entire population," said Haitian Foreign Minister Claudette Werleigh, then with the Washington Office on Haiti, before Congress in July, 1993. "The Haitian people are aware of the great power of the United States in the world. We ask you to use that power to pressure for the resistance of our constitutional government."[3] Flowing from this logic, the recourse to foreign military intervention always lurked—unspoken and denied—just below the surface of the bourgeoisie's agenda.

From the very start of the coup, the U.S. press also raised the "option" of U.S. intervention. On October 3, the *New York Times*' Thomas Friedman complained that the OAS had not gone far enough in its October 2 emergency session. "The question of intervention has bedeviled and paralyzed the organization for the 40 years of its existence," Friedman wrote, apparently unaware of OAS participation in the 1965 Dominican Republic invasion and acquiescence to numerous unilateral U.S. forays from the Bay of Pigs in 1962 to Grenada in 1983 and Panama in 1989. On October 6, the *Washington Post* opined that the only way to guarantee Aristide's "respect for human rights and for a kind of democracy that goes beyond mob rule" was to send "a peace-keeping force sponsored by the OAS" to provide "a lot of Haitians . . . assurance that Mr. Aristide is not going to turn his mob on them."

Meanwhile, the Bush Administration quickly sought to force Aristide to bargain with the coup leaders. Aristide initially refused any deals with Cédras, saying the general and other coup leaders had no alternative but to go into exile or face justice upon his return. Although on the defensive about his human rights record, Aristide remained confident in his ability to play the loopholes in the U.S. agenda, as he had with the elections. The key loophole was that the United States had to support his return and oppose the coup or else it would give a green light to generals throughout Latin America to start a new era of coup d'états against civilian regimes which were still servicing U.S. interests. Underestimating the chasms between the U.S. government's official rhetoric and its true intent, Aristide took his first step down the slippery slope of negotiations.

On October 4 and 5, 1992, an OAS delegation was dispatched to Port-au-Prince supposedly to convince Cédras that resistance was futile and to give up. Instead, the U.S. Embassy set up a tribunal condemning Aristide. "The

United States was ignoring supporters of the elected government," according to French Ambassador Raphael Dufour who was barred from the OAS meetings by then U.S. Ambassador Alvin Adams. The OAS delegation, said Dufour, only "met with a solid line of politicians and businessmen who have been opposed to Aristide . . . I'm not certain the delegation got all the points of view and the view of the Haitian people. The Haitian people are dying under the bullets of the military. Those are the ones who haven't been heard from."[4]

The delegation returned to Washington on October 6 to chastise Aristide for his political behavior and to advise negotiations with Haitian parliamentarians. Aristide could have referred the OAS delegation to the resolution taken by its own October 2 session, and to that taken on October 11 by the UN, rejecting all dealings with confederates of the coup. But Aristide instead assumed a defensive posture, hoping to counteract the media message that he was a political bully.

The parliamentary delegation Aristide met with in Cartagena, Colombia in November, 1991, was almost exclusively made up of coup supporters. Also in attendance, though uninvited, was U.S. Ambassador Adams. The parliamentarians were looking to buy time for the coup to consolidate its grip over a resentful and resistant population. They also hoped to negotiate a lifting of the embargo.

The parliamentarians, with U.S. support, presented an agreement to lift the embargo in exchange for more negotiations, but the document acknowledged neither Aristide's presidency nor his return to Haiti. Aristide had walked into a trap. He refused to sign the document and denounced the "bad faith" of the parliamentarians. They in turn, along with Adams, branded him as an "intransigent," a term which would become familiar to negotiation followers in the months ahead. After offering an olive branch, Aristide was now accused of blocking resolution of the crisis. He had given the pro-coup parliamentarians the moral legitimacy to continue their diplomatic sabotage, when he might have been better off shunning them for their treason.

In November and December, 1992, U.S. Ambassador Adams and OAS special envoy Augusto Ramirez Ocampo, a Colombian diplomat, increased their dealings with the pro-coup parliamentarianism. However, once again, the concessions being formulated were to come from Aristide.

The office of prime minister became the key bargaining chip in their negotiations. It is Haiti's most powerful executive post under the 1987 Constitution, the president being only the formal head of state with power to make appointments and nominations. Reeling under the U.S. media and U.S. government assault on his Administration, Aristide almost immediately sacrificed his popular prime minister, René Préval. This was a giant and crippling concession.

After rejecting Aristide's proposals for compromise candidades, Adams and Ocampo gave Aristide an ultimatum to accept either Marc Bazin for prime minister, or Communist Party head René Théodore, branding Aristide's re-luctance to do so intransigence. Citing anonymous "diplomats," the Decem-ber 28 *New York Times* described what would happen if Aristide did not com-ply: "Failing an agreement...new elections are likely to be held and eventually, the consensus around the hemispheric embargo imposed on Haiti for the last three months will dissipate." Already several tankers had docked in Haiti, giving the putschists ample reserves of oil.

"This is not diplomacy, but just strong-arm tactics," said Paul Dejean, a close Aristide advisor, who heads a human rights group in Haiti. "It is the dic-tatorship of big powers which think they can impose any solution they want."[5]

On January 8, Aristide buckled under the pressure and nominated René Théodore. Despite his Communist credentials, Théodore had long since foresaken any revolutionary principles. He had been a fierce opponent of Aristide and others in the popular sector both before and after the December 1990 election. The moderate Miami-based weekly *Häiti en Marche* described him as the "Theodore bomb" who was part of a "plan carefully conceived on the banks of the Potomac and at Langley."[6] In Theodore, the United States had the perfect combination of a nominal leftist and an Aristide opponent.

"The majority of the people do not want Théodore as prime minister, and their opinion is also mine," said Willy Romelus, the progressive Archbishop of Jeremie, in a December 23 radio broadcast. Numerous statements emanat-ing from the popular sector warned that Aristide was being outflanked and driven into unjustifiable compromises.

The apprehensions of the popular sector of the Lavalas movement were supported by the revelations of a document which was leaked in October by a Haitian U.S.-Embassy security guard, who was assassinated at his home by sol-diers a few days later. [See "The 'Embassy' Memo."] The U.S. Embassy never protested the murder. The document was reportedly written by an anonymous counselor in the U.S. Embassy at the request of Army chief Gen. Raoul Cédras, Senate leader Déjean Bélizaire, and Jean-Jacques Honorat, the first *de facto* prime minister. It outlined a strategy for undermining Aristide's reinstatement. "The United States would agree to recognize a new prime minister and unblock the Haitian government assets in the United States," the document said. "If Aristide comes back, it could not be earlier than a few months from now . . . and only so that he can be sent back, destitute, into exile shortly thereafter . . . The Prime Minister will become the real power in the government." The document also notes that "what is needed presently is a broad, sustained, and very discrete approach from the U.S. policymakers and the media which will counteract and nullify the propaganda of the Lavalas organization." Within a few months, the recommendations outlined in the secret document would become painfully obvious as the broad strategy of the Bush Administration.

Even though the United States tried to smoothly phase in Théodore as prime minister, unruliness from the Duvalierists threatened U.S. plans. On January 25, Duvalierist thugs attacked a meeting being held by Théodore, executing his bodyguard. The oligarchy did not want Aristide's return under any conditions, and Théodore's nomination seemed to be a step in that direction.

The attack almost scuttled the process. Adams was recalled to Washington, and once again the United States began blustering. "Some type of military action might be necessary," warned Howard French in a January 29 article in the *New York Times*. French cited an anonymous American diplomat who predicted that "ultimately the wrath of God will fall"—that is, U.S. military action which could range "from a special-forces type of operation aimed at quickly arresting several officers to a full-scale occupation of the country."

The toughness, however, remained talk. In deeds, the Bush Administration was largely lifting the three-month-old trade embargo against the *de facto* regime. The Treasury Department began to allow shipping by assembly industries with plants in Haiti. On February 4, State Department spokeswoman Margaret Tutweiler tried to sell the measure as a "fine-tuning" of the embargo, arguing that "the sanctions on the assembly sector largely affect innocent Haitians only and have no serious impact on those behind the coup."

"The State Department's decision was prompted by complaints from American companies that relied on Haiti as a source of cheap labor to produce apparel and electronics items," explained the February 7 *Washington Post*. Foreign investors' associations like the Washington-based Caribbean Latin American Action (CLAA) and former Asst. Secretary of State Elliott Abrams lobbied hard behind the scenes. "The Defense Department, . . . convinced the exodus of boat people was largely economic, [was] quickly receptive to CLAA's arguments," the article reported. "The White House also was receptive, especially the office of Vice President Quayle, who heads the Council on Competitiveness."

After Aristide's reluctant acceptance of Théodore for prime minister, the United States began pushing hard for a meeting in Washington. The result was the February 23 signing in Washington of the "Protocol of Accord," the first major agreement to emerge from negotiations. The document was greeted with satisfaction from the U.S. State Department, horror from the popular sector, and contempt from the Duvalierists.

The key elements of the accord were: 1) an amnesty for the Army and other authors of the coup; 2) respect of parliamentary legislation ratified after the coup, which included Cédras' appointment as head of the Army through 1994; and 3) the lifting of the embargo "immediately after the ratification of the prime minister and the inauguration of the government of national consensus." Although it acknowledged Aristide's presidential title, the accord fixed no date for the return of President Aristide.

This ambiguity was of course the element on which coup partisans sought to play. Théodore had said in early February, 1992 that he agreed with Aristide's "political return" to Haiti, but that his "physical return, that is something else." He projected more than one year. Pro-coup Senator Serge Joseph affirmed that it "was not at all a question of President Aristide's return as some have said."[7] Even detached observers said that Aristide had given away a lot for nothing in return.

But within days, the Washington Protocol was defunct. President Aristide interpreted the accord differently than the U.S. State Department and even many of his own advisors. He asserted that there would be in fact no amnesty for Cédras, since "common criminals" were excluded from the amnesty.

The U.S. government and mainstream press cried foul, saying that Aristide was backing out of the accord. In a New York area radio broadcast on March 1, Aristide urged the Haitian community in the United States to not succumb to the "disinformation machine" which characterized him as reneging on the agreement and to "maintain your mobilization and resistance, without which we could not apply pressure at all."

Meanwhile in Haiti, the Duvalierists were taking no chances. In parliament, hard-line deputies and senators brandished revolvers and started fistfights during the sessions which led up to the final non-ratification of the document. Even parliamentarians who had signed the document disowned it, saying, like Senator Eddy Dupiton, that it was just a "proposal." In addition, the Duvalierist-recaptured Supreme Court ruled the agreement to be unconstitutional.

The Duvalierists, having effectively torpedoed the Washington Protocol, went on the offensive. They calculated, with good reason, that Washington was not really enthusiastic about Aristide's return and that they should offer an alternative. This was the origin of the "tripartite meeting" in late May and early June among de facto Prime Minister Jean-Jacques Honorat, de facto President Joseph Nerette, pro-coup parliamentarians, and the Army. The result was the putschists' Villa d'Accueil accord, which called for "a government of consensus," code for a power-sharing arrangement between the Lavalas coalition and hard-line Duvalierists.

The person the putschists chose to head this remodeled civilian front government was one they were sure the United States could not resist: Marc Bazin. He was ratified as the new de facto prime minister on June 10. Bazin, the putschists hoped, would be able to get the embargo lifted and soften up the United States to make Aristide strike a deal for the "government of consensus."

This marked the end of the first phase of the coup d'état. The dirty work of terror and consolidation had been done. Now it was time to try to sell it to the international community.

Until this time, the conflict between the two currents in the Lavalas—bourgeois and popular—remained mostly friction, as the former called for negotiations and the latter for mobilization. Aristide sought to balance the two strategies, saying, with some justice, that they were symbiotic. However,

Aristide, surrounded mostly by advisors from the democratic sector, leaned more towards the bourgeoisie's scheme. He remained basically on the defensive, always trying to seem as reasonable and as inoffensive as possible to the U.S. government. He thus sank ever deeper into a swamp of bargaining and concessions, leaving the people waiting for resolution from talks and never taking the offensive in the streets and mountains.

The logic of reconciliation led inevitably to direct negotiations between Aristide and Cédras. This is what the bourgeoisie counseled, and the popular sector opposed. And this was the beginning of the real division in the Lavalas.

After the Villa d'Accueil accord, the Lavalas bourgeoisie formulated its riposte. Forty-five of the current key representatives went to Miami for a meeting in June, 1992. The "Miami meeting" responded to the Duvalierists' "government of consensus" with a "government of national concord." According to a document issued at the "Miami Meeting" opening, the Lavalas sought "to put in place a real government of concord . . . integrating the political parties, the diverse organized sectors of civil society and all the institutions likely to aid in the national renaissance." The meeting appointed a 10-member "Presidential Commission," a non-official negotiating body, headed by Father Antoine Adrien, which was to be set up in Haiti to search for avenues for negotiations and democratic openings.

The whole project was shrouded in ambiguity. The Lavalas' "concord" seemed almost identical to the Duvalierists' "consensus," which democratic rhetoric did nothing to elucidate. The Presidential Commission had all the trappings of representing Aristide, yet it was distinct from the government *per se*, and Aristide called it an independent initiative. All this double talk was simply to appease the popular organizations, since they were alarmed that one of the principles of the December 16 coalition—"*makout pa ladann*" (Macoutes are disqualified)—was being betrayed. The popular sector—as well as Aristide up to that point—opposed direct negotiations either with Bazin or with Cédras, since this would confer legitimacy upon them and constitute recognition of the coup. Any negotiations with the putschists, the popular sector argued, could only result in a power-sharing deal, and even that deal the coup-makers would double-cross.[8]

But direct negotiations with Bazin—and eventually Cédras—seemed to be exactly what the Lavalas bourgeoisie had in mind when it formed the Presidential Commission. When asked in July if he endorsed negotiations between Aristide and Cédras, Father Adrien responded: "Why not? Why not? We have seen more surprising things than that."[9] Thus, on September 1, 1992, a meeting was arranged between Marc Bazin's "foreign minister" François Benoit and Presidential Commission head Father Adrien at OAS headquarters in Washington, D.C.

At the meeting, Father Adrien in essence asked for the Bazin *de facto* government to prove its good faith by putting an end to the fierce repression still raging in Haiti, so as to open up a "democratic space." The overseers of this project would be a force of "international observers." The first incarnation of this effort was the OAS/DEMOC mission, which, in the blue-prints, was to consist of hundreds of foreigners flooding the country to stay the hand of Macoute violence, by the thinking in the bourgeois Lavalas circles. For popular organizations, the OAS/DEMOC observers could provide the excuse for foreign military intervention if attacked or killed. In any case, the deployment of the OAS observer force during the autumn of 1992 never exceeded more than 20 individuals, who essentially remained ensconced in the luxurious Hotel Montana in the cool heights of the wealthy Port-au-Prince suburb of Petionville.

The ineffectiveness of the OAS observers increased calls by the Lavalas bourgeoisie for a more forceful international role. Since the OAS has no enforcement arm, UN Ambassador Fritz Longchamps began pressing for direct intervention from the UN Security Council. "If the General Assembly judges that the violations of human rights are continuing despite the different initiatives of the UN and that the only way to guarantee and preserve these rights is a 'peacekeeping force,' it will consult the Haitian government...and it can then ask the Security Council to deploy this 'peace-keeping force' so as to stop [the putschists] from assassinating the Haitian people," Longchamps told a Haitian press conference in late November.[10]

The popular sector remained completely opposed to all forms of foreign military intervention in Haiti, whether under the banner of the UN or the United States. Furthermore, it was pointed out—primarily in the pages of *Häiti Progrès*—that the UN Charter explicitly forbids the intervention of the Security Council into the internal affairs of member states.

As the observer mission and negotiations foundered in the autumn of 1992, the Lavalas diplomats figured that the U.S. government's thinly cloaked subversion of Aristide's return was mainly Republican in nature and began to look for salvation in the election of Democrat Bill Clinton. Already the advisors constantly talking to Aristide included such Democratic Party heavyweights as Congressman Charles Rangel (D-NY), former El Salvador Ambassador Robert White, and former Congressman Michael Barnes. Hundreds of Clinton/Gore campaign placards dotted the September 30, 1992 rallies of thousands of Haitians held in New York and Miami.

At the time of Clinton's victory, the Democrats were aware that the Lavalas bourgeoisie expected a radical shift in Haiti policy. This, of course, was not the reality. Even before his inauguration, Clinton reneged on his campaign promise to undo what he called during the campaign Bush's "immoral and illegal policy" of intercepting and repatriating Haitian refugees. In fact, he strengthened the naval blockade against the small wooden sail-boats fleeing Haiti's terror, an act which violates peace-time international law.

Where the Bush Administration did its best to undermine all progress toward Aristide's return, the Clinton team—in particular, new Secretary of

State Warren Christopher—began cautiously working towards Aristide's restoration to power, under the control of UN monitors and "peace-keeping" forces. Aristide, for his part, made the promise of amnesty long demanded of him more explicit than ever, saying at a White House meeting with Clinton in March, 1993 that "the departure of the authors of the coup d'état does not necessarily mean they would have to be in jail or have to leave the country." Clinton approved the statement saying "that sort of attitude on the part of President Aristide is the very thing that should enable us to resolve this in a peaceful way."

The beginning of the process was the deployment in March of a 250-member UN Civilian Mission to monitor and record human rights violations. Many popular organizations complained that the presence of the mission provoked more violence from the Army. "Now instead of beating us during the day, they come and beat us even more savagely at night," a young militant from the Papaye Peasant Movement (MPP) in Hinche explained in June, 1993. "People who had returned to test the mission's effect have had to flee the area once again."[11]

On April 23, President Clinton announced a plan to send a "multinational police force" of 500 to 600 to Haiti to "professionalize" the Haitian Army. This was the first concrete and official proposal by the U.S. government for foreign military deployment in Haiti. In the face of the proposal, Aristide remained enigmatic. This caused an outcry from the popular sector.

On May 17, a coalition of all the major popular organizations sent Aristide an open letter which put him on the spot: "You gave the OAS and UN authorization to send 'civilian observers' into the country, and even though it was strong medicine and a hard blow, we never officially protested because we always believed that you knew what you were doing and that there was a line you would not cross," the letter said. But since the proposal "to send a military police force to occupy the country," the popular organizations continued, "we cannot understand your silence and the silence of your government in this affair . . . We hope that you will immediately take an official public position that is crystal clear in denouncing and condemning this plan."

But the popular sector's warnings went unheeded, especially after the *de facto* government of Marc Bazin collapsed on June 8, 1993. Whether Bazin's resignation was orchestrated from Washington or not is still not known, but its effect was to precipitate Aristide and the Lavalas bourgeoisie to jump into the "void" that was supposedly created. The U.S. government also pointed to the naked rule of the military in Haiti and, along with Haitian Ambassadors Longchamps and Jean Casimir, pushed the matter before the Security Council. On June 16, 1993, the body voted Resolution #841, which called for a mandatory global embargo on oil and arms going to Haiti to take effect June 23.

The day after the vote, President Clinton said in a press conference that he thought that the sanctions would not be sufficient and that the only solution to the problem in Haiti was some kind of multinational peace-keeping force. The Council's seizure of the case of Haiti was the first time since the Korean War that the body had openly intervened in the internal affairs of a country since scenarios like El Salvador, Cambodia, Angola, Namibia and Bosnia were justified as "regional conflicts." The acting Council President had to emphasize the "exceptional" nature of the measures on Haiti. Cuba wrote a letter "opposing with the greatest energy the Security Council's adoption of measures concerning the internal situation" in Haiti because it would create "a dangerous precedent . . . to give this body powers and a mandate which are larger than those granted in the Charter."

On June 23, Ambassador-at-Large Ben Dupuy, the government diplomat most identified with the popular sector, resigned from the government with a letter to Aristide that stated, "without pretending to be more patriotic than anyone else, I think that it is extremely dangerous to put the national sovereignty of the country in the hands of an international organization whose real defense of the peoples' rights, and even its impartiality, can legitimately be put in doubt at this time."

In essence, this was the concern of the popular movement as a whole. They saw the gift of the Security Council's embargo as a trap for Aristide. "By requesting the Security Council to take up the case of Haiti, Aristide has surrendered his leadership and control over efforts for his own restoration to an international body controlled by the very nation which had a hand in the coup which overthrew him," wrote the New York-based Haiti Commission of Inquiry into the September 30th Coup d'État in a June 26 statement. "Having usurped control of the crisis in Haiti, the UN and the United States have begun forcing Aristide into a corner . . . The UN is trying to validate Cédras as a negotiating partner and force Aristide to bargain with him."

The UN now did bring the "two parties" of the Haitian conflict to the bargaining table. Having previously been branded an outlaw by the UN and OAS, Cédras was all too happy to be legitimized by negotiations. As for Aristide, he was in so deep with the UN now, he did not want to hesitate. "Haiti appeared like a country without a government, without a prime minister [after Bazin's resignation], without a president," said Chavannes Jean-Baptiste of the MPP, who was a member of the Presidential Commission, explaining why Aristide accepted the UN invitation. "Thus, you who are the constitutional government, [the UN] writes you to say come, we are going to turn power over to you. If you don't come, it's as if you refuse the power."[12]

The negotiations began June 27, 1993 on Governor's Island, in New York City harbor, to avoid the massive demonstrations of Haitians outside the UN headquarters in Manhattan. The two delegations occupied separate buildings 100 yards apart with Argentine diplomat Danté Caputo, the UN special envoy who took over from OAS special envoy Augusto Ocampo, shuttling between them.

The ensuing document—the "Governor's Island Accord"—was "the direct result of consistent pressure and threats on President Aristide," according to a point-by-point analysis of the accord made by the Haiti Reborn project of the Quixote Center. "There were never any real negotiations, but just the imposition of a plan designed by the international community."[13]

The essential sequence of this 10-point accord was that Aristide would name a new prime minister, the UN would lift sanctions, the parliament would undertake a series of reforms of the police and Armed Forces under the supervision of a UN force, Aristide would decree a blanket amnesty for those involved in the coup, and then Cédras would voluntarily retire at some point before Aristide's return, which was set for October 30, 1993.

"The plan had been conceived with no input from the legitimate government and was shared with the press before reaching negotiators," Haiti Reborn explained. "[Caputo] threatened to have UN sanctions lifted immediately if Aristide did not comply with the plan as proposed."[14]

Dante Caputo called the accord "a model for the future," and President Clinton called it "an historic step forward for democracy."[15] Still, Aristide withheld his signature for almost a full day, which sent UN and U.S. diplomats into a frenzy. One U.S. official called the President "a deal breaker."[16] "Don't think, Mr. President," counseled UN Secretary General Boutros Boutros Ghali in one of the many pressuring phone calls Aristide received that day. "Just sign it."[17]

Even Aristide's own advisors, such as former Ambassador Robert White, pressured him. "It was more important [for Aristide]," said White afterwards, "to get back in four months than to worry about what was essentially a minor problem."[18]

The "minor problem" was that, in addition to many other concessions to the putschists, Aristide agreed to lift the embargo and name his prime minister before the departure of Cédras and before his own return, leaving the putschists fully capable of sinking the process whenever they saw fit. The result: Cédras was legitimized and Aristide's own return was rendered improbable. This was clear enough to the Duvalierists. When Cédras and his delegation returned to Haiti on July 3, he received a hero's welcome from cheering crowds of soldiers and coup supporters at the airport.

"This is not an accord between the military delegation and the constitutional government," said Chavannes Jean-Baptiste, who was part of the government's delegation at Governors Island. "This is an accord between the UN, the OAS, and the 'friends of the Secretary General,'" as the United States, France, Canada, and Venezuela came to be dubbed during the Governor's Island talks.[19] Although the Aristide delegation had stayed up all night on July 2 composing a counter-proposal to what Caputo offered, they were given an "ultimatum" the next day, according to Chavannes, to "take it or leave it."

The bourgeoisie, counting on U.S. good will and support, expressed guarded satisfaction with the accord. "The accord contains the elements of democracy, and return of the truly elected president of the Republic and the relinquishing of their command posts by the leaders of the coup," declared Ambassador Casimir.[20]

But an open letter to President Aristide from ten of the most established popular organizations called the accord "an affront to the heroic struggle of the Haitian people," noting in particular "points 5 and 10 of the accord which accept the entry of foreign troops into the country and gives to the United Nations the right to control the governing of the country."[21]

In fact, the deployment of over 1,200 UN troops, including about 700 U.S. military troops, was one of the State Department's key concerns in drawing up the accord. The soldiers were to be under UN Security Council command, not that of the legitimate government. They were referred to, in official statements, either as "instructors" to "professionalize" the Haitian Armed Forces or "technicians" to help "rebuild the country" by bringing their technical expertise to bear on problems like road construction and justice-system reform. This UN force, with an initial term of deployment of six months, was not restricted in how large it could grow or how long it could stay.

Aristide also went to great lengths to show the United States and Haiti's technocrats that upon his return he would be open to neoliberal economic policies. In July, his government hosted in Miami a "Haiti Government/Business Partnership Conference," with the support of organizations like the CLAA, which had so vigorously fought the embargo. The meeting was well-attended by both the merchant and the technocrat tendencies of Haiti's bourgeoisie. Many of the 200 businesspeople in attendance had helped finance the 1991 coup and break the ensuing embargo. The World Bank, the International Monetary Fund, U.S. AID, and the United Nations Development Programme guided most of the conference with presentations of their plans to revive the Haitian economy, and of the errors that Aristide had made in his first eight months of administration. U.S. AID's $36.5 million "emergency recovery" package, which would largely go to repay bank debts run up during the coup, was the centerpiece of discussion.

Shortly afterwards, Aristide nominated U.S.-leaning Robert Malval as prime minister. Malval was a hybrid between the traditional bourgeoisie and the technocrats, a wealthy printer who was well-connected with the bourgeoisie, the oligarchy, and the Army. Malval was ratified in a ceremony at the Haitian Embassy in Washington, DC on August 30 and installed in Port-au-Prince on September 2. His cabinet also reflected an opening toward the neoliberal technocrat sector.

All of Aristide's political retreats and makeovers had been for naught. He was still not trusted. The project derailed on October 11, when a U.S. troop carrier, the USS Harlan County, carrying the first major deployment of 200 American and Canadian soldiers, turned back from landing when about 100 armed anti-Aristide thugs affiliated with the Haitian military—called "attachés"—demonstrated at the port and threatened foreign diplomats.

The event opened a breach. Conservative sectors in the U.S. government, particularly from the Pentagon and CIA, completely distrusted Aristide and were opposed to the venture of controlling him and the mass movement he commands. Furthermore, if there is to be U.S. military intervention, the conservatives favor the use of "overpowering force," as in Iraq, rather than disguised piecemeal deployments behind the fig-leaf of UN command. After the devastating attack on U.S. troops in Somalia in early October, there was a backlash in U.S. public opinion against U.S. intervention overseas. The Pentagon and CIA used this backlash to try to scuttle the project of returning Aristide.

Many believe that this "hard line" sector was behind the coup against Aristide in the first place. Some U.S. military generals were asked to put pressure on the junta to respect the Governor's Island accord, but in fact they gave reassurance. "An embassy official in Port-au-Prince has described his shock at seeing Marine Maj. Gen. John Sheehan 'yucking it up' with General Cédras at a reception in September," wrote Christopher Hitchens in the November 3 Nation. "'One shot and we're out of there,' a Pentagon spokesman helpfully said of the mission of the good ship Harlan County, almost advising the Haitian military of the paltry risk it would run in breaching the Governor's Island accord."

There is other evidence that the Pentagon and CIA encouraged the attachés to rampage to justify the Harlan County's pull-back. New York Daily News columnist Juan Gonzales was told of the October 11 port demonstration the day beforehand at a Duvalierist meeting at which U.S. Embassy personnel were present. "How can two Daily News reporters who have only visited Haiti on a few occasions learn beforehand of secret plans to sabotage the landing of our troops, while our vaunted officialdom claims it was caught flat-footed?" Gonzalez asked on October 12. "In the weeks to come, we may find out who knew what, and when."[22]

The Clinton/Christopher policy to reconcile Aristide with the Haitian de facto military power was foiled by the U.S. de facto military power. "A member of President Aristide's entourage put it to me bitterly," Hitchens wrote. "All the world knows there has been a military coup in Haiti. But who would believe there has been a silent coup in the United States? This is the Bush Administration policy, determined by the military."

After October 11 and the assassination of Justice Minister Guy Malary on October 14, Aristide's chances of returning on October 30, which had been slim to begin with, evaporated altogether. As Duvalierist violence grew in Haiti, right-wing campaigns in the United States—spearheaded by Senators Dole, Nunn, and Helms—smeared Aristide's psychological health, human rights record, and political affiliations. "The return of Aristide to Haiti is not worth even one American life," said Senator Bob Dole on October 24. Meanwhile, Clinton re-imposed the trade embargo, this time backing it up with a naval blockade.

At this writing in early December, the Lavalas bourgeoisie's strategy of sell-ing Aristide to the United States seems to have failed miserably. Not only did Aristide not return on October 30, but the ministers of his entire government, including Prime Minister Malval, have been unable to perform their duties or even occupy their offices. Headlines announce what the UN has decided to do about Haiti today, while Aristide's calls are relegated to the footnotes.

In addition, Aristide, in siding with the bourgeois sector, has lost his political prestige in the popular sector. "Mr. President," Haiti's principal popular organizations wrote on July 9 after Governor's Island, "today history places us, the popular organizations, at a crossroads where, with or without you, we are going to continue to struggle for the liberation of the country."

On November 9, Aristide himself seems to have finally cast aside all pre-tense as to the option he favors. When asked by a French journalist if he was finally ready to call openly for foreign military intervention he responded: "I am sure that the Haitian people would be happy to be rid of the criminals, but if I ask for an intervention, I will be condemned by my Constitution."[23]

Since Aristide's return via U.S. or UN efforts now seems postponed, if not canceled, so does the military intervention which was needed to restrain the post-coup popular drive for justice. Should popular insurrection or guerrilla war break out and threaten the Duvalierists' present grip on power, U.S. or UN intervention would be quickly mounted. For the time being, however, Warren Christopher has said that the re-establishment of democracy in Haiti is not on the U.S. government's list of priorities.[24]

The coup of September 30, 1991, like all decisive historical moments, provides a litmus test of its actors' convictions. It revealed the true cynicism of the U.S. government and the U.S.-trained Haitian military, as well as the tragic ambivalence of Aristide. In the face of a bloody, unjustifiable coup, Aristide could have rallied the masses to rise up and organize outside of the legalistic confines imposed by the bourgeoisie. For the people of Haiti, and the people of the world, the lines demarcating democracy from dictatorship had never been so clearly drawn and the recourse to self-defense so justified.

But the Lavalas bourgeoisie convinced Aristide that strength lay in the halls of Washington rather than the mountains of Haiti. In two years of negotiations, the putschists have given nothing of the usurped power, and the legitimate government has traded away almost everything. "Meanwhile, Aristide, by stick-ing with these negotiations, has neutralized the only real weapon he has: the man in the street," a bitter Aristide supporter told the *New York Times*.[25]

These set-backs for the bourgeoisie's strategy should not be understood as a defeat for the people's movement overall. The tenacity and patience of the

Haitian people has deep roots. In 1802, Toussaint Louverture, the leader of the successful 1801 revolution to abolish slavery in the French colony of St. Domingue, was captured by French officers when he agreed to negotiate peace at Habitation Bréda. But the slaves of the colony, having tasted a year of freedom, rose up in fury at Napolean's attempt to re-establish slavery. Within two years, the former slave armies had driven the French from the colony and proclaimed independence for the nation of Haiti in 1804.

Today, this past and Haiti's future lies within the Haitian people and their popular organizations, who have learned from the experiences of Habitation Bréda and of Cartagena, Washington, and Governor's Island. The popular organizations place their faith in the people who made the Lavalas possible and continue to defend the movement's original ideals of national independence and democratic rebirth.

NOTES

1. I cite mainly the *Washington Post* and the *New York Times*, the two flagships for the opinion and analysis of U.S. officialdom and finance. However, the campaign against Aristide's human rights record appeared in the columns of all the major urban dailies, including the *Boston Globe*, *Miami Herald*, *Philadelphia Enquirer*, *Los Angeles Times*, and *Chicago Tribune*.

2. Figures given by Jean-Jacques Honorat during an interview in October, 1993. "Democracy Derailed," The 5th Estate, CBC, October 26, 1993.

3. Washington Office on Haiti statement before the House Western Hemisphere Affairs Subcommittee on July 21, 1993.

4. Jean-Jacques Gilles, *Häite en Marche*, January 1, 1992.

5. *New York Post*, October 7, 1991.

6. *The Guardian*, January 22, 1992.

7. *Häiti Progrès*, February 26 to March 3, 1992.

8. In April, 1993, the National Public Assembly (APN), one of the leading popular organizations, proposed a "government of democratic unity," which would comprise all sectors which were anti-Macoute and opposed to the coup, even though they may not have been party to the original Lavalas alliance. "If the traditional bourgeois sector and the petty-bourgeoisie in the Lavalas do not think that they are flirting with the putschists, then they shouldn't make demagogery," the APN said. "They should say loudly to the people, like us, that in the government of concord, Macoutes are not included" because "the Macoutes have never been and will never be interested in democracy." The APN called Macoutism a "sickness without a cure."

9. Interview with Crowing Rooster Productions, July 23, 1992.

10. *Häiti Progrès*, December 2-8, 1992.

11. Interview conducted by the author during a trip to the Central Plateau in June, 1993.

12. *Häiti Progrès*, July 7-13, 1993.

13. "The Challenges Ahead," Haiti Reborn/Quixote Center, July 9, 1993.

14. "The Challenges Ahead."

15. The Caputo quotation is from the Inter-Press Service on July 7, 1993; the Clinton quotation, from IPS on July 22, 1993.

16. Associated Press, July 3, 1993.

17. *Miami Herald*, July 3, 1993.

18. *Newsday*, July 4, 1993.

19. *Häiti Progrès*, July 7-13, 1993.

20. *The Globe and Mail* (Toronto), July 5, 1993.

21. *Häiti Progrès*, July 14-20, 1993.

22. *New York Daily News*, October 12, 1993.

23. Signal FM, November 9, 1993.

24. *New York Times*, November 5, 1993.

25. *New York Times*, October 31, 1993.

THE "EMBASSY" MEMO
Author Unknown

In early 1992, the Washington Office on Haiti, an analysis and information center on democracy and human rights in Haiti, disseminated a "secret" memo reportedly leaked from the U.S. embassy in Port-au-Prince, with the following introductory note: "The text below was transcribed verbatim from a document which surfaced in Port-au-Prince in October 1991, shortly after the coup. This document was reportedly written by a consultant to the U.S. embassy there, as a strategy outline which appears designed to undermine the OAS negotiations and prevent the restoration of Haiti's elected government. While the document's origins could not be verified and the State Department has denied its validity, its contents are startling in light of events since the document was first released in the U.S. in January 1992. A copy of the document from which this text was transcribed is attached."

⌐

1. U.S. and OAS have only one point they insist on, the return of A. The return of A could be for only a brief (symbolic) period of time, he could be returned to be impeached, or he could simply be returned as a figurehead, but they insist that he be returned.

2. Mr. A does not necessarily need to return for some period of time until all guarantees were in place. If the guarantees were not met, then a constitutional process could remove A while he was still out of the country.

3. If A were allowed to return, he would not need to return right away and he would hold no power.

4. A new government of reconciliation would be formed that would include capable people from all the parties except the Lavalas people. The Lavalas people would be excluded from government.

5. A could be returned only to face impeachment, but would be necessary to set the process in place prior to his arrival.

6. The OAS, U.S., Canada and France would guarantee the final arrangement and are willing to provide significant resources and money to resolve the situation. Especially will provide significant package of aid to rebuild military and to ease any concerns the soldiers might have.

7. OAS would put in significant/sufficient international group to guarantee security. U.S. would strongly monitor and support this OAS group so there would be no attempt by any party to challenge it. The group would stay as long as necessary.

8. The OAS, U.S., Canada, France, Venezuela and Mexico are seeing as one.

9. If A refuses to deal or refuses what OAS considers a reasonable deal, he is finished.

10. All OAS countries now believe that A was a very bad guy and no one wants to see him back with any real power, but because of other problems in the hemisphere, they want to see him returned, even if for only one day to resign and leave.

11. U.S. and others believe that negotiation must begin with the Parliament Group's visit to Washington. The Group must look like it is ready to bargain in good faith, otherwise, if the U.S. feels the talks are going nowhere they will impose the sanctions.

12. The Group must put forth its position regarding OAS interference, etc., but it must focus on a resolution and keeping negotiations going. It should compare A to the Ayatollah (and) what would happen if he is allowed to return (but do not dwell on his return). Very important, Group should raise problem that if sanctions are imposed it would lead to impasse, then to civil war and chaos in which A would return and destroy everything and everyone. Imposing sanctions will directly lead to an escalation in violence and a situation that no one can control.

13. If the Group looks like it is bargaining in good faith, the sanctions will be held in reserve, and some solution will be worked out, probably excluding A's return. Absolutely necessary that Group be made up of good negotiators.

There is an urgent need to support and encourage the efforts of the democratically elected Haitian Parliament and all true believers in democracy in Haiti. The next three months are critical. However, given the initial reaction of the Organization of American States (OAS) and the U.S. Government (U.S.) to recent events, the outright encouragement and support for these efforts has become a delicate matter.

What is needed is a comprehensive, sustained and very discrete (*sic*) approach to U.S. policy-makers and the U.S. media that will balance off and negate the propaganda of the Lavalas organization. Clearly, policy makers and their media have already discovered information regarding Aristide that is very troubling. More information must be channeled to them and on a regular basis, and from sources that they will trust and that cannot be directly traced back to anyone in Port-au-Prince. I suggest, therefore, that I be retained to hire a team of four to six people who are influential in Latin American affairs in general and Haitian affairs specifically to do the following:

(1) To educate and encourage a favorable understanding of events in Haiti with the U.S. policy makers and the U.S. media;

(2) To monitor and regularly report on U.S. government and OAS policies and activities that affect relations between Haiti and the rest of the western hemisphere;

(3) To work with and encourage the numerous public policy shaping organizations, namely think-tanks, to elaborate on favorable policy appropriate towards Haiti that will bring a positive outcome to the current situation;

(4) To educate and encourage a favorable understanding in the U.S. Congress on the situation in Haiti.

This suggested strategy would cover the next three months, which will be crucial to resolution of the current situation. To implement this strategy over the three months will require a fee of $50,000 in advance. As everyone is aware, we need to begin as soon as possible.

Keep me informed on your position concerning the strategy described above.

"A second document which appeared at the same time and under the same circumstances reads as follows:"

Diplomatic strategy should include:

1. Yes, OAS and U.S., we will accept Aristide back, how will you guarantee a comprehensive deal? The burden should be put on the OAS and the U.S. to come up with an acceptable plan. If the response is that they will provide an observer group, or unarmed peace-keeping group, then the Haitian delegation response should be that is not sufficient and/or will not work. What else can you come up with that makes sense?

2. It is very important that if the OAS and U.S. want the Haitian delegation now visiting Washington to acknowledge Aristide, then the OAS and the U.S. should agree to recognize the new Prime Minister and (1) to unfreeze Haitian government bank accounts in the U.S., (2) recognize the new Prime Minister's ability to fire Aristide's ambassadors and replace them with new ones. This should be the first step and is very important to be done as quickly as possible.

3. Whatever safeguards the OAS and the U.S. offer should be spelled out in detail, with dollar amounts where appropriate and time frames. For instance, they want to professionalize the military. The U.S. has always wanted this, but has never been able to provide any significant funding to do so (mostly because Congress blocked the money), in this situation there is a good possibility that funds can be found, so the U.S. and other OAS members should be asked to specifically allocate funds for a specific plan to professionalize the military. Such a plan would probably take several years at a yearly cost of $15-20 million.

4. At the same time that the military is being "professionalized," specific commitments on foreign aid and trade benefits should be renewed and where possible accelerated.

5. Additional and significant aid should be given to build an adequate judicial system. Democracy rests on a secure and adequate judicial system. The court system in Haiti needs upwards of $20 million a year for the next five to seven years if it is going to be built into a respectable and self-sustaining institution.

6. The above suggestions should be incorporated into any deal, again putting the burden of success on the OAS and the U.S. to foot the bill for the deal they think is so necessary.

7. The other points of the deal should surely include some of the following: that if A returns it would not be until some time later (months away); that he could be impeached and sent back out; that time was permitted to enact new laws limiting some of his outrageous behaviors and that of his followers; that the Prime Minister become the real power of the government; that the Prime Minister be given adequate economic support to secure his position; that no Lavalas people be included in the new Government; the new Government would be one of reconciliation and made up of able people; and so on.

SELLING OUT DEMOCRACY
John Canham-Clyne

Throughout the crisis in Haiti, the U.S. has used information gathered through its intelligence operations to provide the rationale for American policy—both its lack of support for President Aristide and its opposition to providing sanctuary for Haitian refugees. In *Covert Action Quarterly*, John Canham-Clyne writes that "The claim that the Haitian military was not engaged in systematic repression and the whisper campaign against Aristide have two elements in common. Each rests on the belief that poor Haitians—and their political aspirations—threaten U.S. interests. And each relies on slanted or bogus intelligence collected or created by the State Department, the Justice Department, and the CIA."

Having learned the lessons of the January 6, 1991 failed coup attempt by LaFontant, the military deployed troops under cover of night to prevent mass action in support of Aristide. Within two weeks [of September 30, 1991], the military murdered 1,000 Haitians. By the end of the year another 500 were dead, thousands more summarily arrested and tortured, and tens of thousands in hiding.[1]

President Bush and Secretary of State Jim Baker offered public support for Aristide. Speaking to the Organization of American States, Baker said the coup "has no legitimacy and will not prevail."[2] The U.S. suspended formal assistance, but its commitment to restoring the leftist Aristide quickly revealed itself as largely rhetorical. On October 3, Bush, who had sent U.S. troops to Panama, Somalia, and the Persian Gulf, said he was "disinclined to use American force"[3] to restore Aristide, and only reluctantly joined OAS sanctions against the coup at the end of October.

Behind the facade of pro-democracy oratory, U.S. officials mounted a vicious disinformation campaign against Aristide, which continues today. Within a few weeks, "diplomats" and U.S. officials, usually behind a shield of source anonymity, were painting the deposed leader as a dangerous, violent, mentally unstable zealot. The campaign included a desultory list of actors from earlier wars in Central America. U.S. business interests, for example, enlisted former Assistant Secretary of State and admitted liar Elliott Abrams to lead the charge against the embargo on Capitol Hill.[4]

By late January and early February, 1992, despite the embargo, goods flowed into and refugees flowed out of Haiti. Oil shipments easily evaded the embargo, keeping the military functioning smoothly.[5] On February 4, Bush signalled the end of all but the flimsiest pretense of support for Aristide by excepting the assembly industry from the sanctions. At the same time, the U.S. cracked down on the refugees.

Frantic to avoid thousands of Haitians landing on U.S. shores, the Bush administration set up a processing facility at Guantánamo Bay Naval Base, Cuba, a month and a half after the coup. Haitians picked up by the Coast Guard were taken to the facility for a "prescreening" for political asylum. If Immigration and Naturalization Service (INS) adjudicators determined the refugees had a "credible fear" of persecution, they were screened in to the U.S. for a full-blown political asylum hearing; if not, they were shipped back to Haiti.

The rate of successful applications for asylum had more to do with U.S. policy objectives than the merit of individual cases or actual conditions in Haiti. "It was totally politicized," said a U.S. official intimately familiar with the program. "Whenever somebody from Washington went down to Guantánamo, the rate [of those granted entry into the U.S.] went down, and as soon as they left, it went back up again."[6] Interviewing officers were easily controlled because they lacked an overall understanding of how the program functioned. In early May, "when the interviewing officers found out, to their horror, that the Coast Guard was handing over the manifests [with the names and addresses of all Haitians being sent back] to the Haitian military on the docks, the rate [allowed into the U.S.] went through the roof for a couple of days."[7]

On May 24, 1992, President Bush ended the controversial screening program altogether by ordering the Coast Guard to summarily repatriate any Haitians picked up at sea, with no hearing whatsoever. The new policy forced Haitians seeking asylum to rely on "in-country processing" by hostile INS officers at U.S. Embassy facilities in Haiti, where military thugs carefully observed the process.[8]

Although the policy flagrantly violates the fundamental principle of international asylum law,[9] Bush attempted to justify it by denying that there was systematic repression in Haiti. "I am convinced," he said on May 28 in Marietta, Georgia, "that the people in Haiti are not being physically oppressed. I would not want on my conscience that . . . anyone that was fleeing oppression would be victimized upon return." At the time, the Haitian military was in fact stepping up repression in the countryside, and systematically attacking the grassroots development and social justice organizations which formed the skeleton of Haiti's delicate civil society.[10]

The claim that the Haitian military was not engaged in systematic repression and the whisper campaign against Aristide have two elements in common. Each rests on the belief that poor Haitians—and their political aspirations—threaten U.S. interests. And each relies on slanted or bogus intelligence collected or created by the State Department, the Justice Department, and the CIA.

These two aspects of U.S. policy coalesce in one man recruited from Hitler's military—with a long history of involvement in U.S. covert operations. In late February 1992, the INS dispatched Gunther Otto Wagner, senior intelligence officer at INS's Southeast Regional Headquarters in Dallas, Texas, to Haiti to investigate the reports of targeted persecution against refugees returned by the U.S. Over three months, Wagner and a group of State Department officers interviewed about 3,000 repatriated Haitian refugees.

According to Wagner's 160-page sworn deposition in the Haitian Centers' litigation, he personally interviewed 600 repatriates.[11] During three separate trips, neither he nor his colleagues found a single "credible" case of post-repatriation reprisal by the military. A joint Americas Watch/National Coalition for Haitian Refugees report described this effort as "a wholly slanted undertaking. As an exercise designed to illustrate the premise that repatriates do not face political persecution, the surveys serve a public relations purpose. But as an attempt to discover whether repatriates encounter persecution, the surveys utterly fail."[12]

Wagner's investigative method consisted of checking in with the local military commander, proceeding to a public gathering place, loudly announcing his own identity and asking if anyone knew of any repatriates, particularly any who might have suffered reprisals.[13] Anyone who dared come forward was interviewed in public.

Even under these conditions, two to three percent of those Wagner interviewed reported that they were in hiding or felt threatened. In a grim Catch-22, Wagner dismissed their fears citing the absurd conditions of his own investigation. A person with a credible fear of persecution, he concluded, "would not have been in my presence. Because the individual is out in the street, as far as I am concerned, he is not hiding."[14]

In late March and early April, State and INS produced three unclassified reports that were circulated to asylum officers at Guantánamo who used them to assess country human rights conditions. INS regulations require asylum adjudicators to weigh independent human rights reporting equally with U.S. government sources in evaluating political asylum claims. At Guantánamo, however, screening officers worked long hours, and the resource center holding country human rights reports was housed in a building far from the area where interviewers worked. While it was inconvenient for screening officers to obtain outside reports, INS management distributed Wagner's reports directly to the interviewers. One of Wagner's memos accused independent human rights groups of overstating the number of murders by at least three times.[15]

In early April, Wagner followed up the reports with a briefing at Guantánamo. He told the asylum officers that 95 percent of Haitians seeking political asylum were making "fraudulent claims."[16] Yet, according to his own sworn statement, Wagner had never read asylum law or regulations, was not trained to adjudicate asylum claims, had no training in cross-cultural interviewing techniques, had never been to Haiti before, had not read State Department country reports on Haiti, and could neither identify Haitian political parties nor accurately recall Aristide's popular nickname.[17]

Wagner *should* have been able to identify victims of repression. He devoted the first half of his U.S. government career to helping various dictatorships target them. Wagner was recruited out of Hitler's German Air Force into the U.S. Army's security police in Occupied Germany, with German state and municipal police forces from 1946-51 and as chief investigator with the U.S. Army Security Police Western Area Command from 1951-55. He came to the U.S. in 1955 and was naturalized in 1960.

In 1966, he went to Vietnam as senior Public Safety Adviser under the Office of Public Safety (OPS) of AID. OPS was founded by the CIA in 1962 under an AID umbrella and was often used as a cover for covert operations in Southeast Asia. Wagner was a regional adviser to the Vietnamese National Police Special Branch, a key participant in the CIA-sponsored Phoenix program in which tens of thousands of Vietnamese civilians were summarily arrested, tortured, disappeared, and murdered. He moved on to Managua in 1971 as senior Public Safety Adviser to the Somoza regime, staying on as a consultant when Congress abolished OPS in 1975 after its role in underwriting torture in various countries was revealed.[18] Wagner refused interviews through the INS press office, but according to Douglas Valentine, who interviewed him extensively for his book *The Phoenix Program*, Wagner personally trained Enrique Bermúdez, who later became military commander of the largest Contra force.[19]

State Department officials assisted Wagner. A review of more than 200 pages of unclassified cable traffic from the first half of 1992 between the U.S. embassy in Port-au-Prince and Washington reveals the underlying assumption that Haiti is suffering a plague of liars. The cables concerning persecution of repatriates are often sarcastic—a section of one is titled offhandedly, "Another refugee claim debunked."[20]

Not to be outdone by their State Department and INS colleagues, the CIA weighed in during the summer, dispatching analyst Brian Latell. As publicly acknowledged National Intelligence Officer for Latin America, Latell is the intelligence community's senior analyst on Latin American affairs. In a memo dated July 21, 1992, he offered his "Impressions of Haiti:"

> I do not wish to minimize the role the military plays in intimidating, and occasionally terrorizing real and suspected opponents, but my experiences confirm the community's view that there is no systematic or frequent lethal violence aimed at civilians.[21]

Just a few weeks before Latell's visit, the military had switched front Prime Ministers, jettisoning U.S.-funded human rights activist Jean-Jacques Honorat in favor of failed U.S.-backed presidential candidate, Marc Bazin. Latell gushed about Bazin and the coup leader, Army Chief of Staff Raoul Cédras:

> These meetings reinforced my view that Bazin and his [civilian] supporters are perhaps the most promising group of Haitian leaders since the Duvalier family dictatorship was deposed in 1986. . . . Gen. Cédras impressed me as a conscientious military leader who genuinely wishes to minimize his role in politics, professionalize the armed services and develop a separate and competent civilian police force. I believe he is relatively moderate and incorrupt.[22]

At the time of Latell's visit, several Haitian officers and enlisted men were finishing training courses at Fort Benning, Georgia, despite official denials. As with the 1987 aid cutoff, the Bush administration's "disengagement" from the military was largely fictional. Publicly, Pentagon officials insisted that although Haitians attending classes at the time of the coup could finish up, no additional Haitians could start courses. According to lists obtained by the National Security News Service in Washington, D.C., however, at least ten Haitian officers completed English-language classes begun before the coup, and then began other training courses, most at Fort Benning.[23]

Patrick Elie [head of Aristide's anti-narcotics program] says that shortly after the coup, Aristide supporters monitored radio transmissions in which Col. Joseph-Michel François was heard ordering a company of soldiers to open the airport to receive contraband shipments.[24] François, who promoted himself to national chief of police after the coup and is one of the most powerful junta members, trained at Fort Benning.[25] He reportedly controls thousands of paramilitary *attachés*, and, in Duvalier style, has packed the public payroll with family and friends.[26] Aristide's government told U.S. intelligence officials about the midnight flight, but the U.S. still seems to view the Haitian military as drug warriors. Despite the embargo, the U.S. continues to share "anti-narcotics" intelligence with the Haitian military.[27]

INS's, State's and CIA's analyses—and the Pentagon's continued embrace of the Haitian military—all dovetailed neatly with Bush's assertion that there was little repression in Haiti. Another politician, however, disagreed with Bush and Latell. Three days after Bush announced summary repatriation, Democratic presidential candidate Bill Clinton denounced the move as "another sad example of the administration's callous response to a terrible human tragedy. . . . If I were president, I would—in the absence of clear and compelling evidence that they weren't political refugees—give them temporary asylum until we restored the elected government of Haiti."[28]

Clinton's election spurred another round of smears and phony intelligence. On November 18, the *Miami Herald* warned that "U.S. reconnaissance photos taken over Haiti November 6 show 717 sailboats on the ground. Of those, 610 are ready, and 107 are still under construction. Clearly the means is at hand for a massive exodus of Haitians to South Florida."[29] As

Clinton's inauguration drew near, the boat sightings and expectations for the exodus reached a fever pitch. U.S. Coast Guard commandant Admiral J. William Kime announced that 1,400 boats were ready and another 200 under construction, preparing for an exodus which could involve "several hundred thousand" Haitians.[30]

Coast Guard officials admitted that they gleaned their information from the media rather than from observation. Attorney Michael Ratner of the Center for Constitutional Rights, who actually visited Haiti at the time, believes the reports of boats and impending exodus were wildly exaggerated. "One of the things we specifically set out to do was find boats. We found three boats. Now, we didn't go to every beach, but we fanned out in three teams. The area is so deforested that you can see a lot. I took a car all the way up the coast from Port-au-Prince, stopping frequently. We didn't see any crowds. There are no crowds of people anywhere in Haiti. Even an outpouring of 50,000 people would be so massive for Haiti, given the poverty, number of boats and difficulty in moving around, that it's just not realistic."[31] Indeed, it had taken nine months for 37,000 Haitians to flee after the coup.

The hysteria had a predictable effect. On January 14, under pressure from Florida politicians, Clinton made Haitian refugees the first victims of a series of broken campaign promises, draping the betrayal in a mantle of unctuous humanitarian concern:

> For Haitians who do seek to leave Haiti, boat departure is a terrible and dangerous choice. . . . For this reason, the practice of returning those who flee Haiti by boat will continue, for the time being, after I become president. Those who do leave Haiti . . . by boat will be stopped and directly returned by the United States Coast Guard.

At the same time, Clinton pledged a vigorous effort to restore Aristide, arguing that the ultimate resolution of the refugee crisis lay in solving the political crisis. He then appointed Lawrence Pezzullo, Carter administration Ambassador to Nicaragua, as special envoy. The apparently renewed commitment to Aristide added a new element to the disinformation campaign. As Clinton came into office, the CIA was preparing a National Intelligence Estimate on Haiti, incorporating Latell's analysis of the political situation.[32]

Within a few months, fissures had opened up between the intelligence community and the Clinton administration. In early July, Pezzullo brokered an agreement between Aristide and the military at Governor's Island, New York. Aristide reluctantly agreed to a blanket amnesty for the coup plotters, all of whom except Cédras would be allowed to stay in the military. The military high command agreed to Aristide's return on October 30, and the U.S. agreed to participate in an international effort to train and professionalize the Haitian military.

A month after the agreement was signed, the CIA's psychological profile of Aristide surfaced; it concluded that he was mentally unstable and out of touch with reality. In an article in the *New York Times*, Elaine Sciolino quoted anonymous White House and administration officials downplaying the report. "There is an ideological overlay to some of the official analysis," one senior official told Sciolino, while another dismissed the profile as a "caricature" based on secondhand information."[33] Nevertheless, the allegations helped U.S. officials push Aristide for concessions, portraying his obstinacy as the primary obstacle to peace.

Meanwhile, the Haitian military, while escalating repression throughout the country, began systematically ignoring its commitments at Governor's Island. The junta's recalcitrance was symbolized by the brazen September 11 murder of businessman Antoine Izmery, close friend and financial backer of the exiled President. Thugs in civilian dress dragged him from a church and shot him dead in the street. On October 12, in perhaps the most stunningly ridiculous incident in a story filled with gruesome comedy, a small band of gun-toting, machete-wielding goons faced down the U.S. Navy. The U.S.S. Harlan County, carrying the first detachment of military trainers, turned tail after a small mob of thugs bounced cars and shouted threats from the Port-au-Prince docks. As it became obvious that the Haitian military would not permit Aristide's return, some legislators and commentators began to call for armed U.S. intervention.

On October 20, Brian Latell[34] addressed a gathering of senators, mostly Republicans, at the invitation of Sen. Jesse Helms. According to press reports of the briefings, Latell recycled the lie that Aristide had been hospitalized in Montreal for mental illness in 1980, and the habitual distortions of his human rights record. Based on the briefing, Helms denounced Aristide as a "psychopath" unworthy of support.[35] The disinformation, however, served its purpose: It helped take the steam out of proposals to expand the embargo or intervene.

Clinton administration officials and congressional Democrats lamented the "one-sided" reports. Despite this ineffectual support, the alacrity with which the CIA, State Department, and INS gathered and disseminated flawed "intelligence" suggests that substantial portions of the U.S. foreign policy bureaucracy view Aristide and the popular movement as a threat. The CIA has even rejected intelligence from the Aristide government. Patrick Elie says that the Aristide government-in-exile offered the Agency the services of a nationwide network of Haitian agents to ferret out information on drug trafficking. Unlike the military, notes Elie, "We do have the trust of the Haitian population." Both the CIA and DEA spurned the offer.[36]

Prospects for Aristide's return do not look good. . . . With a powerful pseudo-democracy enhancement apparatus prepared to supplant genuine grassroots organizing, deep institutional ties to the Haitian military, an ingrained mistrust of liberation theology, and powerful business interests determined to maintain Haiti's business climate, the U.S. foreign policy bureaucracy presents a profound threat to Haitian democracy. Balancing the threat are Clinton's tepid personal support for Aristide and the refugees.

Some elements in the actions of the intelligence community and foreign policy bureaucracy are attempting to undermine Clinton's publicly stated support for Aristide. During the 1970s, Sen. Frank Church speculated that the CIA had become a "rogue elephant", but his own investigation, and that of the Pike Committee in the House, found that virtually all covert operations were in fact undertaken at the direction of the President and his Cabinet. Now, nearly two decades later, it appears again that the CIA is undermining the stated policy of a sitting president.

It is easy, however, to overstate the degree of conflict between the president and the national security apparatus. From the outset, Clinton has been unwilling to expend the necessary political capital to combat hardliners, whether in Port-au-Prince, Washington, or Langley. Clinton betrays his own stance on democracy in Haiti with his refugee policy. By returning refugees, he lends credence to the view that human rights conditions in Haiti are tolerable enough to permit in-country processing, which in turn subverts the urgency of returning Aristide. Thus, although the conflict between Clinton and the bureaucracy raises troubling questions of accountability, it is far outweighed by the inherent contradictions within Clinton's own positions.

Haitian emigration, long a focus of U.S. racist fears and paranoia, seems the administration's most vulnerable point. Indeed, when Aristide scheduled an international conference in Miami on January 15 to reexamine refugee policy, the administration went into overdrive, forcing the exiled president to change the focus of the agenda to finding new strategies to revive the corpse of the Governor's Island accord.

Given the hostility to Aristide among the Haitian and U.S. elites, he appears unlikely to return much before the expiration of his term in 1995. At the Miami conference, Jesse Jackson suggested that Aristide's term should be viewed as on hold from the day of the coup until the day of his return. "Cédras and François must know that they will be leaving soon, and when they leave, his term starts up again from that day."[37]

By raising the issue, Jackson spat into the teeth of the disinformation campaign. U.S. officials and journalists often sum up the smears by implying that Aristide is "just like Duvalier." Thus, any attempt to extend his term beyond its constitutional length will likely be met with a furious propaganda volley. As the formal expiration date of Aristide's presidency approaches, the U.S. may push the military again, as it did in 1990, to hold elections. This time, however, the unifying leader of the popular movement will be ineligible, the movement itself will have suffered four years of systematic assault, and U.S. dollars will have a much greater opportunity to promote an acceptably "moderate" candidate.

NOTES

1. "Return to the Darkest Days: Human Rights in Haiti Since the Coup," Joint Report from Americas Watch, National Coalition for Haitian Refugees, and Physicians for Human Rights, December 30, 1991.

2. "OAS Rallies to Haiti's Side," *Miami Herald*, October 3, 1991.

3. "The OAS Agrees to Isolate Chiefs of Haitian Junta," *New York Times*, October 3, 1991, p. A8.

4. Abrams is a board member of Caribbean Latin American Action, an organization that promotes U.S. business development in the region.

5. J.P. Slavin, "Tanker Breaks Embargo, Delivers Fuel to Haiti," *Miami Herald*, January 3, 1992.

6. Author's interview, November 1993.

7. *Ibid.*

8. For an analysis of in-country processing, see *No Port in a Storm: The Misguided Use of In-Country Refugee Processing in Haiti*, Americas Watch/ National Coalition for Haitian Refugees, Jesuit Refugee Services, September 1993.

9. Article 14, paragraph 1 of the United Nations Universal Declaration of Human Rights states, "Everyone has the right to seek and enjoy in other countries asylum from persecution." Found in Walter Laqueur and Barry Rubin, *The Human Rights Reader* (New York: Meridian, 1979), p. 199. The bedrock principle of refugee law is "nonrefoulment," that states shall not return people to areas where they are likely to be persecuted. Article 22, paragraph 8, of the American Convention on Human Rights (1969) reads: "In no case may an alien be deported or returned to a country, regardless of whether or not it is his country of origin, if in that country his right to life or personal freedom is in danger of being violated because of his race, nationality, religion, social status, or political opinions." The U.S. tacitly admits violating this principle by subsequently granting asylum (through in-country processing) to refugees picked up at sea and summarily returned to Haiti.

10. *Silencing a People: The Destruction of Civil Society in Haiti*, Americas Watch/National Coalition for Haitian Refugees, New York, February, 1993.

11. Deposition of Gunther Wagner, *H.C.C. v. McNary*, May 5, 1992.

12. "Half the Story: Skewed U.S. Monitoring of Repatriated Refugees," Americas Watch/National Coalition for Haitian Refugees, June, 1992.

13. Wagner Deposition, pp. 98-100.

14. *Ibid*, p. 130.

15. "Haitian Situation Report: Repatriation," Department of Justice and Immigration and Naturalization Service, HQINT Dallas, Texas. Copy shown to author is undated, but was written after a March 1- 14, 1992 trip by Wagner. At page II: "These credible sources placed the deaths countrywide at between 350 and 500 during and immediately after September 29, 1991, vs. media and activists' estimates at between 1500 and 2000."

16. Deposition of Scott Busby, *H.C.C. v. Sales*. After Wagner's briefing, some asylum officers complained; asylum branch director Greg Beyer instructed Guantánamo management to make certain that asylum officers were exposed to all sources of human rights reporting about Haiti.

17. Deposition of Gunther Wagner, *H.C.C. v. Sales*, May 5, 1992, pp. 40-46, 97.

18. *Latin America and Empire Report*, NACLA, February, 1976, p. 24; Wagner Deposition, pp. 7-11.

19. Pacifica Radio National News, February 12, 1993.

20. Author's review of unclassified Department of State cable from U.S. Embassy, Port-au-Prince, to Secretary of State, February 14, 1992.

21. Christopher Marquis, *Miami Herald*, reprinted as "CIA Memo Discounts 'Oppressive Rule' in Haiti," *Washington Post*, December 19, 1993, p. A21.

22. *Ibid.*

23. "IMET Foreign Military Trainees From FY84 thru FY93," Defense Department Report dated November 15, 1993, provided to author by National Security News Service, Washington, D.C.

24. Elie press conference.

25. Anne Marie O'Connor, "A little known soldier becomes Haiti's police chief: Major received training in Ft. Benning, Ga.," *Atlanta Journal and Constitution*, October 11, 1991.

26. Don Bohning and John Donnelly, "The Enforcers: Who are the *attaches*? They are outnumbered, but have the bullets," *Miami Herald*, October 17, 1993.

27. Douglas Farah, "U.S. Shares Anti-Drug Data With Haiti's Military," *Washington Post*, October 24, 1993.

28. Clinton campaign statement, May 27, 1992.

29. Editorial, "Be firm, fair on Haitians," *Miami Herald*, November 18, 1992.

30. Douglas Farah, "Haitians Preparing Boats Denounce Policy Shift by Clinton," *Washington Post*, January 16, 1993, p. A19.

31. Author's telephone interview, January 19, 1993.

32. Comments of Director of Central Intelligence R. James Woolsey on the Diane Rehm show, syndicated nationally on the American Public Radio network, December 15, 1993. Woolsey refused comment on the content of the estimate, but publicly backed Latell's views.

33. Elaine Sciolino, "Haiti's Man of Destiny Awaits Transition From Political Martyr to Statesman," *New York Times*, August 3, 1993, p. A1.

34. Latell is best known for writing speculative profiles of Fidel Castro, dismissed by one colleague as "psychofiction," and for producing an inflammatory estimate predicting revolution in Mexico in 1984 at the behest of the late CIA director William Casey; see Bob Woodward, *Veil* (New York: Simon and Schuster, 1987), pp. 340-41. Reached by telephone at his home, Latell refused comment on Haiti.

35. R. Jeffrey Smith and John M. Goshko, "CIA's Aristide Profile Spurs Hill Concern," *Washington Post*, October 22, 1993.

36. Elie press conference.

37. "Highlights From the Miami Conference: What Was Said," *Haiti Info*, January 23, 1994, vol. 2, #10, p. 4. *Haiti Info* is published every two weeks in Haiti by the Haitian Information Bureau.

"SHADOW" PLAYS
DIRTY TRICKS IN HAITI
Phil Davison

According to Phil Davison, the original source of much of the inventive anti-Aristide propaganda circulated by U.S. intelligence was Lynn Garrison, a Canadian adventurer who had come to Haiti to "lend a hand" to the coup government. Writing in *The Independent* of London in the fall of 1993, Davison describes Garrison in action.

¬

He likes to be called "The Shadow." That is perhaps because Lynn Garrison, a Canadian, former fighter pilot and Hollywood stunt man, likes to lay low, is close to the CIA and is paranoid to the extreme about being photographed.

Perhaps it is because he shadows Haiti's military ruler, Lieutenant-General Raoul Cédras, the man facing down President Bill Clinton and the international community. Or perhaps it is because of the more than shadowy nature of his work for General Cédras, in a PR role that makes "dirty tricks" sound euphemistic.

Mr. Garrison, who collects vintage airplanes and flew stunts in the film "Those Magnificent Men in Their Flying Machines," is the man behind the recent smear campaign against Haiti's elected but exiled president, Father Jean-Bertrand Aristide. His description of the soft-spoken priest as a "psychotic manic depressive with homicidal and necrophiliac tendencies," and his description of the President's alleged calls for "necklacing" opponents (setting fire to petrol-filled tyres around their necks), formed the basis of CIA reports that caused splits in the United States over policy towards Haiti and may have led Mr. Clinton to back away from his earlier commitment to Mr. Aristide's return home.

There is little hard evidence to back up the allegations against Mr. Aristide, whose unarmed supporters have turned violent only after massacres by paramilitary gunmen, and whose followers see him more as a Gandhi figure than the madman recently portrayed.

How can one Canadian adventurer, who speaks neither French nor Creole, whose own mental make-up is at the very least unusual, have played such an important role in a country whose people are dying of terror and famine? Because, it seems, the CIA took him seriously, and his interpretation of diaries, paintings and medicaments he "liberated" from Mr. Aristide's private headquarters after General Cédras' coup in September, 1991.

Mr. Garrison, who served as a fighter pilot in the Canadian Air Force from 1964 to 1971 before plying his skills in Hollywood, is, by his own account, in contact with the CIA and Republican senators, including Jesse Helms and Robert Dole. It was Mr. Helms who branded Mr. Aristide a "psychopath" on the Senate floor recently. Mr. Dole has expressed similar sentiments to discourage Mr. Clinton from risking the lives of US troops on Mr. Aristide's behalf, democratically elected or not.

Mr. Garrison was called to Haiti by the coup leaders "to lend a hand" the day before they overthrew the populist President in 1991. He came, he insists, merely as a "friend of Haiti," unpaid (although provided with a bodyguard), and has been here since, often sleeping at military headquarters as a security measure.

His first task: to go through Mr. Aristide's private possessions at the palace, according to the rare interviews he has given. He found Mr. Aristide's diaries and handed copies over to a friend, Colonel Pat Collins, the then US military attache in Haiti who is now in Mogadishu. Mr. Garrison kept the originals for his private collection at his Los Angeles home.

Mr. Aristide's doodlings of eight-headed monsters, a common voodoo symbol, led to many of Mr. Garrison's later allegations. Then there were the naive paintings found on Mr. Aristide's walls, some showing people being tortured and killed by what is known here as "Pere Lebrun." Pere Lebrun was the name of a former tire manufacturer in Haiti, whose advertisements showed a smiling black face sticking his head through a tire. In Haiti, the "Pere Lebrun" paintings, like those of voodoo ceremonies that depict the biting off of chickens' heads and people in trances, are common. But Mr. Aristide's collection was apparently what led to the allegations that he advocated what in South Africa is commonly known as "necklacing." Contrary to reports circulated in the US, Mr. Aristide never mentioned "Pere Lebrun" in a speech before the 1991 coup, although he did refer to "that wonderful smell"—which could have been an abstract reference to the practice. His actual words have been non-violent.

Mr. Garrison also keeps the paintings in his Los Angeles collection, along with Mr. Aristide's pajama top, which he claims is of a voodoo design. The fact that his own military and police bosses practice voodoo as much, if not more, than the next man, Mr. Garrison apparently considers irrelevant. Michel François, the Port-au-Prince police chief, recently visited a renowned *houngan* (a voodoo priest) called Dieupere and sacrificed a bull in an eerie night ceremony, according to witnesses. Colonel François was apparently invoking the help of voodoo spirits in his face-off with Mr. Clinton.

Along with General Cédras, Colonel François was supposed to step down and allow Mr. Aristide to return by 30 October under the UN-brokered Governor's Island agreement.

Mr. Garrison has also made much of Mr. Aristide's medicine cabinet, whose contents he keeps in a box at military HQ and claims back up the allegations over the President's mental health. But those who have seen them say the medicine bottles appear designed for a man with heart trouble rather than mental problems.

Nevertheless, Mr. Garrison's one-man campaign may have tipped the balance in the US as Mr. Clinton kept US marines on alert for a possible intervention. While ostensibly continuing to back the exiled President and his return, US officials began using phrases such as a "weird, flaky guy" and Mr. Clinton himself made a faux pas when, in an attempt to back Mr. Aristide, he said, "Look at the alternatives."

Mr. Garrison has also accused Canada's ambassador to Haiti of having irregular links to the Libyan leader, Colonel Muammar Gaddafi. One wonders if it is his influence at work when virtually every Haitian official who is attacking opponents raises some alleged connection to Col. Gaddafi.

A US cameraman, waiting to film an interview with General Cédras last week at military headquarters, was idly twiddling a small automatic camera. "He took your picture," said a Haitian woman who appeared to have a close relationship with Mr. Garrison. The cameraman had not. But the Canadian "friend of Haiti" ripped out and exposed the roll, saying: "A man could die for this." At the cameraman's insistence, he replaced the film with a fresh roll.

HAITI IN THE MAINSTREAM PRESS: EXCESSES AND OMISSIONS

Catherine Orenstein

The CIA and the coup leaders were not alone in promoting an image of Aristide as dangerous and intractable. As Catherine Orenstein documents in *Lies of Our Times*, they were joined by much of the U.S. press. "In its coverage of Haiti," Orenstein writes, "the mainstream media have essentially functioned as the public-relations arm of the U.S. State Department."

⌐

At a demonstration last October against *New York Times* coverage of Haiti, Haitian protesters accused the newspaper of being "the voice of the state department." Their argument had some credibility: a three-month tracking from September 1991 through December 1991 shows that over 35 percent of sources who gave information or commentary in *Times* news articles were U.S. officials. Another 10 percent were unidentified diplomats. This total is almost double the count of all Haitian sources—military, peasant, elite, and Lavalas—combined. Preferential sourcing greatly affects not only the perspective printed, but also the "facts." For example, numbers of deaths attributed to the September 1991 coup ran from "dozens" (U.S. Embassy), to 500 for the week (international human rights groups), to 1,000 (Aristide, citing unreported mass graves). The mainstream media, by depending on State Department sources, run the risk of becoming its mouthpiece.

One of the subtle ways mainstream coverage of Haiti has imposed a U.S.-centric perspective is through an unbalanced use of epithets and adjectives. The media labels assigned to exiled president Aristide play heavily on North American political stereotypes. Aristide has been called a "populist demagogue" (*Los Angeles Times*, 3/18/92), and "a mix of Khomeini and Castro," (*New York Times*, 11/12/90) whose politics "come from Robespierre" (*Washington Post*, 10/2/93). In addition, political labels—"leftist," "socialist," "anti-American"—have been applied exclusively to Aristide and his movement as an unobtrusive and repetitive way of expressing disapproval. In contrast, the *de facto* government is not referred to as rightist. Former *de facto* prime minister Marc Bazin, who was previously the U.S.-backed candidate for president, was labeled, if at all, with the ironic sobriquet, "Mr. Clean" (*Los Angeles Times*, 6/3/92).

There is also an imbalance with respect to the topics the media choose to emphasize. In the days after the coup, newspaper attention focused not on the violence of the army, as one would expect, but rather on Aristide's human rights record. During the two-week period after the coup, the *New York Times* spent over three times as many column inches discussing Aristide's alleged transgressions than it spent reporting on the ongoing military repression. Mass murders, executions, and tortures that were reported in human rights publications earned less than 4 percent of the space that the *Times* devoted to Haiti in those weeks. The *Washington Post* (10/6/91) claimed Aristide organized his followers into "an instrument of real terror," but declined to note the 75 percent reduction in human rights abuses during Aristide's eight months in office reported by many human rights groups, including the National Coalition of Haitian Refugees (NCHR).

If the media reveal themselves in their excuses, what they don't report is just as telling. The failure of the embargo and the deplorable conditions at the Guantánamo Bay refugee camp are two examples. The OAS embargo and U.S. sanctions imposed against Haiti were represented in the mainstream press as forceful blows against the military government. The mainstream press gave little attention to reports of blatant disregard for the embargo. According to the National Labor Committee, for example, $67 million worth of apparel was imported to the United States from Haiti in 1992.

In addition, until a federal court ordered it closed, there was virtually no media coverage of the "temporary" refugee camp at Guantánamo. What little the papers reported gave the impression of a vacation camp: one *Times* article had the preposterous headline "U.S. Base is Oasis to Haitians" (11/28/91). The paucity of mainstream media coverage of Guantánamo—even after a journalist-inspired lawsuit won them limited access—suggests a high degree of self-censorship. This year's unreported events include a hunger strike on January 29, an escape by 11 "inmates" on March 11, and a military crackdown on March 13, in which women were subjected to vaginal searches and 12 barracks were burned down. These reports cast a dark shadow on the U.S. "solution" to the refugee crisis.

In its coverage of Haiti, the mainstream media have essentially functioned as the public-relations arm of the U.S. State Department. The mainstream press has increasingly painted the Haitian situation as intractable, with a choice of outcomes "between mob revenge and anarchy . . . hence the necessity of the U.N. force" (*Newsday*, 5/13). By denying the possibility of an internal Haitian solution, and by ignoring the ambiguous role already played by the United States, the U.S. media suggest that Haiti must once again bow to the traditional "necessity" of a U.S.-determined solution "for its own good."

2

U.S. AID PROGRAMS AND THE HAITIAN POLITICAL ECONOMY

"EXPORT—LED" DEVELOPMENT
Josh DeWind and David H. Kinley III

Over the last several decades, the United States has provided the bulk of the international aid that has gone to Haiti. In *Aiding Migration: The Impact of International Development Assistance on Haiti*, Josh DeWind, director of Latin American and Caribbean Studies at Hunter College, and David Kinley III, an information officer at the World Bank, chronicle the history of that aid. The Kennedy administration cut off aid in 1963 because of corruption and human rights abuses by François Duvalier. According to U.S. government estimates, as much as 80 percent of money earmarked for aid was used up in corruption and mismanagement. The U.S. did not restore aid until the inauguration of Jean-Claude Duvalier as president in 1972, and this was not because Duvalier had corrected human rights abuses or stopped the corruption, but because Henry Kissinger placed more emphasis on a web of international alliances than on any concern for human rights. By 1975, U.S. Agency for International Development (AID) monies to Haiti reached $59.3 million, and by the early 1980s, aid topped $100 million annually.

According to the World Bank, the total volume of international aid committed to Haiti from 1973 through 1981 was $477 million. Eighty percent of this support came from three sources: the U.S. government, the World Bank and the Inter-American Development Bank. Most of the U.S. aid went through AID to different departments of the Haitian government. This aid was generally ineffective at eradicating or alleviating poverty. A 1982 report from the Government Accounting Office, the Congressional research agency, concluded, "The AID program to date has had limited impact on Haiti's dire poverty, and many projects have had less than satisfactory results."

The Haitian government did not carry out the AID projects, and, for its part, AID did nothing to promote change in the power structure, especially in the countryside where it would have been necessary for agriculture projects to have any beneficial effects. DeWind and Kinley note that "while AID's own analysts determined that land concentration had become a major problem in Haiti—with the top 30 percent of the landholders controlling over two-thirds of the cultivable land—no programs to protect small holder land titles or to redistribute land were considered."

In 1981, Haiti, under Jean-Claude Duvalier, came forward with its own ambitious plan for development, which was rejected by the World Bank and U.S. AID as vague and incomplete. Instead, the international donors, led by the World Bank, organized their own scheme which emphasized an export-led development strategy, and pressured Duvalier into accepting it. In *Aiding Migration*, DeWind and Kinley described the plan, which would have an enormous impact on Haiti's future.

⌐

The World Bank has traditionally viewed its role as a bank and international development institution to be the enhancement of the infrastructure upon which private enterprise can flourish.[1] In Haiti, the bank has primarily supported projects such as port development, highways and sewage construction, and the installation of electric power plants. The bank considers these infrastructural projects to be necessary but insufficient for stimulating the private sector's growth. The remaining obstacle to development, from the bank's point of view, results from Haiti's poverty itself. Haiti's population is seen as being too poor to provide a market which can enable the private sector or the government to generate either the earnings or savings needed to sustain development.[2]

The bank believes that, in contrast to Haiti's impoverished domestic market, U.S. and other foreign markets can absorb Haiti's production and yield earnings that will sustain Haiti's economic growth. This vision of Haiti's economic prospects led the World Bank and other international development agencies to design an economic development strategy based upon export production.[3]

In order for Haiti to compete successfully in the international market, the international development agencies believe that its economy must be organized to exploit what AID calls its "comparative advantages."[4] This notion derives from classical 19th century international trade theories, which hold that each nation should develop those resources it possesses and that other nations might lack in the same quantity or richness. What one nation does not produce for itself can be obtained through trade with other nations with different endowments and products. In theory, the result should be an international division of labor in which each nation's population will be able to increase its wealth and satisfy its needs most efficiently.

The international agencies have identified Haiti's greatest international comparative advantage to be its hard-working, low-cost labor force. Other advantages include the country's potentially diversified agriculture, a climate favorable to year-round cultivation, and close proximity to the United States. The World Bank's export-led economic development strategy proposes to employ Haiti's comparative advantages primarily to develop the export potential of two economic sectors: agro-industry and the assembly industry.[4]

Development based on agro-industrial and assembly exports would require a major structural transformation of Haiti's economy and society. Although Haiti has been known historically as an exporter of coffee, cotton, and sugar, contemporary rural agriculture is primarily oriented toward subsistence consumption and local markets. Haitian industry is very underdeveloped and manufactured goods have primarily been produced in artisan shops or imported. Although the assembly industry has grown substantially over the last decade, it still employs only a minor segment of the labor force—approximately 40 thousand workers.

The transformations implied by export-led development can be traced, beginning with the proposed introduction of crops intended to be sold abroad. Marginal hillside lands, which are now producing food for local consumption and suffering from erosion, will be planted with soil conserving trees that yield export crops such as coffee or cacao. Large tracts of flat and potentially more productive land will be re-oriented toward the production of other export crops, such as fruits and vegetables, which can be sold fresh in U. S. winter markets or processed by agro-industrial plants for a more general export market. In total, AID proposes to shift 30 percent of all cultivated land from the production of food for local consumption to the production of export crops.[5]

AID advisors anticipate that such a drastic reorientation of agriculture will cause a decline in income and nutritional status, especially for small farmers and peasants. These problems are expected to last at least until export earnings reach a high enough level to pay for the import of foods no longer produced in Haiti. The agency's planning papers do not consider in detail what impact the development of agro-industry might have on small producers, but one obvious possibility would be a concentration of land holdings and expansion of plantations to attain economies of scale sufficient to supply the new processing plants. Despite the problems of income loss, decline in nutrition, and possible land concentration, AID expects that income from the expansion of export agriculture will in the long run raise the standard of living in rural areas.

Even if the transition to export agriculture is successful, AID anticipates a "massive" displacement of peasant farmers and migration to urban centers.[6] In the judgment of the World Bank,

> Although prospects for agricultural growth do exist, they are not of the magnitude required to sustain even the existing rural population. In addition, if soil conservation and reforestation efforts are to succeed, rural emigration will be needed to alleviate pressure on the land.[7]

Assuming "realistic agricultural development" such as that proposed by AID, the two agencies expect that by the year 2001, Haiti's urban population will have increased by 75 percent due largely to rural-urban migration. The population of Port-au-Prince alone is expected nearly to double during this period, from 850 thousand to 1.6 million people. AID's Food and Agriculture Strategy Team approved of this massive migration as a "mechanism for moving large segments of the population out of poverty."[8]

The growth of Haiti's assembly industry is a key component of the export-led development strategy. The industry's major function is expected to be providing employment and facilitating the absorption of the displaced rural population into urban Port-au-Prince. Another important role for the assembly industry will be to provide foreign exchange earnings needed to pay for imported foods no longer produced within the country. AID describes plans to attract new investments in the assembly industry as "undergirding the entire effort."[9]

Although the export-oriented development programs of the international agencies are not necessarily intended to supplant entirely other programs oriented toward the domestic market production, export programs are being given priority. AID, the World Bank, and the Inter-American Development Bank will continue to fund infrastructural programs such as road and irrigation system construction intended to increase productivity in raising food crops for the domestic market. Similarly, AID and the World Bank are contributing resources to an industrial fund that will finance the production of some manufactured goods for local consumption as well as for export. In the context of export-led development, however, economic measures that are intended to strengthen the domestic economy or are based on import substitution are being pushed aside. A case in point is the World Bank's opposition to tariffs, which the Haitian government instituted to protect local manufacturers against foreign competition. Responding to the tariffs, the World Bank warned:

> While open, the economy has been closing lately at the margin. . . . trade barriers (quotas, prohibitions and custom duties) have been raised and controls over export earnings have been installed. This may direct scarce resources towards less efficient uses in import-substitution. Such an inward-looking policy should be reversed if Haiti is to take full advantage of its comparative advantages.[10]

The reforms recommended by the World Bank would force weak domestic firms to compete with more efficient foreign producers.

Having economic development "led" by export production implies significant cutbacks in the already meager social services that the Haitian government provides for the poor. The World Bank summarizes this tradeoff clearly:

> Private projects with high economic returns should be strongly supported with accordingly less relative emphasis on public expenditures in the social

sectors. . . . Public development expenditures should concentrate on supporting output expansion in the most promising areas and sectors. Temporarily, less emphasis should be placed on social objectives which increase consumption, since the urgent need is to free a major share of GDP [gross domestic product] growth for export.[11]

The World Bank cites government programs that support education, health, and small farms as "examples of misdirected social objectives." Education, the bank admits, is "essential to long-term development," but in the short-term, "it represents a cost. . . . [that] should be minimized." While the bank recommends that programs that support poor farms "are socially desirable given Haiti's widespread rural poverty," the government should allocate its resources to other farms with greater "growth potential."[12]

In other words, the majority of the population that now lives below the level of absolute poverty is being asked to forego improvements in governmental education, health, and rural development programs that might improve their standard of living so that greater investments can be made in the production of goods to be sold and consumed abroad.

In summarizing the overall effects the export-led development strategy will have on the Haitian economy, AID stated:

> What this implies is a more open Haitian economy, with great potential for export manufacturers and processed agricultural products, but with a sharply growing need to import grain and other consumer products. The result will be an historic change toward deeper market interdependence with the United States.[13]

AID welcomes this increased international dependency as a means for Haiti to capitalize on its comparative advantages.

Testifying before the Congress in favor of increased funding to promote the export strategy in Haiti, M. Peter McPherson, then Acting Director of the International Development Corporation and Administrator of AID, predicted that closer ties to U.S. markets would "make the prospects for Haiti as the 'Taiwan of the Caribbean' real indeed."[14] The notion of Haiti's becoming the "Taiwan of the Caribbean" has been widely touted by journalists and promoters of the export-led development strategy.

Comparisons of Taiwan's economic structure with that of Haiti have, however, left some economists less than sanguine about potentials for Haiti's export-led growth. Paul Latortue has cautioned that Taiwan's remarkable spurt in export production from $19 million in 1960 to $8 billion in 1981 was possible only because the export sector was complemented by a strong domestic economy. Taiwan's domestic economy, he argues, is based upon both an agricultural reform, which took place in 1948, and many years of import substitution development prior to the massive growth of export industries.

Because Haiti possesses comparatively weak domestic agricultural and industrial sectors, Dr. Latortue believes that Haiti's imports will exceed exports and create a structural imbalance in trade that will be impossible to sustain. Casting doubt on whether the export strategy will ultimately help the poor, Dr. Latortue has pointed out that "Haitian workers are being asked to pay for imports at Miami prices on the basis of wages set at $2.80 a day."[15]

The Haitian government's 5-year plan for 1981-1986, which was criticized by the international agencies, does not call for export-led development. The plan lists increasing national production as its first objective and emphasizes the production of agricultural and manufactured goods for local consumption.[16] In pushing the Haitian government to modify the 5-year plan, the World Bank stated that "priorities are required to be defined" and listed the choice between "production for export vs. import substitution" as being an issue of "paramount importance."[17] It is not apparent from World Bank documents whether or not the Haitian government ever resisted adopting an export-led strategy. What is clear, however, is that the Haitian government was not offered much of a choice.

The World Bank's *Country Program Paper* issued in May 1983, one year after the bank proposed export-led development, indicates that the international development agencies coerced the Haitian government into accepting their new strategy.

Under strong pressure from the international financial community and from governments of traditional donor agencies, the President of Haiti and the group surrounding him were made to understand that continued aid to Haiti would require major policy corrections.[18] . . .

The Haitian government formally accepted the export-led strategy at the first subgroup meeting on Haiti Held by the World Bank's Caribbean Group for Cooperation in Economic Development, which met in June 1982. . . .

NOTES

1. Edward S. Mason and Robert E. Asher, *The World Bank Since Bretton Woods* (Washington, D.C.: The Brookings Institution, 1973), pp. 460-81.
2. World Bank, "Economic Memorandum on Haiti" (Report No. 3079-HA), May 25, 1982, p. 28-a; and "Economic Note for the Haitian Subgroup," November 23, 1983, pp. 5-7.
3. *Ibid.*
4. World Bank, "Country Program Paper, Haiti" (Review Draft), May 20, 1983, p. 5. The World Bank originally proposed that tourism be developed as an important component of this strategy, but tourism to Haiti has fallen in recent years and no related major projects have been "identified" or proposed by the Haitian government or the international development agencies (World Bank, 1982, p. 26).
5. U.S. AID, "Country Development Strategy Statement, Haiti, FY 1984," 1982, p. 89.
6. U.S. AID, "Food and Agriculture Sector Strategy for Haiti, Final Report," 1982, p. 172.
7. World Bank, 1983, p. 16.
8. U.S. AID, "Food and Agriculture Sector Strategy for Haiti," 1982, pp. 170-71 and Table IV.

9. U.S. AID, "Country Development Strategy," 1982, p. ii.

10. World Bank, 1982, p. v.

11. World Bank, "Haiti: Policy Proposals for Growth" (Report No. 5601-HA), June 10, 1985, pp. vi, 45.

12. *Ibid.*, pp. 45-46.

13. U.S. AID, "Country Development Strategy," 1982, p. ii.

14. Peter M. McPherson, "Economic Support Fund Assistance for Latin America and the Caribbean, Attachment A ("Current Economic Situation of Key Caribbean Basin Countries: Haiti"), Statement before the Committee on Foreign Affairs, House of Representatives, April 21, 1982.

15. Paul Latortue, Presentation at the "Conference on New Perspectives on Caribbean Studies: Toward the 21st Century," Hunter College, New York, N.Y., September 1, 1984.

16. Joint Commission for the Implementation of Foreign Assistance, *Acte Final de la VIIIeme Reunuion de la Commission Mixte pour L'Implementation des Programmes de Cooperation Externe en Haiti* (Washington, D.C.: Organization of American States, Inter-American Economic and Social Council, 1981), p. 147.

17. World Bank, 1982, pp. 21-22.

18. World Bank, 1983, p. 4.

SWINE AID
Paul Farmer

The exodus from Haiti's countryside, so eagerly desired by the international banking and aid agencies, was not easily engineered. Living on tiny plots of land was a long-established way of life in Haiti, but the international agencies' program received an important boost due to a fortuitous epidemic of swine fever. In 1978, African swine fever was detected in the pigs of the Dominican Republic, and that caused the United States to launch an investigation of pigs in Haiti, some of whom were found to be infected with the disease, although the actual numbers appear to have been small and the Haitian pigs seemed to be resistant to the disease. At any rate, if African swine fever ever made its way to the United States, the University of Minnesota estimated it would wreak $150 million to $5 billion worth of damage. And so, at the behest of North American experts, a great pig massacre began—an event which Bernard Diederich described as "the worst calamity ever to befall the peasant." Paul Farmer, a physician and anthropologist who has worked in Haiti for over a decade, describes the pig debacle in his book *AIDS and Accusation: Haiti and the Geography of Blame.*

᥎

In 1978, the appearance of African swine fever in the Dominican Republic led the United States to spearhead an epidemiologic investigation of the porcine stock in neighboring Haiti. Haitian pigs in the Artibonite Valley were found to have been infected. Curiously, however, few Haitian pigs had died. Some veterinary experts felt that this might be because the *kochon planch*, as the Haitian pig was termed, had become remarkably resistant to disease. Some peasants were sure there had been no swine fever, that the entire epidemic was a sham staged so that the North "Americans could make money selling their pigs."

North American agricultural experts feared that African swine fever could threaten the U.S. pig industry, and bankrolled PEPPADEP (Programme pour l'Eradication de la Peste Porcine Africaine et pour le Développement de l'Elevage Porcin), a $23 million extermination and restocking program. This would be no small task, as there were an estimated 1.3 million pigs in Haiti, and they were often the peasants' most important holding. The significance of the Creole pig, as it was called after its extermination, is well known to anyone who has studied the rural Haitian economy:

> The peasant subsistence economy is the backbone of the nation, and the pigs were once the main components of that economy. With no banking system available to him, the peasant relied on hog production as a bank account to meet his most pressing obligations: baptism, health care, schooling, funerals, religious ceremonies, and protection against urban-based loan sharks who would grab his land at the first opportunity.[1]

The Haitian peasantry was shaken cruelly by this latest twist of fate. Years later, it became clear that PEPPADEP had further impoverished and "peripheralized" the Haitian peasantry, if such a thing were possible, and had generated an ill will whose dimensions are underlined by Elizabeth Abbott: "PEPPADEP, the program to eradicate every last one of these Creole pigs, would be the most devastating blow struck [to] impoverished Haiti, but until there were actually no more pigs, the awesome consequences of PEPPADEP were neither understood nor predicted."[2] Initiated in May 1982 (well after the abatement of any clinical disease in Haiti), the pig slaughter ended in June of the following year. By August 1984, with no pigs left, the nation was declared free of African swine fever.

It is unlikely that a single Haitian peasant celebrated this veterinary victory. [Do] Kay [a rural village of about 1,000 people near Haiti's central plateau] resident Luc Joseph refers to the slaughter of the pigs as "the very last thing left in the possible punishments that have afflicted us. We knew we couldn't have cows. We knew we couldn't have goats. We had resigned ourselves, because we at least had our pigs." "I don't know how we're going to get over this one," said Dieugrand, another of the water refugees [who were forced to move to Do Kay from more fertile land nearby that was flooded as the result of a new dam], in the spring of 1984. "This hill is just too steep to climb." He is echoed by a Haitian economist, who observes that, although the value of the destroyed livestock has been estimated at $600 million, "the real loss to the peasant is incalculable.... [The peasant economy] is reeling from the impact of being without pigs. A whole way of life has been destroyed in this survival economy. This is the worse calamity to ever befall the peasant."[3] As apocalyptic as such evaluations sounded, they were soon revealed to be true:

> School opening that October, the first after PEPPADEP's final eradication of the nation's pigs, revealed that [school] registration had plunged as much as 40 to 50 percent. Street vendors of cheap notebooks and pencils went hungry. The Lebanese and Syrian dry goods merchants had unsold stockpiles of checkered cotton for the traditional Haitian school uniforms. Deschamps Printing Company's orders for Creole and French textbooks plummeted. All over Haiti children stayed at home, understanding that something was happening to them and that times were suddenly much harder.[4]

In Do Kay, the number of children reporting for the first week of school was down by a third, and Mme. Alexis, headmaster Mâitre Gerard, and mission treasurer Jésula Auguste spent days bringing uniforms and other "classical furnishings" to the homes of the no-shows. They were all determined that not a single child would be prevented from attending school because of the pig disaster, and with Père Alexis [local priest of the Eglise Episcopale d'Haiti] were actively planning to restore the pigs to the peasants.

Working with USAID and the Organization of American States, the Haitian government announced a pig replacement program, act two of PEPPADEP. As "suspicious" Haitians had predicted, the replacement stock was purchased from U.S. farmers. In order to receive Iowa pigs as a "secondary multiplication center," program participants were required to build pigsties to specifications and also demonstrate the availability of the capital necessary to feed the pigs. This effectively eliminated the overwhelming majority of peasants. Père Alexis decided that helping villagers to replace their lost pigs was an undertaking that fell squarely within his mission, despite his distaste for USAID. In the space of two months, he and his team had erected a sturdy tin-roofed sty that was, as many noted, "better than the homes of Christians." The priest's plan was to breed the pigs and distribute *gratis* the piglets, with the request that one piglet from each subsequent litter be returned to the project. In that way, he announced, the cycle could be continued until everyone had pigs. Since the new pigs were promised by North American agronomists to have litters of six to ten piglets, the proposal was greeted with satisfaction by the community. Dozens of villagers watched with delight as more than a score of sturdy piglets were delivered in the summer of 1985.

It did not take long for this auspicious beginning to go awry. The pigs looked little like the lowslung, black Creole pigs that had populated Haiti for centuries. Although the new pigs, soon termed *kochon blan* ("foreign pigs"), were very large, they were manifestly more fragile than their predecessors. They fell ill and required veterinary intervention; they turned their noses up at the garbage that had been the mainstay of the native pigs' diet. The *kochon blan* fared well only on expensive wheat-based, vitamin-enriched feed—a commodity also sold by the government. Although public proclamations assured the people that the price of pig feed would be controlled, artificially created shortages soon led to a thriving parallel market that netted fortunes for a few in the Duvalier clique and its successors. The cost of feed each year for an adult pig ran between $120 and $250, depending on the black market.

There were, in addition to technical difficulties, dilemmas of a more cultural order. With the help of his staff, Père Alexis had decided that the first litters of pigs should go to the community councils of Do Kay and surrounding villages, where they were to be held communally. This idealistic plan was approved in a large public meeting held in Do Kay shortly after the introduction of the new livestock, and well before the arrival of the first litters. Once distributed, the pigs did very well in two or three of the ten villages with which the Kay-based staff was working. In many of the others, however, there soon were difficulties. In some settings, the pigs simply did not thrive. Villagers admitted that they were unaccustomed to caring for communally held property. In at least two villages, one member of the community council attempted to claim ownership of one or more of the pigs. In Vieux Fonds . . . machetes were drawn during the course of pig-related arguments. In a community outside the limits of Alexis's sphere of action, the priest and his co-workers were accused of "spreading communist ideas," an accusation that was to recur in 1987. Père Alexis concluded that his error had been to exaggerate the local population's enthusiasm for the idea of shared property. There would be less division, he was sure, when pigs were distributed to individual households. But the slow process of distribution meant that for well over two years, some had pigs and some did not. Others had lost their pigs to sickness or bad business deals. The setting was ripe for hard feelings. . . . The next eruption of anger was expressed less directly, in *kola* accusations.

Kola is a root believed, in Do Kay at least, to be particularly noxious to pigs. When mixed with millet or corn stalks, it may be used as a pig poison. If its native toxicity is deemed insufficient, many feel that *Kola* may be "fixed" by an *amate*, a specialist in malicious magic. Magically enhanced *kola* is a far more efficacious poison. In this case, the poison is termed "not simple" (*pa senp*), a distinction that is invariably made when accusations of pig poisoning are brought up. . . . There seemed to be a *kola* accusation for every pig death.

Père Alexis threw up his hands, saying, "I give up! The only way to please everyone would be to import one thousand healthy adult Creole pigs and distribute them simultaneously!" A tour of the communities surrounding Do Kay convinced him that the "white pigs" were simply not suited to Haiti. The new pigs would not eat their predecessors' fare, and the cost of wheat shorts was subject to black market control and well beyond the reach of the rural poor. The dissension and *kola* accusations discouraged him, and the priest recommended that the pig project be closed down. But Mme. Alexis was insistent that "everybody have at least one pig," and decided that henceforth she would oversee the project.

Mme. Alexis focused her distribution efforts on individual families in Do and Ba Kay, rather than working through community groups. She too met with little success. Although several poor villagers sold their pigs for handsome profits, many of the *kochon blatn* did not fare well outside the complex. Some died, others simply failed to thrive. Sows came into heat infrequently and bore small litters. Less than four years after the inauguration of the pig project, Mme. Alexis also declared herself "ready to close down the project. It's a waste of time. These pigs will never become acclimated to Haiti. . . . Next they'll ask us to install a generator and air conditioning. . . ."

NOTES

1. Bernard Diederich, "Swine Fever Ironies: The Slaughter of the Haitian Black Pig," *Caribbean Review* 14(1), 1985, pp. 16-17, 41.
2. Elizabeth Abbott, *Haiti: The Duvaliers and Their Legacy* (New York, McGraw Hill, 1988), p. 241.
3. Diederich, p. 16.
4. Abbott, pp. 274-275.

SWEATSHOP DEVELOPMENT
The National Labor Committee

For some Haitians, the killing of pigs appeared to be part of a larger U.S. development plan to push the peasants off their tiny subsistence farms into the cities, where they could take jobs in the burgeoning U.S.-owned plants that assembled toys and clothing for the U.S. market. And whether or not one cares to accept this as part of a cynical plot, the pig fiasco does fit in remarkably well with the overall redirection of the Haitian economy.

As part of the redirection of aid, the Reagan Administration's Caribbean Basin Initiative was intended to boost the production of goods in the region by offering free access to the U.S. market. U.S. AID helped to establish promotional offices in the Caribbean to lure investors to the region and concentrated on boosting assembly operations.

The results of this project are best chronicled in *Haiti After the Coup: Sweatshop or Real Development?*, a report by Charles Kernaghan, Barbara Briggs, and their associates at the New York-based National Labor Committee Education Fund in Support of Worker and Human Rights in Central America. U.S. investment represents 90 percent of total foreign investment in Haiti, and 95 percent of the country's light manufacturing exports are destined for U.S. markets. Foreign companies pay no taxes in Haiti, and, as the U.S. Commerce Department rhapsodized in 1985, "Both foreign and Haitian businessmen share the same views on the environment for doing business in Haiti. All fully appreciate the low-cost labor and strong work ethic of the Haitian people."

As reported by the National Labor Committee delegation that visited Haiti in March of 1993, many Haitian assembly workers make the equivalent of U.S.14 cents an hour. And while U.S. AID programs worked to encourage American corporations to locate in Haiti's free-trade zone, they fought against Aristide's efforts to raise the minimum wage—to 37 cents an hour.

┐

SKIRTING THE EMBARGO

Two days after the September 30, 1991 Haitian military coup ousted democratically elected President Jean-Bertrand Aristide from power, the Organization of American States (OAS) imposed a commercial embargo on Haiti. The Bush administration did not comply with the embargo for a full month, and then gave U.S. companies until December to start clearing out their inventories.

Just as the embargo was getting underway, U.S. companies began a lobbying effort directed at the Bush Administration to end U.S. compliance with the international embargo. On December 23, 1991, corporations with business interests in Haiti bought space in the *Washington Post* to publish an open letter to President Bush. They argued that, "By lifting the U.S. embargo you will save lives and lay the economic groundwork for a permanent, stable democracy. . . . Please Mr. President," stated the corporations, "give the American and Haitian workers the *best Christmas present yet* by allowing them to go back to work."

On February 4, 1992, George Bush lifted the embargo on U.S. companies assembling goods in or sourcing production from Haiti. State Department spokeswoman Margaret Tutwiler stated that the Foreign Assets Control office of the U.S. Treasury Department would grant special licenses for U.S. companies on a case-by-case basis. "But if one of those companies is, in fact, owned by an individual actively supporting the coup, we do not believe that Treasury would issue a license." One hundred and fifty licenses were issued.[1]

But the Treasury Department did, in fact, hand out licenses to companies controlled by well known coup organizers. . . .

The Mevs family is well known in Haiti. It is described in the *Journal of Commerce* (March 4, 1993) as one of the "handful of families who rose to great wealth during the dictatorship of François (Papa Doc) Duvalier with a monopoly on the country's sugar industry."[2] The monopoly, known as the Haitian Sugar Company and owned by Fritz Mevs Sr., was one of the corporations that appealed to President Bush to lift the embargo as a "Christmas present" for the workers.

The *International Business Chronicle* (March 15-28, 1993) reports that "a small clique of rich import-export merchants, with close ties to the military authorities in local ports, have profited from the embargo by smuggling banned goods."[3] The Mevs family has its own private pier in Port-au-Prince. Haitian Senator Bernard Sansaricq recently accused Fritz Mevs, Sr. of running contraband cement illegally imported from Jamaica and Cuba. According to Senator Sansarich, Mevs made four million dollars on each of nine illegal cement shipments beginning in June 1992.[4] Fritz Mevs, Sr. is also "said to share the military's disdain for Mr. Aristide,"[5] according to the *Journal of Commerce*. . . .

The Bush Administration repeatedly turned to this same Mevs family to seek help in breaking the political deadlock in Haiti. The *Journal of Commerce* noted that Dante Caputo, the UN/OAS Special Envoy to Haiti, "resents the U.S.-Mevs contacts. He says they reinforce the view that Washington is coddling anti-Aristide forces, the very people Mr. Caputo says must cede to international pressure to restore democracy."[6]

The Mevs family also owns over 2.5 million square feet of factory and warehouse space—60 buildings—spread out over three industrial parks housing assembly industries that target the U.S. market. The Mevs' assembly operation near the national airport is said to be one of the largest privately-owned industrial parks in the Caribbean.[7]

THE MODEL FACTORY: .14 CENTS AN HOUR

Aware that we were a labor delegation, a very decent representative of a Haitian manufacturers association still arranged for us to visit a Haitian assembly factory. We knew they would show us the top of the line. The Vetex factory, we were told by the manager who was showing us around, was a joint venture between the Mevs family and RSK Industries, Inc., an apparel firm headquartered in New York.

The Vetex company consisted of two adjacent plants where approximately 500 sewing operators, inspectors, folders and packers—overwhelmingly women—were assembling children's wear and women's undergarments for export to the U.S. market. The children's matching outfits, the swimsuits and the little girls dresses were particularly colorful. These women were sewing for Sears—some of the children's wear labels we saw were Silver Unicorn, KV Kids and Electric Kids. The factory also assembles clothing for J.C.Penny and Wal-Mart. Other labels we saw were Devant and Seabell.

The plant was clean and well lit, despite the fact that there were few windows. Piped-in "Muzak" was playing over loudspeakers. It was hot, but not stifling since there were fans, though it was not air conditioned like the front office.

The legal minimum wage in Haiti is H$3 a day. The Vetex manager, who had been educated at Rutgers University in New Jersey, explained in perfect English that he paid his workers H$5 a day. He also told us that they were turning out 228,000 panties and bras a week for shipment to the States.

The factory operated on a five-and-a-half day schedule, 6:30 a.m. to 3:30 p.m. Monday through Friday and 6:30 a.m. to 12:30 p.m. on Saturday—a 45-hour work week, not including lunch break.

A Haitian dollar equals 5 gourds. So a wage of H$5 would amount to 25 gourds a day. At the current exchange rate of 13.5 gourdes to one U.S. dollar, the Vetex workers would be making US$1.85 a day, or 23 cents an hour. For a 45-hour week they would earn $11.11.

However, even these claims by management turned out to be inflated. We were a fairly large delegation, 10 people, including our two translators. Members of our delegation were able to break off from the main group, staying far enough behind to be able to speak privately with the workers.

A different story emerged. The majority of workers told us that they were paid H$3 a day. This amounts to *US$1.11 a day*. Incredibly, this is less than *14 U.S. cents an hour*.

One woman we spoke to was a single mother with two children. She told us that she made H$3 a day—US$1.11. How did she make ends meet? She said it cost her the U.S. equivalent of 44 cents a day for transportation to and from work—there is no public transportation. The workers use the colorful, but dangerously over-crowded "tap-taps," which are small pickup trucks outfitted with covered wooden cabs and benches. She also spent about 30 U.S. cents for lunch. This meant that she went home at the end of a nine-hour day with the equivalent of 37 U.S. cents in her pocket. . . .

An extremely competent looking woman in her late thirties who had worked in the plant for four years as an inspector made H$4 a day. No one we spoke with made more than this. Four Haitian dollars is the equivalent of

US$1.48 a day. Travel cost her 52 U.S. cents a day and she spent 37 cents a day on food. That leaves 59 U.S. cents. To make H$4.00 she works a nine hour day. She has two sons, eight and ten. She told us, "The money goes very fast. Often there is nothing left for the weekend."

As we were about to walk away she looked at us and said, "We want our president back."

A young man was sewing Electric Kids outfits. He had worked in the plant for four years. He was making H$3 a day. He had a wife and two children, aged one and four-and-a-half. It cost him 41 U.S. cents a day for transportation and he skipped lunch. This meant he could go home with 70 cents a day.

He and his family can afford only one meal a day. His home is a one-room straw hut. There is no water, no electricity. When it rains, the house becomes flooded and everything is drenched. For such a house for his family, he pays US$115 a year rent. What else can you afford on wages of 14 cents an hour?

We asked, was there ever a union here? He told us, "There used to be a union before the coup. After the factory re-opened, all the union members were fired."

As we were leaving the factory, some of us trailing far enough behind the manager could hear the workers telling us in a loud, persistent whisper, "Three dollars a day. Only three dollars a day." They wanted to set the record straight. . . .

LET THEM EAT SUGAR CANE WATER AND BREAD

A researcher gave a Haitian woman friend of hers H$15 and together they went off to the La Saline market, which is located in a poor slum area. She wanted to see what and how much food the woman could buy with the H$15, which is about $5.55 U.S.

The Haitian woman was an experienced shopper. This is what she was able to purchase before the money ran out:

- A small basket of 12 plantains
- four onions
- four tomatoes
- about 3 cups of cornmeal
- four bouillon seasoning cubes
- a cup of sugar

That was it. She explained that since the coup, market prices had quadrupled.

The most common meals for working families are cornmeal with onions or some boiled plantains with beans—when beans can be afforded. Almost everyone is down to one meal a day. Most have to borrow what they can to survive. Many working families have only bread to eat and rely upon sugar cane water to fill themselves up. The poor are barely surviving, but they are getting sicker.

At the "model" apparel factory owned by one of the richest families in Haiti, the highest paid workers received H$4 a day—US$1.48. The average transportation cost to and from work was 44 cents a day, while a meager breakfast and lunch came to 33 cents. This left 71 U.S. cents to bring home at the end of an eight or nine hour day. Multiply this by six days and you have $4.26 to meet a family's expenses for a week. According to USAID, food typically accounts for 64 percent of the cost of a basic "basket" of necessities needed for the minimal survival of a poor Haitian family.[8] This means that a working family would have approximately $2.73 a week with which to feed themselves—a little less than half of what our experienced Haitian shopper had to spend. The remaining $1.53 would have to cover rent and all other expenses. . . .

THE "MOST DYNAMIC SECTOR" OF THE ECONOMY

RSK, J.C. Penney and Wal-Mart can do better than this. Sears can do better than this. It doesn't have to contract out work for 14 cents an hour. In 1990, Sears Roebuck's gross revenue totaled *$56 billion*. This was 34 times the size of Haiti's entire gross domestic product in 1991.

We watched the workers at the Vetex plants attaching Sears "Kid Vantage" price tags to the children's clothing they had sewn. The price for one child's outfit was $9.99. The label proudly advertised that it had been printed on recycled paper. Standing in that factory in Haiti, this play toward the environmental consciousness of the U.S. consumer seemed hollow, even plain cynical. . . .

The National Labor Committee knows of 66 U.S. companies importing mostly assembled goods from Haiti. In 1992, despite the OAS international embargo, U.S. apparel firms and retailers—"under a loophole benefiting U.S.-owned exporters"—imported *$67,629,000*-worth of clothing sewn in Haiti.[9]

We had the chance to visit another apparel plant, which wasn't the top of the line. It wasn't owned by the Mevs like the Vetex plant, but conditions were a little better.

At this plant, 400 women sewed eight hours a day assembling women's undergarments for Rocky Mount, TNB/NY and State Nightwear labels. The base pay was H$4.50. With overtime the women could earn H$6.50 a day.

But even H$6.50 is only US$2.41 for a nine hour day—27 cents an hour. Workers and owner agreed, you cannot survive on that pay.

We questioned the owner, "Why can't you pay more?" He explained that when the embargo was lifted many U.S. companies let it be known that they would continue contracting assembly work to Haiti only if their costs were lowered. The owner claimed he could not pay more and survive in the business. What were other assembly companies paying? He told us that many he knew of were paying H$2.00. That would be only 74 U.S. cents a day, *nine cents an hour*. Had his factory ever been inspected for compliance with state occupational health and safety or environmental regulations? "Never," he responded. Does his company pay taxes? "No, none of the companies do." Are there any health or pension benefits for the employees? "No, not now. The companies pay nothing." Was there a union in his plant? "There was a union before the coup, but afterwards the repression was too great. The military was hunting them. They were afraid and fled Port-au-Prince. Now, we have no union."

He was a factory owner. He was obviously doing quite well for himself. We asked if assembly operations like his, which sewed cut fabric shipped from the U.S., were the way to develop Haiti's economy. Again he answered, "No. There is no tie-in between these assembly operations and the domestic economy. We get the pieces, the labels, the plastic wrappings and the hangers from the U.S. All we do is sew and then ship. This is not going to build real industry in Haiti."

Later, we were told by a representative of a manufacturers association that the "value added" by the garment assembly sector in Haiti to the products exported was 13 percent. No component of the garment is produced locally in Haiti. The only value added to the clothing is the cost of the labor to sew it. At a wage of 14 cents an hour with no benefits, no corporate taxes and factory rents of US$1.25 per square foot per year, that does not leave much money behind in Haiti. According to the U.S. Commerce Department, Haiti exported $177.9 million worth of apparel to the U.S. in 1989.[10] USAID maintains that Haiti's assembly sector is the "most dynamic sector" of the economy. But the real value of Haiti's apparel exports in 1989 was only $23.1 million dollars—the labor value added in Haiti—not $177.9 million. Most of this apparel "trade" comprised U.S. components going back and forth.

MILITARY STEALS THE WORKERS' PENSIONS

ONA, the National Office of Old Age Pension, was created in 1967. It was to function as a social security system to cover workers who retired or were incapacitated. Two percent was deducted from the employee's wage, and the employer was supposed to match that two percent.[11]

Businesses—including U.S. companies—stopped paying social security benefits after Duvalier fled in 1986. This is confirmed by U.S. Department of Labor "Foreign Labor Trends" reports on Haiti. The Labor Department states in its Key Labor Indicators that from 1986 through 1989 "supplementary benefits as % of manufacturing earning" in Haiti were "negligible."[12] In other words, as standard practice assembly companies in Haiti were paying no benefits for their employees.

Even when the money was being collected by ONA, it was deposited at the National Bank at zero percent interest rate. The funds sometimes served as a pool of no interest/no payback loans for Duvalier's business cronies.

Now that the military is in charge, what is left of the ONA fund is being totally plundered. The Port-au-Prince Chief of Police, Lieutenant Colonel Joseph Michel François appointed his girlfriend Margareth Lamur to run the ONA pension fund.

Another of Lt. Col. François' businesses was reported on in 1992 by the London-based *Economist Intelligence Unit*:

> One operation was providing a group of officers with $500,000 a month through racketeering in cement from the state factory; the group was said to involve the Chief of Police, Colonel Michel François, who is reported to be a multi-millionaire. Some are said to have become millionaires by exploiting shortages resulting from the embargo."[13]

A Haitian Army captain's salary is US$160 a month, but by plundering the poorest country in the Western Hemisphere—their own—the military leaders live like—and are—millionaires.

It is this same police chief who banned all street demonstrations, no matter how small and orderly.

Lt. Col François was trained at the U.S. military's School of the Americas in Georgia at U.S. taxpayers' expense.

Haitian workers are also supposed to have health insurance. The public agency is called OFATMA, the National Insurance, Worker Accidents, Illness and Maternity Office. By law, the employer is mandated to pay the equivalent of three percent of the company's payroll to OFATMA. Again, no one does, including the U.S. companies.[14]

If you enter a state-run hospital in Haiti, you must bring your own sheets and purchase your own food while you are there. Often more than one person is in a bed. Patients have to buy their medicines as well as any needles that might be used. A foreign religious worker who had been working in Haiti for over a decade told us that at the state-run hospital in Hinche, Haiti's fourth largest city, there is blood on the floors and sheets, and the stench is unbearable.

After the coup, the military destroyed the union at the state-owned telephone agency, Teleco. Some unionists were killed, others fled. The military then fired both the workers who represented the union as trustees overseeing the workers pension fund along with management. Once the union was gone, the military could start plundering the estimated $2.6 million telephone workers' fund.

A former high official in Teleco told us that it was standard practice—even during the short Aristide government—for several military leaders to receive "paychecks" every fifteen days.

WHAT USAID KNEW: EXPORTS UP, WAGES DOWN

USAID knew that legally mandated worker health and pension benefits were not being paid by either domestic or U.S. companies operating in Haiti.[15]

USAID also knew that Haitian wages, expressed in U.S. dollars, had fallen 39 percent from 1983 to 1991.[16] But even this underestimates the severity of the wage cuts. Since benefits were also not being paid, the dollar value of Haitian wages had actually fallen 56 percent between 1983 and 1991. And this wage decline coincided with a virtual doubling of Haitian apparel exports to the U.S.

By 1989, there were 100 U.S.-Haitian joint venture apparel operations employing 15,000 sewers assembling clothing for the U.S. market. Haitian apparel exports to the U.S. grew from $81 million in 1983 to $177.9 million in 1989. This represented an average 14 percent annual increase. In 1989, apparel comprised 47 percent of Haiti's total exports to the U.S. In 1989, Haiti was the third largest exporter of apparel to the U.S. in the entire Central American and Caribbean region.[17]

USAID knew that each job in the assembly export sector in Haiti feeds an estimated five to seven people.[18] In 1990, an estimated 70 percent of the Haitian workforce was either unemployed or underemployed.

How do seven people survive on a wage of 14 U.S. cents an hour? Even the highest paying jobs at the Vetex apparel plant owned by Mevs and RSK, Inc. left the worker with $2.73 (U.S.) to spend on food for the week. Divide that by seven, and you get 39 cents to feed a person for a week, or six cents a day.

USAID also knew that transportation costs cut deeply into the workers' wages. A study done in the early 1980s found that some assembly workers spent as much as one-quarter of their daily wage, and two hours of time, just getting to and from work. "Transportation to and from work is a major problem for employees in Port-au-Prince," according to the U.S. Commerce Department, which went on to note that, "It is both expensive and unreliable."[19]

In fact, the U.S. government knew a lot about the reality of the Haitian assembly jobs USAID was promoting. In 1989, the U.S. Commerce Department summarized the working and living conditions of Haitian assembly workers this way:

> Health and sanitation facilities at all socioeconomic levels are either limited in degree of sophistication or nonexistent. The vast majority of the population, including most of the relatively better-off factory employees in Port-au-Prince, does not have ready access to safe drinking water, adequate medical care, or sufficient nutritious food. There are essentially no unemployment or social assistance programs. Education is relatively expensive and thus out of reach for much of the population.[20]

WOMEN GET SPECIAL TREATMENT FROM USAID

In 1986, USAID put $7.7 million into an Export and Investment Promotion Project "to recruit assembly contracts and attract overseas investors" to Haiti. USAID felt that "medium and smaller-sized American compan[ies], which often do not have overseas offices, have to be reached through aggressive outreach efforts." Haiti's "large pool of productive, competitive labor seeking employment" would be one of the "factors enhancing" this promotional effort.[21]

According to USAID, one of the primary objectives was to help Haitian women. USAID observed that, "Assembly industries in Haiti have a tendency to create a relatively greater demand for female workers who are believed to be better qualified for work which requires detail, dexterity, and patience. This carries a particular advantage in that increased employment for women in urban areas provides additional income which will more directly bear on the welfare of infants and children."[22]

USAID carried out a "social soundness analysis" showing that "the project will have a strong impact on women . . ."

In 1984, USAID was writing the same thing: "The assembly industries constitute one of the most dynamic economic activities in generating jobs for women. To date, they have created some 60,000 jobs locally, 85% of which are occupied by women."[23]

Only here, USAID admits that, "Although the importance of women in the industrial sector of Haiti is unquestionable, the conditions under which they work are not generally conducive to realizing their productive capacities nor adequately safeguarding their children's welfare."[24]

USAID's public stance was that its real target in working with and financing Haiti's business sector was always to create decent paying jobs that would allow Haitian families to live in dignity and health. How odd then, that USAID has no empirical studies clearly documenting the number of jobs created in Haiti's assembly export sector, no studies on what percentage of these jobs went to women, whether or not the minimum wage was paid, how many hours were worked, whether overtime and benefits were paid, what working conditions were, how people traveled to and from work, what it cost and how long it took, and how families could afford to live on the wages paid. In 1984, USAID observed, "Haiti has no reliable work force data."[25] In 1992, the U.S. Commerce Department again noted, "No reliable data exists" on wages and that, "Reliable data on employment are nonexistent in Haiti."[26] USAID never bothered to document the most basic working and living conditions of those very people whom they were supposed to be assisting. What little information exists has to be pulled from between the lines, or sought in other places than USAID reports.

However, USAID was funding studies as early as 1980 that were proving that it was far cheaper for U.S. companies to produce in Haiti than in the U.S., despite the costs of relocation, setting up production, freight and customs. A survey of Haitian and U.S. electronic assembly plants operating in Haiti established that 38 percent of the companies enjoyed savings of between 20 and 40 percent over U.S. production, while 20 percent enjoyed savings of between 40 and 60 percent. This study may also have pinpointed the real interest in women assembly workers; that is, "Women workers tend to be quieter." Also, "Traditional management prerogatives such as the right to hire and fire are respected by the government. There are no profit sharing schemes or feather-bedding requirements." Only quiet women who "are young and highly motivated" and who "adapt easily to industrial discipline" are strong candidates for employment.[27]

USAID never wavers. In June of 1991, USAID allocated another $5 million to continue its 1986 investment promotion efforts aimed at attracting assembly industries to Haiti. No need for another "social soundness analysis," for "The impact of this project on Haiti's poor was demonstrated in the original economic and social soundness analyses" back in 1986 (despite the fact that there was no reliable data, starting in 1984 through 1992, concerning the actual living and working conditions of assembly workers).

USAID could still go on to note in mid 1991 that, "Most of these jobs will be for low-income citizens with a large proportion of these going to women. As citizens enjoy employment opportunities, they can then secure their shelter, provide necessary nutrition for their families, place their children in schools and provide adequate health care for their families. With improvement in the social status of its citizens, Haiti's new democracy will be strengthened and the participation of its population assured."[28]

No sooner had this been said, then USAID set out to oppose the Aristide government's attempt to raise the pitifully low minimum wage in Haiti's export assembly industry.

USAID OPPOSES WAGE INCREASE

A factory employee who worked for Wilson Sporting goods in Port-au-Prince during the period President Aristide was in office told us that he worked ten hours a day for US$12.22 a week. This would make an annual wage of $635.29. Even if this was only nine hours of work, allowing an hour for lunch, it would still amount to only 27 US cents an hour, $2.44 a day, without benefits. This was a little above the minimum wage, which has been set at 15 gourdes a day since 1984. At the 1991 market exchange rate of 8.5 gourdes to one U.S. dollar, the minimum daily wage for an eight hour day was US$1.76, or 22 cents an hour. Wilson's extra five cents an hour meant it was paying 23 percent above the minimum wage. This must be what the U.S. Commerce Department meant when it stated, "Although no reliable data exists, wages in the assembly sector, which are based mainly on piece-work, are higher than the minimum . . . "[29]

On April 2, 1991, just two months into the new administration, President Aristide invited Haiti's private sector leaders to the National Palace for a meeting. He appealed to them: "The country needs you." President Aristide requested their help.[30] Something had to be done to begin to improve the miserable conditions destroying the Haitian people. A year earlier the Haitian Chamber of Commerce had warned that "the execrable living conditions of our workers" would eventually lead to social upheaval.

The U.S. Commerce Department was saying that, "In real terms the minimum wage declined 45 percent"[31] in Haiti since 1985. But it was worse still, because health and pension benefits were not being paid. And as USAID observed, in 1990, "essential services and infrastructure have deteriorated significantly" because of military corruption preceding the Aristide government. USAID pointed out that, "Haiti is one of the world's least developed countries and is the poorest country in the Western Hemisphere."[32]

President Aristide, who was elected by over 67 percent of the popular vote, proposed raising the daily minimum wage from 15 gourdes to 25 gourdes. The Haitian Senate called for a new minimum wage of 28 gourdes.

If President Aristide's reform measures had gone through, the new minimum daily wage in U.S. dollars would have been $2.94 a day, or 37 cents an hour. The Aristide government also pressed to reform the corrupt national workers' health and pension benefit agencies. Had Aristide's plan been accomplished, and had real benefit payments been made by domestic and foreign companies, the fully loaded minimum daily wage would have been $4.03, or about 50 cents an hour.

Had the Haitian Senate's wage package been approved the fully loaded minimum hourly wage would have been 53 cents an hour.

Though the new minimum wage under the Aristide government would have still been less than one-eleventh of the average U.S. apparel wage (50 cents versus $5.85 an hour), USAID opposed this increase and orchestrated opposition to it.

USAID GOES ON THE ATTACK AGAINST REFORMS

In the middle of the constitutional government's short reign, USAID was declaring that "signals" from the Aristide Administration "to the business community have been mixed." USAID went on the attack saying that, "decisions have been made which could be highly detrimental to economic growth, for example in the areas of labor and foreign exchange controls."[33] USAID was displeased with the fact that the democratically elected government wanted to place temporary price controls on basic foodstuffs so the people could afford to eat.

But USAID's real wrath was targeted on labor reform efforts. According to USAID, the proposed minimum wage increase would price Haiti right out of the low wage assembly market. We are told that "wage systems should not be the forum for welfare and social programs." USAID warned that "high distortion in labor costs"—i.e. the 50 cent hourly wage proposed by the constitutional government—"for example, can lead to capital intensive, rather than labor intensive responses to opening of markets."[34] Haiti might turn into Switzerland or Denmark.

The Haitian government had to understand this one thing: "Haiti has comparative advantage in its location and in its highly productive, low-cost labor force." USAID set the game rules: "The business sector in Haiti has been a dynamic force since the mid-1970s with exporters, primarily in the drawback assembly sector, diversifying products and markets to capitalize on Haiti's comparative advantages in the world marketplace." USAID threw its full weight behind "stimulating the growth of demand for labor."[35]

USAID had work to do. In 1991, USAID stated, "Labor remains a major problem in business development and expansion in Haiti. While Haitian labor is generally highly productive at the worker level, frequent disruption caused by strikes, unexpected holidays and labor actions impede overall productivity in Haiti." Also, "With the proposed minimum wage, Haiti's pricing of exported goods will exceed that of the Dominican Republic, Jamaica, El Salvador and Honduras."[36]

This was not true, and USAID knew it. A study commissioned by USAID showed that even if Haiti's manufacturing wage were increased to 75 cents an hour, well above what the Aristide Government was proposing, this would still be 15 percent lower than Jamaica; 35 percent lower than Cost Rica; 50 percent lower than Mexico; and 64 percent lower than Barbados. The only country Haiti would surpass if a 75 cent an hour wage was achieved would be the Dominican Republic,[37] USAID's proclaimed showcase of a successful—and USAID sponsored—development strategy.

Also threatening was that, according to USAID, the Haitian "labor courts have been viewed as predominately biased in favor of labor." USAID would therefore, "address these judicial issues and work with the business community to document handling of labor disputes for dialogue with the government."[38]

Just how threatening to the investment climate in Haiti was the labor movement? To answer this we will quote at length from USAID itself.

> The army, always a corrupt element that routinely loots the society, has been allowed to run out of control. The old privileged elites of the Duvalier era are still largely in place, and rapacious new ones have arisen to seize hold of the Haitian economy. These entrepreneurs have a 19th century approach to making money and have moved in to take advantage of the country's massive and cheap labor pool. They run sweatshops, pay starvation wages and oppose any effort to improve the lot of the average impoverished Haitian. It is this new economic class that Haiti's incipient trade unions now battle against on behalf of their members. The most that can be said for the unions' progress is that they have a toehold in the society . . . [39]

This could have been written by the Haitian labor movement, by the National Labor Committee, by Americas Watch, by the Washington Office on Haiti, or by Amnesty International. However, it was written by USAID in August 1990 for a 1991 Haiti project it was funding.

For the last decade, the U.S. Commerce Department has essentially portrayed worker rights conditions in Haiti as unchanged. The following, written by Commerce in 1991 is typical of its yearly reports:

> Haitian labor unions remain weak for social, historical, and economic reasons. Union contracts do not yet exist; rather, informal, unofficial, mostly unwritten agreements, and in some cases, tacit acceptance allow the presence of unions in plants. Although unions have become relatively more active in grievance negotiations, formal management recognition of unions as bargaining agents is not yet the norm. Even with no government interference, the relatively new phenomenon of trade unionism has developed erratically in Haiti, where unemployment or under employment is estimated to affect at least 50 percent of the available work force, and where many employers would prefer not to work with unions.[40]

In summary, USAID sees Haiti's unions as having a tiny "toehold" in an economy dominated by rapacious elites left over from the Duvalier era, while the U.S. Commerce Department sees Haiti's unions as weak in a society "where many employers would prefer not to work with unions."

One might conclude from this that USAID would be supportive of labor unions. Unfortunately, nothing could be further from the truth.

USAID LONGS FOR A "GOOD INVESTMENT CLIMATE"

Under the Aristide government, USAID observed, "Businesses are postponing investment and reducing inventory while waiting to see the future directions of the new government before making significant business growth decisions."[41] USAID, which had spent tens of millions of U.S. tax dollars since 1980 to foster offshore investment in Haiti's low wage assembly sector, stopped promoting investment in 1991.

Three months before the coup d'état that toppled the democratically elected government, USAID was musing: "If Haiti's investment climate can be returned to that which existed during the CNG or improved beyond that and the negative attitude toward Haiti appropriately countered, Haiti stands to experience significant growth."[42] The CNG was the National Council of Government headed by Lieutenant General Henri Namphy, a Duvalier loyalist, who took power after Duvalier fled.

Looking back on these military juntas, *The Economist* noted in December 1990 that:

The spirit of the Duvaliers lives on among the military tyrants who have, since 1986, continued to repress the poor, black majority in the interest of a tiny, rich, light-skinned elite. Public housing, health, education and transport have grown steadily worse.[43]

In July of 1987, under the CNG government, 139 peasants were hacked to death with machetes because they were demonstrating in support of land reform efforts.

U.S. General Accounting Office researchers visiting Haiti in 1988 found, "A constraint frequently cited by U.S. officials and some private-sector representatives is the lack of investor confidence in the country's stability following the ouster of the Duvalier dictatorship."[44]

Of course, "The organized labor movement in Haiti" under Duvalier was "almost non-existent." In 1982, the U.S. Labor Department was able to state that:

> An abundant supply of labor is one of Haiti's major attractions for foreign investors. Together with political stability and proximity, it gives the country a strong comparative advantage in labor-intensive primary and assembly industries and in the provision of tourism services for North American markets.[45]

No unions and a 34-year dictatorship created political stability and a good investment climate in Haiti, according to AID and the Labor Department under the Bush Administration.

USAID PLAN CALLS FOR THE USE OF FRONT GROUPS

As soon as President Aristide came into office, a USAID/Haiti Mission internal staff assessment concluded that the incoming Aristide Government "could benefit from position papers staking out the issues" in order to suggest "possible policy solutions" to direct economic development. The USAID study continued, "However, in view of legitimate political sensitivities, greater policy ownership by various Haitian interest groups may be more important than more donor produced studies and reports." The "donor," USAID, was supposed to go backstage. Rather, "Enhancing indigenous policy dialogue capacities within the private sector may be the most productive course of action." The internal assessment suggested that "an *ad hoc* committee of business organizations under the umbrella of USAID's export and investment promotion project . . . could not only propose and oversee the preparation of policy papers but could entertain proposals from a variety of private sector interest groups."[46]

According to AID, "Policy reform will be more effective in the emerging democratic and nationalistic environment if many diverse internal interest groups are assisted in understanding and articulating policy positions."[47]

USAID next set out to open a dialogue with these "many diverse internal interest groups." The USAID internal working paper mentioned above was completed in February 1991, the month President Aristide assumed office. By April, USAID had a team of experts on the ground in Haiti. The team included Charles Beaulieu, the former governor of the Haitian Central Bank. (USAID was quite familiar with Haiti's banking system, having allocated over $53 million to private banks in that country since the early 1980s.) USAID had chosen the Stanford Research Institute, working with Ernst & Young, to carry out this research. These were two very trusted USAID contractors. In 1991, the Virginia-based Stanford Research Institute received $1,227,000 in USAID contracts to assist the "Agency in Economic Policy Analysis and Assessment of Science and Technology Policies,"—while the Washington, D.C.-based firm of Ernst & Young collected $6,149,445 in contract fees.

The purpose of their mission was made explicitly clear. According to their report, "The emphasis of the study team was placed on listening to business people, learning about their problems and constraints and looking for solutions to the problems." The "many diverse internal interest groups" were to be drawn exclusively from the business community. The Stanford Research Team reported back to USAID that the government's proposed minimum wage increase:

> . . . is generally not being very well received by the business community in Haiti. Many business leaders fear that the large minimum wage increase will lead to higher wage demands from semi-skilled and skilled workers, which will be beyond the companies' capacity to pay, given the high cost structure in Haiti for non-labor cost factors such as port charges, electricity and telecommunications."[48]

Given the source of funding for the contract, it should not come as too much of a surprise that the Stanford Research Institute is in full agreement with USAID: "One of Haiti's main assets is its large pool of disciplined and competitively priced labor," which "can be used for targeted promotional efforts, as the business climate is improved."[49]

For USAID and the Stanford Research Institute, Haiti's future is being jeopardized by "the new wage bill" which "is expected to reduce the overall competitiveness of Haiti."

USAID's next move was to quickly allocate $26 million to the "ad hoc committee of business organizations"—under USAID's control—to help keep "Haitian production competitive in world markets."[50]

A USAID internal working paper—referred to above—recommended that an "ad hoc committee of [Haitian] business organizations" be organized and placed "under the umbrella of USAID's export and investment promotion project (Prominex)." Prominex, the Center for the Promotion of Investment and Exports, which receives 99 percent of its funding from USAID, is in fact a USAID front group. . . .

What sort of an organization was Prominex? In 1989, Haitian press reports indicated that U.S. officials were irritated by the behavior of Prominex Chairman Joel Thebaud, who was using U.S. tax dollars on too many first class plane trips and lavish dinners. There were also allegations that $2 million in USAID funding had been misappropriated.[51] This is something only USAID could confirm. However, in 1991, before pouring another $5 million into the project, USAID scrapped the Prominex label, renaming its project Probe— Promotion of Business and Exports.

Prominex was created by USAID in 1986 "to recruit assembly contracts and attract overseas investors" by mounting "a marketing effort that identifies the country as a serious contender for overseas investment." Two of Haiti's strong points were "a large pool of productive, competitive labor seeking employment" along with "a sophisticated and aggressive group of successful entrepreneurs."[52] In fact, this appears to be central to USAID's development strategy for the entire Central American and Caribbean region. In country after country, USAID's strategy is based on working with local business elites in order to more efficiently utilize the large pools of low wage labor available across the region. . . .

Chosen as president of USAID's Prominex project was Andre Apaid, a wealthy Haitian businessman. Apaid owns Industries Nationales Reunies, S.A. (INR), a contract assembly firm employing over 1,700 workers in 1990. INR's most successful division is Alpha Electronics, S.A., which assembles electronic products for Sperry/Unisys, IBM, Remington and Honeywell. Alpha-supplied components end up in U.S. government computers and U.S. Defense Department sonar and radar equipment.[53]

At the December 1991 Miami Conference on the Caribbean—sponsored annually by Caribbean/Latin American Action and attended by over 1,000 business and government leaders—Andre Apaid addressed a "Haiti Strategy Breakfast." Asked what he would do if President Aristide returned to Haiti, Apaid vehemently responded, "I'd strangle him!" The tone of the breakfast meeting was such that the British ambassador to Haiti got up and left.

Alpha Industries was one of the companies that urged President Bush to lift the embargo to give the "best Christmas present yet" to the Haitian workers.

Alpha Industries is also now exporting assembled goods to the U.S., despite the fact that Apaid is a known sympathizer with the coup, and, in fact, is a major financial contributor to de facto Prime Minister Marc L. Bazin. Apaid is one of the chief lobbyists in the U.S. for the military government in Haiti. . . .

CAN YOU TELL AN ORGANIZATION BY ITS FRIENDS?

Corporations and their owners in Haiti, USAID's partners, pay no taxes. A 1989 U.S. Department of State country report on Haiti noted, "Tax evasion is a time honored tradition in Haiti."[54] Commenting on the situation in Haiti in 1990 the U.S. Department of Commerce stated, "Corporate and income taxes are largely evaded, so much of the burden is on the taxpayers in the form of consumption taxes."[55] In other words, one of the poorest countries in the world—where the vast majority of the population earns under $150 a year—also has one of the most regressive tax structures. The Haitian government tries to get by on a 10 percent sales tax.

What about U.S.-sponsored reform efforts? After a 10-year relationship, and after USAID had poured over $100 million into Haiti's private sector, USAID was forced to admit in 1992 that: "Most tax assistance efforts have failed in the past because top GOH [Government of Haiti] officials' commitments were too often compromised by illicit arrangements with taxpayers and strong taxpayer resistance in paying taxes because such funds were too often wasted or misappropriated."[56] If it sounds dismally corrupt, it is, but it also gets worse. And what about the U.S. taxpayer who was footing the bill so USAID could pour more than $100 million at this corrupt business elite?

Illegal trade was also rampant. According to USAID, in 1990 Haiti's "contraband trade is estimated to be about $300 million per year, or about 50 percent of total imports."[57] We are informed that "Customs outside Port-au-Prince remains out of control." By a conservative estimate, the Haitian government, which is so badly strapped for revenue, is being cheated out of at least $60 million dollars a year in customs duties due to this illegal trade. . . .

The best thing that can be said about USAID's 10-year attempt to work with the "progressive elements of the private sector" is that it was a miserable failure.

In 1988, the U.S. General Accounting Office—the investigating arm of Congress—reported that Haiti's economy is "dominated by a rich elite of closely associated family groupings who control export-import trade, tourism, construction, and the formal manufacturing sector."[58] A year later the U.S. Department of Commerce observed the same: "Haitian society is highly personalized. Friendship and social connections, therefore, may carry more weight than legal rights and responsibilities."[59]

In short, the old boy network continues to reign and completely controls the economy. USAID's programs did not make a dent in the "time honored tradition in Haiti" of corporate and income tax evasion. USAID was unable to even slow down the growth in contraband trade. Nor did they even scratch the surface of the graft and corruption which permeate Haiti's business climate.

After over $100 million spent, and after a decade of working with Haiti's private sector, it is a legitimate question to ask, what if anything has USAID accomplished? . . .

Writing in 1992 the U.S. Commerce Department stated that, "The United States is by far the largest foreign investor with an estimated $120 million [$90 million excluding inventory] invested in Haiti as of early 1991. With the exception of several oil companies and banks (Texaco, Exxon, Bank of Boston, Citibank), U.S. investment is almost entirely in the assembly sector."[60] U.S. investment is estimated to represent over 90 percent of total foreign investment in Haiti. Also, 95 percent of Haiti's light manufacturing exports are destined for the U.S. markets.

What have been the social results accompanying this U.S. investment? In 1982, the U.S. Labor Department observed that, "There is a long history of government repression of the labor movement in Haiti." Not surprisingly then, "The organized labor movement in Haiti is almost non-existent." However, "investment and assembly-type opportunities in Haiti are excellent because of Haiti's low labor costs."

If we leap ahead to 1990, the U.S. Labor Department is still convinced that "dexterous, low-cost unskilled labor [all] remain selling points for labor-intensive assembly operations in Haiti." Nor has the labor rights situation changed all that much. According to the Labor Department's 1990 report "Worker Rights in Export Processing Zones:"

> It appears that while freedom of association, the right to strike, and to organize are legally provided to all workers in Haiti, in reality few workers enjoy such rights whether employed in export processing operations or local firms."[61]

To the Labor Department, "It appears that many employers of the export industry are not in fact willing to bargain with trade unions." Also, "many employers, domestic and foreign, still question the legitimacy of unions."[62] In fact, there is not one single collective bargaining agreement in effect in Haiti's assembly sector.

Once again, what happened to the progressive element of the private sector that USAID was nurturing? During the 1980's USAID spent millions to promote foreign investment in Haiti's assembly sector, while the continuing violation of internationally recognized worker rights in the export processing zones remained nearly untouched. Given that USAID was working with U.S. companies and U.S.-Haitian joint ventures, the job of promoting worker rights should not have been insurmountable.

DEJA VU

In April of 1992, in the midst of the violent intransigence of the military regime in Haiti, the U.S. Commerce Department calmly noted:

> After an internationally recognized government is reestablished, the best long-term prospect for U.S. business will continue to be investment in ex-

port assembly operations. Haiti's proximity to the United States, its access to Generalized System of Preferences (GSP), Caribbean Basin Initiative (CBI) and Section 807 U.S. Customs benefits, as well as its abundance of low-wage, productive labor should make it a good location for assembly operations when the country achieves some level of political stability. Best prospects for U.S. exporters include imports for the Assembly Sector: textiles, electronic components, packaging materials, and raw materials used in the manufacture of sporting goods and toys.[63]

Notice that the Commerce Department cannot bring itself to mention the restoration of the elected constitutional government of President Aristide.

We heard this in 1982 from the U.S. Department of Labor: "An abundant supply of labor is one of Haiti's major attractions for foreign investors." Of course, they are referring to "Haiti's low cost labor."[64]

In 1984, the Commerce Department believed that "Haiti's major economic resources are the abundance of unskilled and semi-skilled labor and a sophisticated and dynamic private sector."

In 1985, Commerce observed that, "Both foreign and Haitian businessmen share the same views on the environment for doing business in Haiti. All fully appreciate the low cost labor, and strong work ethic of the Haitian people. Absenteeism is low and work stoppages are rare . . . "[65]

In 1986, USAID explained that, "A large part of productive, competitive labor seeking employment in industry and agriculture" was one of the key "factors enhancing" U.S. investment in Haiti.

By 1991, nothing has changed. USAID believes, "Haiti has some strong factors which make it a prime candidate for increased international trade and competitive production." Those factors just happen to be: "highly productive, low cost labor; proximity of major markets through U.S. ports; entrepreneurial management. . . ."[66]

NOTES

1. "Haiti," *Caribbean UPDATE*, March 1992.
2. "Attorney for Wealthy Haitians Criticized for Role in US Talks," *The Journal of Commerce*, March 4, 1993.
3. "Haiti Embargo Busters," *International Business Chronicle*, March 15-March 28, 1993.
4. "Haiti," *Caribbean UPDATE*, November, 1992.
5. "Attorney for Wealthy Haitians Criticized for Role in US Talks," *The Journal of Commerce*, March 4, 1993.
6. *Ibid.*
7. "An industrial park on the way up," *Hispaniola Business*, October 15, 1990.
8. M. Catherine Maternowska, Ph.D. candidate at the Anthropology Department of the Columbia University, New York, New York. Also see *Concept Paper Economic Recovery Assistance II*, USAID/Haiti, November 1986.
9. Conversation on April 22, 1993 with Nina Gressens from the U.S. Department of Commerce.
10. "Haiti," *Foreign Economic Trends and Their Implications for the United States*, U.S. Department of Commerce, International Trade Administration, April 6, 1992.
11. *Investment in Haiti*, Ministry of Economy, Finance, and Industry; Investment Promotion Division (Haiti), 1983.
12. *Haiti: Foreign Labor Trends Report*, 1989-1990, U.S. Department of Labor, Bureau of International Labor Affairs.
13. "Haiti," *EIU Country Report No. 4, 1992*, The Economist Intelligence Unit.

14. *Investment in Haiti*, Ministry of Economy, Finance, and Industry; Investment Promotion Division (Haiti), 1983.

15. *Haiti: Foreign Labor Trends Report*, 1989-1990, U.S. Department of Labor, Bureau of International Labor Affairs.

16. "Haiti," *Foreign Economic Trends and Their Implications for the United States*, U.S. Department of Commerce, International Trade Administration, April 6, 1992.

17. "Haiti," *Project Paper/Promotion of Business and Export Project* (Amendment Number 1/Project Number: 521-0186), USAID, June 29, 1991.

18. *Strategic Options for Haiti's Promotion of Business and Exports (Probe) Project*, USAID, June, 1991.

19. *Foreign Economic Trends and their Implications for the United States*, U.S. Department of Commerce, May 1989.

20. *Ibid.*

21. "Haiti," *Project Paper/Export and Investment Promotion*, (Project Number: 521-0186), USAID, August 8, 1986.

22. *Ibid.*

23. *Country Development Strategy Statement: FY 1986: Haiti*, USAID, January 1984.

24. *Ibid.*

25. *Ibid.*

26. "Haiti," *Foreign Economic Trends and Their Implications for the United States*, American Embassy Port-Au-Prince, U.S. Department of Commerce, International Trade Administration, April 6, 1992.

27. *The Electrotechnical Industry in Haiti*, The Ministry of Economy, Finance, and Industry; Investment Promotion Division (Haiti), 1981 (Estimated).

28. "Haiti," *Project Paper/Promotion of Business and Export Project* (Amendment Number 1/Project Number: 521-0186), USAID, June 29, 1991.

29. "Haiti," *Foreign Economic Trends and Their Implications for the United States*, American Embassy Port-au-Prince, U.S. Department of Commerce, International Trade Administration, April 6, 1992.

30. "Haiti," *Caribbean UPDATE*, May, 1991.

31. *Haiti: Foreign Labor Trends Report*, 1989-1990, U.S. Department of Labor, Bureau of International Labor Affairs.

32. "Haiti Macroeconomic Assessment," *Staff Working Papers*, USAID, February 1991.

33. *Ibid.*

34. "Haiti," *Project Paper/Promotion of Business and Export Project* (Amendment Number 1/Project Number: 521-0186), USAID, June 29, 1991.

35. *Ibid.*

36. *Ibid.*

37. *Strategic Options for Haiti's Promotion of Business and Exports (Probe) Project*, USAID, June 1991.

38. "Haiti," *Project Paper/Promotion of Business and Export Project* (Amendment Number 1/Project Number: 521-0186), USAID, June 29, 1991.

39. *LAC Regional/Project Paper, American Institute for Free Labor Development*, United States International Development Cooperation Agency; Agency for International Development, August 8, 1990.

40. *Haiti—Economic Policy & Trade Practices*, ETP910200, U.S. Department of Commerce, International Trade Administration, 1991.

41. "Haiti," *Project Paper/Promotion of Business and Export Project* (Amendment Number 1/Project Number: 521-0186), USAID, June 29, 1991.

42. *Ibid.*

43. "Priest-President," *The Economist*, December 22, 1990.

44. *Caribbean Basin Initiative: Impact on Selected Countries*, United States General Accounting Office, July 1988.

45. *Labor Profile: Haiti*, Department of Labor, Bureau of International Labor Affairs, July 1982.

46. "Haiti Macroeconomic Assessment," *Staff Working Papers*, USAID, February, 1991.

47. *Ibid.*

48. *Strategic Options for Haiti's Promotion of Business and Exports (Probe) Project*, USAID, June 1991.

49. *Ibid.*

50. "Haiti," *Project Paper/Promotion of Business and Export Project* (Amendment Number 1/Project Number: 521-0186), USAID, June 29, 1991.

51. "Financial Scandal at Prominex: US$2 Million Stolen in 2 Years," *Petit Samedi Soir*, February 11-17, 1989.

52. *"Haiti," Project Paper/Export and Investment Promotion* (Project Number: 521-0186), USAID, August 8, 1986.

53. "Alpha Electronics sets new standards of excellence," *Hispaniola Business*, October 15, 1990.

54. "Country Report on Economic Policy and Trade Practices," Department of State, May 1989.

55. *Haiti—Economic Policy & Trade Practices*," ETP910200, U.S. Department of Commerce, International Trade Administration, 1991.

56. "Haiti Macroeconomic Assessment," *Staff Working Papers*, USAID, February 1991.

57. *Ibid.*

58. *Caribbean Basin Initiative: Impact on Selected Countries*, United States General Accounting Office, July 1988.

59. *Haiti—Commercial Activities Report '89*, CAR8902, The American Embassy, U.S. Department of Commerce, February 1989.

60. "Haiti," *Foreign Economic Trends and Their Implications for the United States*, American Embassy Port-Au-Prince, U.S. Department of Commerce, International Trade Administration, April 6, 1992.

61. *Worker Rights in Export Processing Zones*, Bureau of International Labor Affairs, U.S. Department of Labor, August 1990.

62. *Ibid.*

63. "Haiti," *Foreign Economic Trends and Their Implications for the United States*, American Embassy Port-Au-Prince, U.S. Department of Commerce, International Trade Administration, April 6, 1992.

64. *Labor Profile: Haiti*, July 1982, Department of Labor, Bureau of International Labor Affairs.

65. *Doing Business With Haiti*, Libby Colen Roper, Overseas Business Reports, OBR 85-11, U.S. Department of Commerce, International Trade Administration, June 1985.

66. "Haiti," *Project Paper/Promotion of Business and Export Project* (Amendment Number 1/Project Number:521-0186), USAID, June 29, 1991.

A "FAKE KIND OF DEVELOPMENT"

Interview with Antoine Izmery

Shortly before he was assassinated in Port-au-Prince, Antoine Izmery, a leading Haitian businessman and strong supporter of Aristide, talked to the Haitian Information Bureau about how the international aid programs systematically corrupted the nation's economy by pumping money not into development, but into the hands of an indolent oligarchy. "They let you steal your own country," he said, "Just provide a little protection." Izmery was murdered by *attachés* of the military on September 11, 1993, after being dragged out of the church where he was attending a memorial service for the victims of a 1988 massacre.

┐

The development will be a kind of fake kind of development that will only implant the American way in which they will be selling the country to the foreigners. It's not a matter of privatization, we are talking about people taking control of Haiti, through the financial means that they have. And in my business way of thinking, this country has never been so cheap to buy, in terms of value. And that's one thing that we always say—"Haiti is for the Haitians. We cannot sell this country like they did in the Dominican Republic."

There is, for example the "emergency project" that they have for starting the economy [the "Emergency Economic Recovery Plan," put together by consultants from the World Bank, International Monetary Fund, USAID, and International Development Bank, along with Haitian consultants, including Madame Rey), which is based on borrowed money, grants . . . which goes to a private sector that should not be called "private" sector, but "mafia" sector.

That same mafia sector will use the money, stolen through corruption, to buy this country with a kind of legal veneer.

In all those talks, they plan to put US$30 million into the assembly plants. The owners and investors in those assembly plants will profit from that, but they never say a word about the 16-gourde per day salary, which represents something like US$32 per month . . . It's about $1.12 per day for 30 days. If we start talking about a 35-gourde minimum salary, representing about US$70 a month . . . we will be immediately against [Haitian Prime Minister] Malval.

My views are that we have to put all the development process in favor of the people, mostly in agriculture, schools, medical services and also in roads, even if they have to be gravel roads.

You can help them through financing cooperatives or whatever, to start giving what the people need—first of all, food, to be able to eat at least once a day; programs for the kids to be able to go to literacy classes; work in agriculture; roads, and hospitals for their minimum needs—headaches, toothaches, like that.

If you don't start like that, you will be starting wrong. Again, the same people will be making the same money. You will give $10 million to the rich, who will pass on $3 million to the poor and keep the $7 million.

It will be a development with what they want to see for working class people, but for me it is not a working class if it is based on 16 gourdes. It will be a "slave state," "a slave class." I do not think that Malval can respond to that and I do not think the international community wants to respond to it.

Remember, the destabilization process against Aristide was accentuated by meetings of the American ambassador with the private sector through Citibank and USAID. They were against the 35-gourde minimum wage and they bought people out in parliament to go against those increases, because their minds are not set to develop Haiti. It is just to use the work of those people to keep them as dumb as they can with a minimum salary.

There is another problem here—monopolies. There is no competition in Haiti. Let's take an example—cooking oil. They receive the cheapest oil there is—palm oil, which is not recommended for human consumption. They use it, and even if there are five producers, they all fix their prices together, so there is no real competition. Each one has his share of the market.

"Don't interfere in my market. I have ten percent, you have 20. I leave you with your 20, leave me with my ten. But I work five hours a day, I make enough money to live, quietly."

It's the same thing with tomato paste—the tomato paste factory. They have sales of 220,000 cartons per year. They only make $10 per carton—they make $2 million, and they only work four hours a day. So that's what we have to start changing, too! Just because the monopolies don't exist on paper does not mean they do not exist!

So to break that, for example, you get all the buyers of cooking oil and have them organize themselves into a partnership to make their own factory. The monopolists cannot live if they do not have the intermediaries. If the buyers make their own thing and they already have the distribution in their hands, they can make money out of the production and the distribution, and then they will force the other ones . . . they will be able to break their backs! That's the only way that you can beat them!

But that has to be understood and built up by the government, through encouraging and by helping organize and provide credit to the people who need it and stopping the credit to people like [Clifford] Brandt. But you will never find this in the capitalist who is under the imperialist way of thinking. Remember that your first enemy is not the private sector; it's the imperialist. . . .

Another thing also is that this country is so corrupt, that the Americans do not have to do the corruption. They let you steal your own country, just giving you a little protection. . . .

SUBVERTING DEMOCRACY
Haitian Information Bureau

There is another side to American aid in Haiti. Along with the economic programs, aimed at transforming agriculture into a new industrial base, American foreign policy sought to export to Haiti, as it has elsewhere in the hemisphere, a centrist democratic political state to underlie and run the new economy. That endeavor has led the U.S. to intercede directly in Haitian domestic politics. The Haitian Information Bureau describes the subterranean politics of "democracy-building."

On March 5, 1994, Parliamentarian Samuel Madistin and two other parliamentarians were forced into hiding when they discovered a truck-load of armed men were looking for them. One parliamentarian reported finding a dead body near his home, a sign that he had been targeted for assassination.

The reason for the repression was clear—at a packed press conference held the previous day, Madistin denounced two U.S.-based organizations for intervening in Haitian affairs: the U.S. government-linked Center for Democracy (CFD) and a small, right-wing outfit, the Nation Freedom Institute (NFI), briefly associated with Oliver North and the Iran-Contra scandal. "Because the international community, the people who were putting pressure on the president . . . did not have success here, they organized the departure of a group of parliamentarians to go to Washington," he said, so that parliamentarians could meet with "group[s] whose function . . . is to destabilize democratic movements in Latin America."

CFD, NFI and a half dozen similar organizations which can trace their origins to the bowels of the U.S. Central Intelligence Agency and the National Security Council have quietly been operating in Haiti for a decade to ensure that the inevitable decline of Duvalierist rule would not lead to the installment of a popularly oriented government—exactly the sort represented by the administration of President Jean-Bertrand Aristide. After Aristide was elected in December 1990, these groups—either official U.S. agencies or organizations which receive U.S. government funding and work in tandem with domestic and international agencies—actively worked to undermine his domestic and international support. And, since the September 1991 coup that ousted Aristide, they have dutifully toiled to hinder his return, or to ensure that if he does resume power, he will not be postitioned to implement significant social and economic reforms.

NED AND "DEMOCRACY" IN HAITI
The National Endowment for Democracy (NED) is a Congressionally created "private" organization designed to promote what its by-laws define as democ-

racy "consistent . . . with the broad concerns of U.S. national interests." In practice, this means that "A lot of what [NED] do[es] today was done covertly 25 years ago by the CIA," NED's first president and current CFD head Allen Weinstein told the *Washington Post* in 1991.

NED got involved in Haiti in 1985, just before Jean-Claude (Baby Doc) Duvalier fled. As with its operations in many countries, in Haiti, NED and its spin-off organizations, which share many common board members and affiliations, are interlocked with official government institutions such as the U.S. Agency for International Development (AID).

Between 1986 and 1990, NED funneled over $2.3 million in funds into Haiti.

A 1988 study commissioned by AID noted that Haiti had between 800 and 1,500 "non-governmental organizations," with U.S. funding reaching at least 400.

At a time when the democratic and popular movement was picking up steam, the study recommended more support for "the independent sector" and listed possible recipients.

AID and NED each helped found institutions which later received sizable grants. One of those, the Haitian Institute for Research and Development (IHRED), played a very partisan role in the eighties and especially in the 1990 elections when it was allied with Marc L. Bazin, the U.S. government's preferred candidate, and helped him create his coalition.

(Bazin later served as the second illegal prime minister of the post coup d'état regime, overseeing rampant corruption and repression. Another NED grantee—Jean-Jacques Honorat from the Haitian Center for the Defence of Rights and Freedom (CHADEL)—served as the first illegal prime minister of the regime.)

Today, IHRED is still active but much more quietly. It is known to be funding "civic education" for health monitors working in Cité Soleil for the Centers for Health and Development (CDS), a health organization run by Bazin-backer Dr. Reginald Boulos and generously funded by AID.

Because they hold the power of virtual life or death over the poor Cité Soleil residents, the CDS monitors function like ward captains or even a small-time mafia. Popular organizers report the monitors are attempting to replace grassroots neighborhood organizations with groups they create, and predict the monitors will be crucial in "get-out-the-vote" drives for CDS- and U.S.-favored candidates in future elections.

Other NED funding recipients included the "yellow" Workers Federation Union (FOS), founded in 1984 with Baby Doc's approval so that Haiti, which previously had crushed union-organizing attempts, would qualify for the U.S. Caribbean Basin Initiative economic package.

AID AND "DEMOCRACY ENHANCEMENT"

Jean-Bertrand Aristide's election took U.S. policymakers by surprise, as they had been counting on Bazin, the candidate they backed and funded, to win. Following Aristide's election, in an effort to channel the Haitians' popular upsurge, Congress hastily approved $24.4 million for a five-year "Democracy Enhancement Project" (DEP) for Haiti. According to AID documents, the DEP's purpose was to work in a "non-partisan" way with elected officials, unions and popular organizations to support "effective and sustainable programs with democratic values; promote pluralism and broad-based participation."

AID documents written a few months after Aristide's inauguration state that funds should be used for "civic education" especially before the 1992 and 1994 regional and local elections where there would not be "a presidential strongman to carry other candidates."

The AID documents betray their clear bias against Haiti's popular nationalist president who was attempting to intoduce reforms into Haitian society and institutions, and although AID claims its grants are awarded in a "non-partisan" manner, Haitian recipients, like those in other countries, will no doubt be what AID and NED call "moderate" and "centrist," and who firmly oppose popular or revolutionary movements.

After being briefly cancelled following the 1991 coup, DEP is now back in full swing, with hundreds of thousands of AID funding dollars going to groups for organizing, and for media and "education" campaigns.

Recent NED funding is unknown, because as a "private" organization it discloses only what it wants to, but many recent AID grantees are known. As revealed by the National Labor Committee, many of the groups on the grantee list are renowned not for their embrace of *lavalas* and the vibrant Haitian popular movement, but rather for being in the so-called "moderate" camp and sometimes even in the opposition.

For instance, one grantee ($300,000 in two years) is the Ecumenical Center for Human Rights. The Center's director, Jean-Claude Bajeux, is a high-level member of the CONACOM political party, which only reluctantly supported Aristide's presidency and openly broke with Aristide and the political front which supports him, the FNCD, in March 1994.

Another grant recipient is the Development and Democracy Foundation (FONDEM) ($190,000 in six months), which has been carrying out massive radio campaigns urging people to be "proud of Port-au-Prince" and to respect human rights, and saying "democracy is discipline" while the army and paramilitary groups continue to shoot, rape, rob and terrorize the unarmed population. Although closely linked to Aristide ally Port-au-Prince Mayor Evans Paul, many in the democratic movement believe the FONDEM messages are deliberately meant to demobilize the population.

Other grants go to two so-called "national platforms" of popular organizations with the acronyms PLANOP and CONAPOP which frequently hold press conferences and issue statements. Both say they represent a broad base of dozens of smaller organizations, but most of the groups did not exist before the coup and it is unlikely, given the repression preventing more than a few people from meeting at one time in poor neighborhoods, that the "platforms" really represent who they claim.

AID also gave $1.6 million to two NED spin-offs—the National Democratic Institute for International Affairs (NDI) and the National Republican Institute for International Affairs (NRI), associated with the two major U.S. parties—to work with Haitian parties as well as civilian and military leaders, but their work to date has not come to light.

THE CENTER FOR DEMOCRACY

The most active grantee of the past few months is Weinstein's CFD, which received more than $620,000 from AID for work in Haiti, and an unknown quantity from "private funders," which may include NED, its traditional principal supporter.

In the past, the CFD has been very active in countries like Nicaragua and the Philippines where the U.S. government was anxious to establish what it defines as "moderate" or "centrist" governments in the face of strong progressive, popular and democratic movements.

For its Haiti work, the CFD has contracted Steve Horblitt, a longtime Haiti watcher known for his "moderate" politics and also a former Aide to former U.S. Representative Walter Fauntroy, an open and avid supporter of U.S.-favorite Bazin.

CFD documents say it will be working to "strengthen" the legislature, but also that it has embarked on a "privately funded" effort to work with "Haitian entrepreneurs."

The outcome of this effort—which included bringing four Haitian delegations to Washington for a series of meetings—is a new private sector group, the Center for Free Enterprise and Democracy (CLED).

The new group, made up of young, right-wing businesspeople, is steered by right-wing "political analyst" Lionel Delatour, who worked for the U.S. State Department as a translator and escort while a student in Washington, D.C. in the 1970s and later as a charge d'affaires for the Haitian embassy during Jean-Claude Duvalier's regime.

CLED first announced itself to the public in June 1993, when it released a 29-page "Economic Policy Proposal" calling for a number of severe neoliberal adjustments to Haiti's economy, including "zero tariffs" and an across-the-board 20 percent income tax for all Haitians—those earning $150 per year and those earning $1.5 million. CLED also recommended massive public sector lay-offs, privatization and a freeze on Haiti's minimum wage "to improve the attractiveness of Haiti as a source of imports and as an investment destination."

The CLED proposal says the group favors democracy and respects the will of the majority, but notes, quoting Thomas Jefferson, "to be rightful that will must be reasonable" and says it sees democracy as "free elections, free speech, free enterprise and free trade."

After June, CLED seemed to fade from the political scene, but 1994 has seen its reappearance with a vengeance.

When 15 private sector groups announced a 12-day "strike" intended to force the lifting of the embargo in late January 1994, the spokesperson for the groups was CLED's Bernard Craan, a pharmaceuticals importer.

Resolutions issued by the groups following the strike sought to virtually order President Jean-Bertrand Aristide to have the embargo lifted.

On February 24, Parliamentarian Evans Beaubrun (from a party which openly supported the 1991 coup d'état) announced he was working on a new amnesty law which would cover all sorts of crimes and even include a "fiscal amnesty." On the radio the following day, Craan explained that he and Beaubrun had met twice to prepare the law, and called for "the most diligence possible to vote for this law."

The CFD itself jumped into the fray when it funded the February 7 visit to Washington of a delegation of parliamentarians, half pro-coup and the other half mostly luke-warm supporters of President Aristide, ostensibly to discuss the embargo and ways to resolve the crisis.

On February 19, the parliamentarians announced "their plan" and wrote a letter to United Nations Secretary General Boutros Boutros Ghali outlining the steps: President Aristide names a prime minister, who in turn creates an even broader cabinet than that of Robert Malval, the moderate prime minister appointed by Aristide; the United Nations lifts the embargo; coup leader Lt. General Raoul Cédras (but no other officer) retires; and, at an unspecified time in the future, Aristide returns.

U.S. and U.N. officials called the plan—firmly and immediately rejected by Aristide and dozens of popular organizations and leaders from the democratic movement—the "parliamentary plan." But on March 9, under extensive questioning on Capitol Hill, U.S. Special Advisor on Haiti Lawrence Pezzullo revealed that the parliamentary delegation, led by former Ton Ton Macoute and self-proclaimed neo-Duvalierist Parliamentarian Robert Mondé, was hand-picked by himself and U.S. Ambassador to Haiti William Swing, and that the plan originated not with the Haitian parliamentarians but as a State Department memo last December.

State Department officers apparently provided the memo to the CFD, which then flew the parliamentarians in for three weeks. The delegation adopted the plan (although one democrat, Senate President Firmin Jean-Louis, defected and returned to Haiti) and announced it as "home-grown." It was a maneuver used repeatedly during the 1990 Nicaragua campaign, where U.S. teams would write press releases and hand them to UNO presidential candidate Violeta Chamorro to read.

The CFD covered the parliamentarians' travel and housing costs, Pezzullo also acknowledged on March 9. An AID representative also present said that the U.S. government funds had probably been used "incorrectly."

(On March 4, CLED's Craan was on the radio again, calling the "parliamentary plan" and the Chamber of Deputies' ratification of it "an act of patriotism.")

ESCAPING THE U.S. GRIP

When Pezzullo admitted that the State Department actually wrote the "parliamentary plan" and that parliamentarians' trips were paid for by the CFD, he almost certainly was only revealing the tip of an enormous iceberg. The State Department and the CIA, directly and indirectly via a number of "private" organizations which they control, are deeply involved in complex and multifaceted efforts to shift power from Aristide and the popular movement he represents to a "moderate," business-led coalition that will govern the country according to U.S.-approved precepts of free markets, free trade and economic liberalization.

Beyond the "non-partisan" program descriptions, the neatly typed grant descriptions and the publicized overt activities, there are very likely other monies flowing to those individuals and organizations which can best support U.S. "interests" in Haiti. Just as the CIA has admitted it has military "assets" (such as Cédras and other army leaders), it probably has civilian "assets" being groomed for upcoming elections, whether or not Aristide returns.

For Haiti to achieve the true democracy that its people demanded when they voted on December 16, 1990, it will take more than the return of the exiled president. Haiti must escape the insidious, multi-year plan which has been drawn up in Washington and Langley, Virginia, where the CIA is headquartered. Until the vicious tentacles of the "democracy enhancement" octopus are cut off, the Haitian people—and others the world over—will be struggling against not only the opponents of justice, dignity and human rights in their own countries, but also against well-equipped and well-funded international professionals.

3

DRUGS: THE HAITIAN CONNECTION

PRESS BRIEFING ON THE HAITIAN DRUG TRADE
Patrick Elie

Beginning in the mid-1980s, a steady stream of evidence emerged linking the Haitian military leaders to the drug trade. In early 1994, Patrick Elie, Aristide's coordinator for Haiti's anti-drug program—who was living in hiding in the U.S. under death threats from the coup government—delivered a briefing at the Haitian embassy in Washington. Elie argued the drug business in Haiti had become the "engine" that drove the military and overwhelmed the island's commerce, providing the basis for the local numbers business, generalized smuggling, and a brisk money-laundering operation.

Although the DEA—along with other U.S. government agencies—is now downplaying the size of the Haitian drug trade, Elie estimates it is worth about $250 million a year. After the 1991 coup, Elie said, the business took a "quantum leap," involving government agencies devoted to "public service," and government corporations such as the Port Authority (which controls imports and exports as well as access to both military and international airports) and a state-owned flour mill.

⌐

Alix Silva was deputy commander in chief of the Haitian army at the time of the coup. He disappeared. No one seemed to care. He had been, after 1986, the key officer waging the war against drug trafficking and, more precisely, exposing the involvement of the Haitian military in protecting and profiting from it. . . .

As time went on, the drug business boomed. Drugs, mainly from the Colombian Cali cartel, would come into Haiti, sometimes exiting through the Dominican Republic, ending up in Puerto Rico. The Colombians would send their own agents to oversee the operation and paid their Haitian collaborators by giving them part of the shipment. The Haitians then could sell those drugs inside Haiti and export small portions strapped to a courier or mule's body into Miami or New York. . . .

[Elie said that efforts to interdict drug shipments were often frustrated because the military refused to help.] The U.S. [Drug Enforcement Agency] became aware through intelligence in Latin America that a large shipment of cocaine was coming in [on May 31, 1991]. When [Tony] Greco [the resident DEA agent in Haiti, who later had to be withdrawn after receiving death threats] tried to reach the Haitian military, it so happened that the officer [in charge] had turned off his radio and could not be reached. Consequently, Greco had to go and watch the drop of 400 kilos, about one hour's drive from Port-au-Prince. After that he indicated to me that not only were the Haitian military conspicuously absent at a moment when they knew they were going to be needed but there was evidence that the drugs were actually retrieved by two boats of the so-called Haitian navy. . . .

[In March 1989, under American pressure, General Prosper Avril, who briefly headed a Haitian military government, sacked 140 officers because of their involvement in the drug trade.] A week later he was the victim of an attempted coup involving the two most powerful units of the Haitian army, namely the Leopard, a counterguerrilla unit formed by the U.S., and the palace guard. There is your network.

[While Elie has no evidence that either Colonel Michel François, who heads the police, or army chief General Raoul Cédras were engaged in drug trafficking before the coup, he says they were drawn into the business afterward because so many of the top men in the military were in the business.]

Our relationship with the DEA and CIA was one that was just starting to develop. Up to that point, they had had a long tradition of only working through the Haitian military. This was the first time they were dealing with an elected government. It appears that the same things that were worrying us were worrying DEA and CIA. In both cases, they were very unhappy with the inability of the Haitian military to fight drug trafficking. . . .

SENATE HEARINGS ON HAITIAN DRUG TRAFFICKING

Senate Foreign Relations Committee, Subcommittee on Terrorism, Narcotics and International Operations

In 1988 Massachusetts Senator John Kerry—who had become known for his investigations into drug trafficking and the Iran contra scandal—chaired a Senate subcommittee which held hearings on the drug trade in Haiti and Central America. Among the witnesses interviewed by Kerry was George Morales, then in prison on drug charges.

┐

Senator Kerry: Have you ever been to Haiti?

Mr. Morales: Many times.

Senator Kerry: Did you use Haiti as a trans-shipment point for drugs?

Mr. Morales: I used the Isle of Haiti mainly as a parking lot, as a place that I would place my aircraft so they could be repaired and also so that I could leave the city of Port-au-Prince without having to do the paperwork necessary to get permission to fly an aircraft over the island, so I could leave the island without having to follow the flight plan.

You know what I mean by this? When you prepare a flight plan, the control tower not only of Haiti but Jamaica or any other Caribbean island has to send the record to the control tower in the city of Miami. When they send the record to the city of Miami, the surveillance authorities can then see that one has left Haiti and has seen what the place of destination is so we could do that without having a flight plan.

Senator Kerry: Do you know whether or not Haiti is a major transshipment point for drugs?

Mr. Morales: Lately we have seen in the papers that Haiti—

Senator Kerry: I don't want to ask you about the papers or the reports. I just want to know from your knowledge when you were trafficking drugs.

Mr. Morales: From my own knowledge, from what I did?

Senator Kerry: Did you transship through them?

Mr. Morales: Yes, I did.

Senator Kerry: Do you know if others were transshipping through Haiti?

Mr. Morales: Yes. It is something which is done fairly commonly, Senator.

Senator Kerry: Was a plane that you kept at the airport in Haiti a plane you later contributed to the Contra effort?

Mr. Morales: Well, I will repeat that we used Haiti as a parking lot. That particular airplane was a DC-3, and we had parked it there at the airport. It is a fairly large international airport, and we kept that DC-3 airplane there in Haiti, and at the time I was using it together with other aircraft which the Government of Haiti and especially the Duvalier family [sic]. . . .

In April 1994, Kerry's Foreign Relations subcommittee took the testimony of another federal prisoner, former Medellín cartel operative Gabriel Taboada. Taboada provided more corroboration of drug dealing in Haiti, including the involvement of important members of the coup government.

Senator Kerry: What else have you learned about the nature of the cartel's use of Haiti?

Mr. Taboada (as translated): I learned later on that the cartel used Haiti as a bridge so as to later move the drugs toward the United States . . . They took planes out of Colombia. They landed in Haiti, protected by the Haitian military . . . In 1984, in one of my visits to Pablo Éscobar's office in the town, in Medellín, Gustavo Gaviria introduced me to an officer, a member of the Haitian police whose name is Michel François. Mr. François was in that office, and I was able to talk to him for 30 minutes.

I mentioned to Mr. François when he told me that he was Haitian, and a Haitian officer, that in 1982 and in 1984 I had imported two cars through the Haitian ambassador, a Mercedes and a Ferrari, that I was in the car business with diplomats and I was making good money, and he told me that—he said, well, why wasn't I in the drug business if the drug business made good money, and I said at that time I was not in the drug business. I asked him what he was doing and what his business was, and he said that at that time he was in Medellín arranging a cocaine deal with Gustavo Gaviria and Pablo Éscobar.

Senator Kerry: And you know for a fact that this was Michel François of Haiti?

Mr. Taboada (as translated): That's right, 100 percent sure.

Senator Kerry: Did you subsequently, in your work with the cartel when you started to deal with cocaine, learn anything more about drugs and Michel François?

Mr. Taboada (as translated): Later on I learned that approximately 32,000 kilos of cocaine went in through Haiti in 1987, and that in that same year, top military in Haiti and Mr. François, too, were at the Naples ranch with Pablo Éscobar—in other words, Rodrigues Gonzales Gacha, the Mexican, and other members of the Medellín cartel.

Senator Kerry: Did you learn something about any drug shipments to Haiti?

Mr. Taboada (as translated): Yes, 32,000 kilos of cocaine that went into Haiti and later continued their course to the United States.

Senator Kerry: And did Mr. François, to your knowledge, have anything to do with that shipment?

Mr. Taboada (as translated): Yes . . . he protected the drugs in Haiti, and he then allowed the drugs to continue to the United States.

Senator Kerry: You know for a fact that these drugs reached the United States?

Mr. Taboada (as translated): In fact, yes, it did reach the United States. . . . Most of it went in as cargo through the airport in Miami.

Senator Kerry: Well, I'm not going to go into further detail on that transaction, on the 32,000 kilos at this hearing now, but besides Michel François, have you seen other Haitian military figures meet with members of the cartel in Colombia?

Mr. Taboada (as translated): At that same time, when I stayed at that office, at Gustavo Gaviria's office—because that was, or is, rather, a house, because it's still standing, and on the first floor of that house there were billiard tables. On the second floor, there were two offices, and at that same time I met, or rather, I saw—I saw, because he was not introduced to me, another Haitian military figure who later, when I returned a week later, Gustavo Gaviria told me that he was General Prosper Avril. . . .

DRUGS AND THE HAITIAN MILITARY

Senator John Kerry

In late 1993, Senator Kerry, who had by then made a considerable study of the Haitian role in the drug trade, issued a memorandum on what his inquiries had turned up to date. Kerry concluded that "there is a partnership made in hell, in cocaine, and in dollars between the Colombian cartels and the Haitian military."

┐

FUNDAMENTAL POINTS

Since the mid-1980s, the U.S. has had clear evidence of the involvement of senior members of the Haitian military in controlling drug trafficking through Haiti. Haiti has been used to tranship drugs by air and sea through Port-au-Prince.

We heard testimony about how the leading members of the Haitian military viewed control of the drug trafficking as a kind of "perk" that went with being the top military personnel in the country. The drug trafficking "perk" to the Haitian military is like getting your stars when you become an American general—it goes with the promotion. Right now it is controlled by the Port-Au-Prince Police Chief, Lieutenant Colonel Michael François.

In the 1980s and early 1990s, the Administration kept certifying that human rights and the drug problem we had with Haiti were getting better. They weren't and haven't. We have had a succession of military figures running the drug trade. As the Clinton State Department acknowledged in April, corruption of Haitian officials continues to be a major problem.

Recently, we learned that there are more than 1,000 Colombian nationals living in Haiti. They aren't there to play soccer. There is only one reason for a Colombian to live in Haiti, which has no functioning economy. That reason is the drug trade. There is a partnership made in hell, in cocaine, and in dollars between the Colombian cartels and the Haitian military. This partnership has to be broken.

Since April, the State Department has also acknowledged publicly that we have received credible reports indicating involvement of government and military personnel in Haiti in narcotics trafficking. In fact, our own chief Drug Enforcement Administration agent in Haiti had to leave the country last year after he received a life-threatening phone call directed at his family from a member of the Haitian military. The problem was our DEA agent had arrested a lower-level Haiti official who was a member of the drug organization run by the high-ranking member of the Haitian military.

Haitian President Aristide is right when he says that one of the reasons the Haitian military will not let go is that their life-style depends on the drug trade. They have been making a hundred million dollars or more on provid-ing sanctuary for drugs coming to the U.S. They do not want to lose that money. And they don't want to be prosecuted for their criminal activity.

DETAILS

The last time the U.S. made a big push to get rid of the drug traffickers in the Haitian military, the result was that the military leader of Haiti, Lt. Gen. Prosper Avril, dismissed 140 officers, mostly for drug trafficking. This in turn brought about a coup attempt at Avril, who then stepped down. The drug traffickers are among the most powerful people in Haiti.

There is relatively little direct evidence that Haitian military leader Lt. Gen. Raoul Cédras is involved with the drug trade. But obviously, there is an arrangement between him and people like Police Chief Lt. Col. Michael François, who clearly controls the trade.

We have specific witnesses, living in South Florida, who have told us that the Haitian military has been continuing to protect drug deals, and that they believe the highest levels of the Haitian military, including François, are involved.

The principal Colombian who controls Haiti is Fernando Burgos Martinez. We have a witness who was arrested in Haiti after a marijuana drop, and had to make a payoff to Fernando Burgos Martinez to be released. The witness complained that he wasn't getting good service in Haiti and made a $20,000 payoff. Hours later, his pilots were flown home.

HOW ARE OUR CURRENT ANTI-DRUG EFFORTS IN HAITI GOING?

We have two DEA agents in Haiti. They are confined to the U.S. embassy. They gather intelligence as they can. They cannot make cases. They are not able to do anything of significance right now. Their work is effectively shut down.

Both the State Department and DEA have publicly acknowledged that: "Corruption within the anti-narcotics services, which are staffed by the military at all levels, is substantial enough to hamper any significant drug investigations focused on dismantling Colombian organizations operating in Haiti."

IMPACT OF THE EMBARGO ON THE DRUG TRADE

The broad-scale, world-wide economic set of sanctions against Haiti imposed by the United Nations at our request not only puts pressure on the Haitian military to permit the restoration of the Aristide government—it also has the salutory effect of making Haiti less attractive as a drug-transshipment point. Since we are not letting anything in or out of Haiti, Haiti is not going to continue to be as important a drug-transit site so long as the embargo is in place. No boats will be going in, no boats will be going out.

Unfortunately, the border between Haiti and the Dominican Republic can't be adequately patrolled by the Dominicans. During past embargoes, the drugs continued to flow. They were dropped off planes in Haiti, smuggled across the border to the Dominican Republic, and smuggled to the U.S. from there. The cocaine trade slows, but it doesn't stop.

WHAT CAN BE DONE ABOUT THE PROBLEM?

So long as the military runs the police, there is no solution for Haiti's drug corruption problem. We need to rebuild the police force from the ground up.

We can't begin those kind of reforms until the Aristide government is back in place. At that point, he has to reclaim the police department from the military and start fresh, with support from the United Nations and from the United States. . . .

CIA FORMED HAITIAN UNIT LATER TIED TO NARCOTICS TRADE

Tim Weiner, Stephen Engelberg, and Howard W. French

Over time, ample evidence has emerged to show the involvement of Haitian military rulers in the drug trade. In November 1993, the *New York Times* revealed that the Haitian Intelligence Service, an elite unit created and trained by the CIA in the mid-1980s to combat the drug business and to monitor internal Haitian politics, had actually become involved in trading drugs, machinating against the Aristide government, and "committing acts of terror against Aristide supporters."

 ⌐

The Central Intelligence Agency created an intelligence service in Haiti in the mid-1980s to fight the cocaine trade, but the unit evolved into an instrument of political terror whose officers at times engaged in drug trafficking, American and Haitian officials say.

American officials say the C.I.A. cut its ties to the Haitian organization shortly after the 1991 military coup against Haiti's first democratically elected President, the Rev. Jean-Bertrand Aristide.

Three former chiefs of the Haitian unit, the National Intelligence Service, known as S.I.N. from its initials in French, are now on the United States Treasury Department's list of Haitian officials whose assets in the United States were frozen this month because of their support for the military leaders blocking Father Aristide's return to power.

ANALYSES ARE CRITICIZED

The disclosure of the American role in creating the agency in 1986 comes amid increasing Congressional and public debate about the intelligence relationship between the United States and Haiti, the richest and poorest countries in the Western Hemisphere.

Supporters of Father Aristide contend that the C.I.A. is undermining the chances for his return with analyses skewed by a misplaced trust in his military foes.

The agency paid key members of the junta now in power for political and military information up until the ouster of Father Aristide in 1991. A review of the C.I.A.'s activities in Haiti under the Reagan and Bush Administrations, based on documents and interviews with current and former officials, confirms that senior C.I.A. officers have long been deeply skeptical about the stability and politics of President Aristide, a leftist priest.

C.I.A. HELP FOR ARISTIDE

No evidence suggests that the C.I.A. backed the coup or intentionally undermined President Aristide. In fact, the agency has acted to help him at times, for example through a program that is now training bodyguards to protect him should he return to Haiti from his exile into the United States.

Though much of the C.I.A.'s activity in Haiti remains secret, the emerging record reveals both failures and achievements in recent years.

Having created the Haitian intelligence service, the agency failed to insure that several million dollars spent training and equipping the service from 1986 to 1991 was actually used in the war on drugs. The unit produced little narcotics intelligence. Senior members committed acts of political terror against Aristide supporters, including interrogations that included torture, and threatened last year to kill the local chief of the United States Drug Enforcement Administration.

On the other hand, United States officials said, one senior Haitian intelligence officer dissuaded soldiers from killing President Aristide during the 1991 coup. The C.I.A. also helped to save the lives of at least six Aristide supporters after the coup, evacuating them in a late-night rescue that involved the Navy's elite SEAL unit, officials said.

The C.I.A. also had a mixed track record in analyzing the fall of the 30-year Duvalier family dictatorship in 1986. The agency's analysts did not foresee the political violence that led to the collapse of elections in 1987 and the 1991 coup. But the analysts, contradicting the White House and the State Department, correctly predicted this year that the Haitian military would block President Aristide's scheduled return in October.

Members of the Congressional panels that oversee the C.I.A. say the agency's intelligence-gathering helped American policy makers bewildered by the political chaos that followed the fall of the Duvalier dictatorship, including a series of military coups, and by Father Aristide's overwhelming victory in the December 1990 election.

LAWMAKER CITES C.I.A.'S "BUM RAP"

"The problems in Haiti are problems of policy, not intelligence," said Representative Dan Glickman, a Kansas Democrat who heads the House intelligence committee. "In some cases, intelligence gets a bum rap. From the interviews we've had with the agency, I don't get any feeling that our goal was to preserve military dictatorship in Haiti."

But Senator Christopher J. Dodd, a Connecticut Democrat on the Senate Foreign Relations Committee who received extensive briefings from the agency, asserted last week that the C.I.A.'s view of Haiti was distorted by its ties to the Haitian military. "A lot of the information we're getting is from the very same people who in front of the world are brutally murdering people," Senator Dodd said.

One crucial source of information for American intelligence over the years, according to two Government officials, was Lieut. Gen. Raoul Cédras, who leads the Haitian armed forces. The officials said he provided the United States Government with reports critical of Father Aristide. The officials did not provide details from those reports. Nor did they say whether the general was paid.

In 1957, François Duvalier rose to power in Haiti. A corrupt dictator, he consolidated his power with the aid of a 10,000-member gang known as the Tonton Macoute.

Four years later, he was threatened by a C.I.A. covert operation in which the agency supplied arms to opponents plotting a coup, according to a 1975 Senate report. The plot failed.

On his death in 1971, Mr. Duvalier bequeathed his regime to his son, Jean-Claude, who received nearly $400 million in American economic aid until a popular revolt toppled his Government and he fled the country in February 1986.

Shortly afterward the C.I.A. created the Haitian intelligence service, S.I.N. The agency was staffed solely with officers of the Haitian Army, which was already widely perceived as an unprofessional force with a tendency toward corruption. The stated purpose was to stem the flow of hundreds of millions of dollars' worth of cocaine through Haiti, a crucial transit point for drug traffickers.

MODEL FOR AGENCY DESPITE AID CURB

The United States would gain information on the Haitian military by creating the unit; the Haitian military would obtain money, training and equipment from the C.I.A.

In intelligence parlance, it was a "liaison" relationship. The C.I.A. does not normally report to Congress on such relationships, citing the sensitivity of other nations to disclosures of secrets. That reduces the role of Congressional oversight.

S.I.N. received $500,000 to $1 million a year in equipment, training and financial support from the C.I.A., United States and Haitian Government officials say. The money may have sent a mixed message, for Congress was withholding about $1.5 million in aid for the Haitian military regime at the same time.

By late 1988, the agency decided to "distance itself" from the intelligence service, a senior United States official said. But the ties continued until October 1991, just after the September 30 coup against Father Aristide, he said.

A 1992 Drug Enforcement Administration document described S.I.N. in the present tense, as "a covert counternarcotics intelligence unit which often works in unison with the C.I.A. at post."

The Haitian intelligence service provided little information on drug trafficking and some of its members themselves became enmeshed in the drug trade, American officials said. A United States official who worked at the American Embassy in Haiti in 1991 and 1992 said he took a dim view of S.I.N.

"It was a military organization that distributed drugs in Haiti," said the official, who spoke on condition of anonymity. "It never produced drug intelligence. The agency gave them money under counter-narcotics and they used their training to do other things in the political arena."

U.S. DRUG OFFICIAL GETS DRUG THREAT

"The money that was spent to train these guys in the counter-narcotics field boggled the mind—half a million to a million a year," the official said. "They were turning it around and using it for political reasons, against whatever group they wanted to gather information on."

In September 1992, the work of United States drug-enforcement officials in Haiti led to the arrest of a S.I.N. officer on cocaine charges by the Haitian authorities.

A few days later, the Drug Enforcement Administration's chief in Haiti, Tony Greco, received a death threat on his private telephone line in the American Embassy. The caller identified himself as the arrested intelligence officer's superior, United States Government records show. Mr. Greco immediately left Haiti and has not returned.

Three former chiefs of the Haitian intelligence service—Col. Ernst Prudhomme, Col. Diderot Sylvain and Col. Leopold Clerjeune—were named by the United States Treasury Department in a November 1 order for seizure of their assets in the United States. The document named 41 people "who seized power illegally," helped anti-Aristide forces or "contributed to the violence in Haiti."

Haitian officials say those S.I.N. officers persecuted Father Aristide's supporters and used their C.I.A. training to spy on them.

"They were heavily involved in spying on so-called subversive groups," an exiled member of the Aristide Government said. "They were doing nothing but political repression. Father Aristide was one of their targets. They targeted people who were for change."

Between 1 A.M. and 3 A.M. on November 2, 1989, Colonel Prudhomme, who headed S.I.N. and held the title of chief of national security, led a brutal interrogation of Evans Paul, the Mayor of Haiti's capital, Port-au-Prince, according to a sworn deposition taken from Mr. Paul in connection with a Federal lawsuit filed against senior Haitian military officers in 1991 in Miami.

Colonel Clerjeune also was present at the interrogation, which left Mr. Paul with five broken ribs and internal injuries, the Mayor said.

Mr. Paul, who opposed the military regime, was arrested by soldiers, beaten and taken to the police headquarters in Port-au-Prince, where the beatings continued, according to sworn statements. When Mr. Paul lost consciousness, he said, he was revived by soldiers holding a flame from a cigarette lighter under his nose.

"Prudhomme himself never touched me," Mr. Paul said in an interview from Haiti. "He played the role of the intellectual, the man who searched carefully for contradictions in your account—the man who seemed to give direction to the whole enterprise. He wanted to present me to the world as a terrorist."

"He seemed to have so much information about my life, all the way from my childhood," the Mayor said. "It was if he had been following me step by step."

Last summer, Mr. Paul met his interrogator again. Colonel Prudhomme was part of the military delegation led by General Cédras at talks mediated by the United Nations in July at Governors Island in New York. The accord reached at that meeting called for General Cédras to step down by October 15 and allow Mr. Aristide to return on October 30. The military reneged on the accord.

But S.I.N. also produced a success story: Col. Alix P. Silva, who led the Haitian intelligence service from 1986 to 1988. In 1988, Colonel Silva compiled a list of 18 senior Haitian military officials whom he said should be cashiered for unprofessional conduct, corruption or cocaine trafficking. At the head of the list was Lieut. Gen. Prosper Avril, who seized power in a 1989 coup.

Forced into hiding when General Avril took power, Colonel Silva resurfaced after the 1990 election, in which Father Aristide won 67.5 percent of the vote in a field of 10 candidates. The colonel then served as Deputy Commander in Chief of the army under General Cédras, who betrayed President Aristide by ousting him in September 1991.

It was Colonel Silva, current and former American officials say, who persuaded Haitian soldiers not to shoot Father Aristide on the night of the coup. Although briefly a member of the Cédras junta, Colonel Silva was among a handful of Aristide supporters who were evacuated shortly after the coup in a clandestine flight from Haiti that was coordinated by the C.I.A. and a team of Navy commandos, the officials said.

Though derring-do may be part of the C.I.A.'s image, the agency's most important task is helping American leaders understand what goes on in the world. Its intelligence analysts, not its spies, hold sway in Washington.

The agency's leading analyst of Latin American affairs, Brian Latell, traveled to Port-au-Prince in July 1992 and recorded his trip in a three-page note that he later shared with members of Congressional intelligence committees. He met with General Cédras, who he said impressed him as "a conscientious military leader who genuinely wishes to minimize his role in politics."

That impression, Father Aristide's supporters say, contributed to the faith placed in General Cédras by the United States policy makers, a faith broken when the general abrogated the Governor's Island accord.

Mr. Latell also reported that he "saw no evidence of oppressive rule" in Haiti.

RIGHTS REPORT TELLS A DIFFERENT STORY

"I do not wish to minimize the role the military plays in intimidating, and occasionally terrorizing real and suspected opponents," the analyst said, but "there is no systematic or frequent lethal violence aimed at civilians."

That conflicts with a State Department report for the same year, which said, "Haitians suffered frequent human rights abuses throughout 1992, including extra-judicial killings by security forces, disappearances, beatings and other mistreatment of detainees and prisoners, arbitrary arrests and detention and executive interference with the judicial process."

Mr. Glickman, chairman of the House Intelligence Committee, defended Mr. Latell's work and said that no institutional bias afflicted the agency's reporting on Haiti.

But he said he had questions about "this whole counter-narcotics involvement of the agency" and what good, if any, it achieved in Haiti.

(Based on reporting by Stephen Engelberg, Howard W. French, and Tim Weiner; written by Tim Weiner)

"GREYMAIL" WARNING ON
HAITIAN DRUG PROSECUTIONS

Memo from Mark M. Richard, U.S.
Deputy Assistant Attorney General

By late spring 1994, there was increasing pressure on the Clinton administration to remove the Haitian coup leaders—and prosecution for drug trafficking was one of the strategies open to the U.S. for accomplishing this. In April the U.S. Department of Justice issued a confidential memorandum to top officials in the CIA, National Security Council, National Security Agency, Drug Enforcement Agency, FBI, State Department, Treasury Department, and Pentagon. The memo informs these agencies of impending prosecution of leading Haitian military and civilian figures. The implicit task of the memo is also to provide a warning to any U.S. agents in place or officials who might be compromised by the potential prosecution of the Haitian figures.

┐

April 8, 1994

RE: Request for Document Search by Intelligence Agencies and Components Regarding Haitian Government Officials Targeted in U.S. Attorney's Office, SD/FL [Southern District, Florida], Criminal Investigation

This letter will serve to notify your respective agencies of a criminal investigation currently underway in the Southern District of Florida in which are targeted a number of officials within the Haitian government. This investigation is still at a preliminary stage and thus indictments that may result from the investigation will not occur in the immediate future. We request therefore that the information in this letter not be disseminated except as is necessary to perform the tasks described below.

As the information below reflects, the investigation focuses on the trafficking of cocaine through the country of Haiti under the control and/or protection of these government officials. That information also reflects a strong likelihood that classified information will become at issue in this case. We therefore wish now to establish a liaison with the various components of the intelligence community to avoid problems that ensue when these types of issues are thrust upon all of us after indictment. . . .

The investigation that gives rise to this search request has been conducted by the Organized Crime Drug Enforcement Task Force in Miami for approximately the past three years and has been directed at various Haitian drug trafficking organizations. Within the past few months, the focus of the investigation has narrowed to certain Colombians traffickers and Haitian government officials responsible for transshipment of cocaine through Haiti.

Through debriefing various cooperating witnesses the U.S. Attorney's Office in Miami has established that the Haitian military has been closely involved in the facilitation of drug trafficking since at least the early 1980s. We understand that the military are paid to protect the off-loading of planes as well as the loading of ships, freighters being a principal mode of importation from Haiti; in addition, the military sometimes seize cocaine, then sell it to Haitian traffickers who ship it to the United States.

According to reports published in the media, shortly after Jean-Claude Duvalier fled Haiti in 1985, the Central Intelligence Agency assisted the new Haitian government in establishing the National Intelligence Service, a counter-narcotics/intelligence agency known by its initials in French, S.I.N. (hereafter SIN). Specifically, the CIA was reported to have provied financial support for start up and maintenance, training for SIN's personnel, and equipment for use by SIN personnel. We expect that several of the individuals investigated in this matter would likely have been associated with any such organization.

Attached to this letter are a list of persons currently targeted by the U.S. Attorney's Office in Miami. As you will note, each of them is a member of the Haitian military with the exception of MAX PAUL, who [is] director of Ports in Port-au-Prince. From recent experience in other CIPA cases, we believe that one or more of these persons may assert a defense of 'public authority,' or some variation thereof, by claiming their criminal acts were done with the knowledge of and at the behest of American authorities. At the very least, intelligence equities that are known to these individuals will be at risk in the event of an indictment, and any joint operations that were under taken between the U.S. and Haiti will be cast in the worst possible light.

Experience certainly suggests that it is best to grapple with any difficult issues early, before an indictment invokes both severe time constraints and public debate. Therefore, we ask that you read these requests broadly to address problems before they become urgent.

In order to guage appropriately, and to thwart effectively, a 'public authority' defense or a 'greymail' defense at the earliest possible moment, the Department of Justice and the U.S. Attorney's Office, Southern District of Florida, would appreciate your assistance in researching your indices and files as to each of the names in the attached Addendum and as otherwise necessary to assist us in answering the following questions: . . .
[Approximately one and a half pages of questions appears in the memo at this point.]

Addendum:

List of Haitian Military and Civilian Personnel/Entities To Be Researched in Agency Indices
1. General Jean-Claude Duperval
2. Col. Jean-Claude Paul (deceased 1988)
3. Col. (FNU) [first name unknown] Cazime
4. Lt. Col. Andre Claudel Josaphat (DOB: 08/17/56)
5. Maxime Antoine (Haitian Military, rank unknown)
6. Col. FNU Oxyl
7. Capt. (FNU) Mintord
8. Col. Hyppolite Granpetard aka Hippolite Granpetard
9. Col. Antoine Atouriste
10. Col. Diderot Sylvain
11. Capt. Gerald Larochel (DOB: 04/04/58)
12. Capt. (FNU) Lamour
13. Capt. Jean Jaccuse Jouenice aka Jackson Joanis (DOB 10/25/58)
14. Col. Michel Francois, Chief of Police, Port-Au-Prince, Haiti
15. Max Paul, Director of Ports 1 (civilian)
16. National Intelligence Service (SIN)

1. Max Paul's brothers, Colonel Jean-Claude Paul (deceased) and of Antonio Paul, and sister-in-law, Mirielle Mireaux Paul (deceased), were indicted in the Southern District of Florida in 1988 for conspiracy and cocaine trafficking. After that indictment, both Antonio Paul and Mirielle Paul, Colonel Paul's wife, made contact with American authorities at the U.S. Embassy in Port-au-Prince, Haiti in an unsuccessful effort to resolve these charges.
[Not long after this memo was sent, Antonio Paul was found innocent of cocaine trafficking charges by a jury in Miami.]

4

HUMAN RIGHTS AND THE REFUGEE QUESTION

TERROR PREVAILS IN HAITI

Human Rights Watch/Americas–National Coalition for Haitian Refugees

By early 1994, torture and repression had become endemic in Haiti, though it was frequently "ignored or downplayed" by the U.S. government. In an April 1994 report, *Terror Prevails in Haiti: Human Rights Violations and Failed Diplomacy*, Human Rights Watch/Americas (formerly Americas Watch) and the National Coalition for Haitian Refugees documented the brutal activities practiced by the Haitian military and FRAPH, with the support of the coup government.

┐

Terror, intimidation, and the nightmare of reborn Duvalierism have become the Haitian citizens' daily reality as military rule continues for a third year. As successive internationally sponsored efforts to negotiate President Jean-Bertrand Aristide's return have failed, the army has come to believe that it can retain power indefinitely. To this end, it has reneged on successive agreements and used armed civilian thugs to drive off United Nations-backed U.S. and Canadian military instructors. Although the Armed Forces of Haiti (*Forces Armés d'Haiti*, FADH), remain nominally steady at some 7,000 men, their strength and sway has grown since the coup with the addition of tens of thousands of civilian attachés.[1] In the second half of 1993, these bands of thugs were fashioned into the quasi-political organization known as the Front for the Advancement and Progress of Haiti (*Front pour l'Avancement et le Progrès d'Haiti*, FRAPH). FRAPH, which sounds like the French word for "hit," has been nurtured by the military since its emergence in September 1993.

The Clinton administration, while more active than the previous administration in pushing for the restoration of democracy to Haiti, has failed to make respect for human rights a central component in its policy toward Haiti. Throughout the year, the administration carried out an indiscriminate and inhumane policy of forcibly repatriating Haitians fleeing well-documented persecution. And, in order to defend its refugee policy, the administration alternatively ignored or downplayed human rights, despite the obvious deterioration in the human rights situation.

The administration continued to ignore human rights during the Governors Island negotiations, when it refused to support proposals that would hold human rights violators accountable or guarantee respect for human rights in the future. The administration's public reaction to an alarming increase in reports of political killings in Cité Soleil in February and March, for example, was limited to a weak press statement issued only in Haiti that failed to blame the army and its supporters for the murders.[2]

As a political solution appeared more and more remote, political violence continued unimpeded, with seventy-one murders committed between February 1 and mid-March, in Port-au-Prince alone, under investigation by the United Nations/Organization of American States' International Civilian Mission. There has also been an increase in reports of disappearances, politically motivated rapes, and arbitrary arrests during the first months of 1994. Residents of Port-au-Prince's Cité Soleil, who are perceived by the military and its backers as Aristide supporters, have been particularly targeted by the heightened violence, especially since the December 27, 1993 massacre there.

The recent violations are only the most recent attacks in the consistent campaign of terror against Haitians. In the first half of 1993, the military continued to restrict basic freedoms in Haiti—banning public support for Aristide, barring most meetings, and intimidating the independent media with violence and threats. Arbitrary arrest, beatings, and torture, including rape, while in detention continued to be the rule rather than the exception. The deployment of the International Civilian Mission (MICIVIH) beginning in February led to certain modifications in the repression, particularly outside the capital. Consistent intervention by observers on behalf of people illegally arrested or mistreated in detention led to releases from prison and somewhat fewer arrests. It also persuaded the military to make greater use of civilian attachés, making it more difficult to implicate the army in illegal acts. The presence of the mission emboldened local groups to organize pro-Aristide rallies in some cities (most of which were swiftly repressed) and communal meetings in several rural areas.

Human rights conditions began to deteriorate immediately following the signing of the Governors Island Agreement in New York on July 3, 1993. The military, aided by its attaches or armed civilians, began a deliberate campaign of heightened terror and violence. Killings, forced disappearances, illegal arrests, beatings, and torture increased sharply in July and August. Conditions deteriorated further after the inauguration of the short-lived constitutional government of Robert Malval and the lifting of the international oil and arms embargo. In the two months before President Aristide's scheduled return on October 30, the army increasingly collaborated with gangs of armed civilians who kidnapped, tortured, and killed Aristide supporters. Armed civilians made nightly visits to many neighborhoods of Port-au-Prince, firing their guns in the air, threatening and arresting residents. Similar bands prevented the Malval government from functioning and blocked the implementation of measures approved at Governors Island that would have led to a restoration of President Aristide's government.

The parameters of the crisis are geographically demonstrated by the rising death toll following the Governor's Island agreement. Using figures for political killings or suspicious murders from the International Civilian Mission for the months of May through September 1993, and February 1994, and from Haitian human rights groups in the intervening period, the pattern of violence in relation to political developments is clear.

Political Killings and Suspicious Murders
May 1993-February 1994[3]

May 9
June 5
July 34
August 33
September .... 60+
October .... 80+
November .... 70+
December .... 55+
January .... 30+
February .... 50+

Many of the victims were community leaders or members of groups favoring Aristide's return. Others, such as the people killed in the December 27 arson attack in Cité Soleil,[4] died because they lived in the shantytowns where there existed considerable support for Aristide.

Throughout 1993, civil society continued to fall victim to repression, as it had in the first year after the coup, as HRW/Americas reported in *Silencing a People*.[5] Restrictions on the rights of free speech and free assembly and the virtual ban on meetings by popular organizations, even nonpolitical ones, led to fragmentation and increased demoralization that had a negative impact on grassroots development and self-help projects. The fledgling efforts to organize demonstrations in support of Aristide's return, strengthened by the arrival of the International Civilian Mission, collapsed with the renewed terror that began in September. The only public demonstrations tolerated by those in power since then have been organized by FRAPH and other like-minded groups.

The repression since the Governor's Island Accord has created increasing numbers of internally displaced people, described as "in hiding" or marronage. The forced displacement of tens, if not hundreds of thousands of Haitians is part of the military's strategy to destroy all forms of organization or opposition. The high level of internal displacement has resulted in severe economic hardship as families are separated and lose their already limited sources of income.

Pressures on the independent media, in the form of threats, intimidation, arrests, and violence, have forced provincial radio stations to shut down and caused radio and television stations in Port-au-Prince to practice increased self-censorship. Journalists have been forced into hiding, further impeding the flow of information both locally and internationally. . . .

NOTES

1. Attachés are civilian, paramilitary troops supported and armed by the Armed Forces of Haiti.

2. A March 18, 1994 press guidance prepared by the State Department could be interpreted as indirectly blaming President Aristide for the killings. The guidance states, in part, "We believe this repression is a result of the pressure put on all sectors of Haitian society by the existence of a political vacuum and the continuing crisis in the country." The State Department has frequently criticized President Aristide for not appointing a Prime Minister, and therefore creating a political vacuum.

3. The presence of the International Civilian Mission around the country made it possible for the first time to obtain relatively comprehensive figures on the numbers of victims of human rights violations. Figures from May through September 1993 and February 1994 come from the Mission.

4. The Justice and Peace Commission reported the identities of 36 people killed during the incident, as well as 25 people disappeared or unaccounted for, and four injured. Investigations into the massacre are continuing, and another credible estimate has put the number of people dead as high as 102.

5. Americas Watch and the National Coalition for Haitian Refugees, *Silencing a People: The Destruction of Civil Society in Haiti* (New York: Human Rights Watch, 1993). See also the following Americas Watch/NCHR reports: *No Port in a Storm: The Misguided Use of In-Country Refugee Processing in Haiti* (1993), *Half the Story: The Skewed U.S. Monitoring of Repatriated Refugees* (1992), *Return to the Darkest Days: Human Rights in Haiti Since the Coup* (1991), and *The Aristide Government's Human Rights Record* (1991).

HAITI HUMAN RIGHTS REPORT
U.S. Embassy, Port-au-Prince

The U.S. government's "downplaying" of human rights violations in Haiti was confirmed by a cable sent from the embassy in Port-au-Prince to top officials in Washington on April 12, 1994. The cable—reportedly drafted by Political Officer Ellen Cosgrove, and signed by Ambassador William L. Swing—describes how "the Haitian left, including President Aristide and his supporters in Washington and here, consistently manipulate or even fabricate human rights abuses." The cable suggests that abuses were being invented as a propaganda tool for Aristide, and also to gain credence for the asylum claims of Haitian refugees, most of whom were merely seeking to escape "economic conditions," and not political terror. (Names of individuals, which were originally included in this cable despite the additional danger it might cause, were blanked out before the cable was disseminated by organizations.)

┐

1. Confidential, entire text.

2. This is an action message—see para. 24.

SUMMARY

3. Human rights abuses have increased recently because the army and its allies believe that they have "stared down" the USG [United States government] and can act against their adversaries, and frighten the Haitian people into submission, with impunity. The right-wing FRAPH movement, and the current climate of intimidation, took root after both the Harlan County and the UN observer mission beat a retreat. Some FRAPH members are former Aristide supporters.

4. The Haitian left manipulates and fabricates human rights abuses as a propaganda tool, wittingly or unwittingly assisted in this report by human rights NGOs [non-governmental organizations] and by the ICM. Migration is primarily caused by economic conditions, but is aggravated by violence. Institutions which ordinarily guarantee human rights, like an independent judiciary and professional law enforcement entities, do not/not exist in Haiti [sic].

5. The means envisaged by the Governor's Island Accord to begin creating such institutions, the UNMIS, was never deployed because of the October 11 Harlan County Departure. Both Aristide and Cédras are profiting from the resulting vacuum, Aristide to decry abuses and cement his influence in Washington, Cédras to tacitly condone their commission and cement his influence in Haiti.

6. If the US and UN choose to remain engaged with Aristide, they must also remain engaged in human rights monitoring and institution-building in Haiti, otherwise Aristide will continue to use lawlessness in Haiti to force his own agenda of intervention. Demarches and press statements can only do so much; we welcome the return of the Inter-American Human Rights commission, and urge that the remaining OAS observers still in the DR [Dominican Republic] return to Haiti ASAP. End Summary.

ABUSES ARE INCREASING

7. Since the departure of the Harlan County October 12, the army has acted on the assumption that the U.S. government and, most importantly, its military forces will not intervene in Haiti. The army's control of the strategic fuel reserve and contraband activities insure that they will be hurt least (and benefit most) from the current embargo. Cédras and the central staff tacitly condone both widespread police criminal activity and the persecution and elimination of Aristide partisans, confident that the international community will be unable to do more than deplore and condemn the acts of violence. Such violence has not been confined to Port-Au-Prince slums.

FEAR AND BRUTALITY IN THE PROVINCES

8. For example, following February's army-fabricated "Lavalas commando attack" in Les Cayes, local military terrorized and beat citizens and torched neighborhoods, allegedly "searching for suspects," in actuality ensuring that the populace remains cowed and frightened. According to the RMA office in Les Cayes, one elderly man was so badly beaten—numerous broken ribs, broken jaw, internal bleeding—that he died of his injuries. The victim had never sought political asylum, but other beating victims who survived have since sought asylum status. The army corporal allegedly responsible for many of the beatings, a corporal Minsroux, remains on active duty in the Les Cayes area.

THE ONLY INSTITUTION IS THE "GWO NEG"

9. Haiti has no functional institutions, especially outside of Port-Au-Prince. In their absence, Haitians gravitate, for assistance and protection, toward whomever is seen to be the "Gwo Neg" (Big Man). The "Gwo Neg" traditionally dispenses favors and collects protection money. Under Aristide, the "Gwo Neg was usually the local Lavalas leader, or a politically-appointed "delegue" dispatched from the interior ministry in Port-Au-Prince. After the Coup, the local constables called "section chiefs" regained their former power (embassy has reported in detail, and extensively, on this problem).

THE IGM BEAT FEET IN OCTOBER, 1993

The deployment of ICM observers to Haiti's provincial capitals in March, 1993 introduced a mediating force into this volatile mix. In the absence of an impartial justice of the peace or law enforcement representative, rural Haitians told their stories of stolen livestock, family disputes, and the local army extorsion [sic] racket to the ICM observers, who listened patiently and sought to help where they could. The October, 1993 retreat of the UN police and judicial training presence, and the subsequent flight of the ICM observers to the Dominican Republic, where they remained until February of this year, left a vacuum that has been filled by FRAPH.

FRAPH MOVED RIGHT IN

11. There is currently a FRAPH office and FRAPH bullies in virtually every town and city in Haiti (ref C and previous reporting). Assuming that thousands of FRAPH members are not clandestinely flown into Haiti each night from abroad, it seems obvious that FRAPH is recruiting on the ground among poor slum dwellers and peasants. At least some of the current, large, FRAPH "membership" were once part of President Aristide's 37% of the electorate. This is understandable; FRAPH hands out food, money, favors and a vague sense of purpose. People tolerate (or are too scared to protest) brutal local extortion rackets run by FRAPH. The present climate of intimidation is made even worse because, according to the ICM, a number of former Lavalas partisans have defected to FRAPH, in the process fingering their former pro-Aristide confederates to FRAPH's thugs.

LAVALAS AND FRAPH: SAME M.O., OVERLAPPING MEMBERSHIP

12. In addition to having many of the same "members," FRAPH has essentially the same modus operandi as the Lavalas "comites de quartier" that were sanctioned, and encouraged, during the Aristide presidency. The key difference is that the amorphous expression of popular discontent that is FRAPH is an instrument of the military, whereas the "comites de quartier" were the instruments of the executive. FRAPH is already grooming candidates, and wooing/terrorizing potential voters, in anticipation of local and parliamentary elections scheduled for this December.

VIOLENCE AS PROPAGANDA

13. The Haitian left, including President Aristide and his supporters in Washington and here, consistently manipulate or even fabricate human rights abuses as a propaganda tool. Their justification for doing this is that they are an unarmed force arrayed against an armed and brutal military. Under these circumstances they see the truth as a flexible means to obtain a worthy political end.

THE RAPE EPIDEMIC — EQUATING HAITI AND BOSNIA

14. A case in point is the sudden epidemic of rapes reported both by pro-Aristide human rights activists and by the ICM (ref. F). For a range of cul-

tural reasons (not pleasant to contemplate), rape has never been considered or reported as a serious crime here. Hardline ideological Aristide supporters here regularly compare the human rights situation in Haiti to the carnage in Bosnia. Some have called recent violence in Port-Au-Prince slums "political cleansing," equating this with "ethnic cleansing" against muslims by Bosnian serbs. An Aristide confidant recently offered, as an example of "political cleansing," the fact that FRAPH thugs force the drivers of tap tap buses to change their signs from "Cite Soleil" to "Cite Simone" (the first name of Mrs. François Duvalier, and the original name of the area under Duvalierism). We are, frankly, suspicious of the sudden, high number of reported rapes, particularly in this culture, occurring at the same time that Aristide activists seek to draw a comparison between Haiti and Bosnia.

"JOSEPH Y," HIGH-PROFILE HUMAN RIGHTS VICTIM

15. Political propaganda and economic migration join in the case of _____, who spoke with Senator Dodd during his recent visit here (Ref. E) in a meeting arranged by the embassy. The alleged kidnapping of _____'s four-year-old son (ref F) had generated media attention here and was reported in an April 7 New York Times article in which _____ was identified as "Joseph Y." _____ told both Senator Dodd and the New York Times reporter that he had been "beaten with wet towels" at the Port-Au-Prince anti-gang police station as part of a campaign of harassment against him that culminated in the abduction of his child. Because the _____ case resembles hundreds of asylum cases seen each week at these refugee processing centers in Haiti, it is worth examining closely.

TRUST US, THEY DON'T BEAT YOU WITH WET TOWELS AT ANTI-GANG

16. Out of a brutal and untrained municipal police force of roughly 1,200 men (reinforced by civilian attaches), three of the worst police companies are the 22nd company (also called Delmas 33 and "Fort Dimanche"), the 4th company (also called "cafeteria") and the anti-gang unit. All operate attache activity directed against Aristide activists. Elements of the 22nd company have shot suspected Aristide supporters on sight in the streets of Port-Au-Prince (Ref K). Suspects "brought in for questioning" at the anti-gang unit are regularly brutally beaten, but with fists and clubs, not, to our knowledge, with "wet towels." If the beating gets out of hand, as reportedly often happens, the victim is finished off and the body is dumped in an area called "Titanten," a marshy no-mans-land pitted with ravines, which is located north of Port-Au-Prince. Alternatively, the body is simply dumped in the street. The beaten and disfigured bodies found in Cite Soleil (ref G) in recent weeks could well be victims of police brutality; dumping them in

Cite Soleil also sends a clear and terrifying message to the ghetto neighborhood's inhabitants.

WE BELIEVE "JOSEPH Y" IS PRIMARILY AN ECONOMIC MIGRANT

17. In addition to his account of having been "beaten with wet towels," _____ displayed a small keloid scar located behind his right ear, visibly several years old, as evidence of his mistreatment at anti-gang. His young son, reportedly recently kidnapped by frightening strangers and held for seven days without food or water, was plump, extroverted and playful. The child only evinced discomfort when he was questioned about his alleged ordeal, turning his back and replying to questions in monosyllables. _____, who said to the New York Times reporter "We must get out of this country," later declined expedited asylum processing, saying that he preferred to wait for asylum in Canada, because he preferred a French-speaking country.

THE NGOS AND THE ICM: TRUTH, LIES, AND POLITICS

18. The _____ nun who sheltered the _____ family _____ and brought the case to our, and the ICM's attention is also a registered nurse. We have to assume that she knows more about old and recent scars, about child psychology, and even —having lived among Haiti's poor for five years—about beatings at anti-gang then we do. Certainly she believed the _____'s account of their troubles, as did the ICM. The problem is that we do not believe it, chiefly because we know all too much about the way the police and army really handle suspected Aristide supporters— and it is not with wet towels.

MOST BOAT PEOPLE/ASYLUM SEEKERS NOT/NOT POLITICAL VICTIMS

19. While some of the killings reported by the ICM are probably the result of rising criminality in a society that is disintegrating economically under sanctions, the army and right wing elements are unquestionably committing numerous, serious human rights abuses, including murders of suspected Aristide partisans. The majority of Haitian boat people, and the majority of asylum applicants, remain, however, intending economic migrants. Over 50,000 migrants have been returned to Haiti since the beginning of 1991; slightly more than half since the September, 1991 coup d'état. What this figure indicates, in our view, is that political disruption increases existing high levels of economic migration, because unsettled conditions and/or violence contribute to an intending economic migrant's decision to leave, whether or not the individual is persecuted.

20. We base this, in the case of the repatriated boat people, on their own accounts of hunger, poverty and despair. In the case of the majority of asy-

lum seekers, we base this assumption on what we know of this anarchic society and its corrupt, brutal police and military—many of the applicants' accounts simply do not correspond to reality. We should bear in mind that 980 Haitians, and their families, have been granted political asylum since February, 1992 because they had a credible claim of persecution.

INSTITUTIONS AND OBSERVERS CONTROL VIOLENCE

21. What are we saying? We are saying that there is a high level of structural, or endemic, violence in Haiti because law enforcement and the judiciary are absent, or corrupt, or are the actual perpetrators of violence and injustice. The political crisis has worsened a bad situation by adding ideology to existing tensions. The prescriptive measures intended to deal with this problem in a lasting way were the un-sponsored police and judicial reform presence and the UN civilian observers. Both of these forces retreated when they should have stood fast. So ICM observers finally returned, but during their four month absence from Haiti's provinces, the military and their armed civilian allies (loosely identified as attaches or FRAPH) took over.

ARISTIDE/RIGHTS MONITORING/INSTITUTION BUILDING

22. The departure of the Harlan County, the flight of the ICM to the Dominican Republic, and the resulting vacuum greatly benefited both the Aristide camp and the army. President Aristide and his lobbying apparatus in Washington have increasing substantiation for charges that the human rights situation here is getting worse—and what they cannot substantiate, they will fabricate. The army has cemented its hold on power, its financial tentacles in embargo contraband and state industries, and its ability to intimidate a frightened population.

23. If the US and UN choose to remain engaged with President Aristide, they must also remain engaged with institution-building and human rights monitoring in Haiti. Backing away from institution-building and rights monitoring, while supporting Aristide, has contributed to the present deteriorating human rights situation here and the exploitation of the tragedy by Aristide and his Washington lobbying apparatus. Opting for an easier ride early on has led to a very rough ride in the here and now.

AGAIN, SEND MONITORS AND OBSERVERS

24. Embassy Demarches—both at the working level on individual cases and to general Cédras on the overall problem—can only do so much. Press Communiques condemning the violence and calling on the military to halt it can draw attention to the problem, but cannot decrease the violence. Embassy appreciates Washington's quick support of our recommendation that the OAS

Inter-American Human Rights Commission visit Haiti urgently to report on the situation (ref A), and again urges that the remaining OAS observers still on stand-by in the Dominican Republic be dispatched back to Haiti as soon as possible. The only meaningful, peaceful way to control human rights abuses, at this point, is to position more monitors and observers on the ground. Embassy also reiterates, with this message, our previous request (ref D) for TDY assistance with human rights and repatriate monitoring.

NO PORT IN A STORM

Human Rights Watch/Americas– National Coalition for Haitian Refugees–Jesuit Refugee Service USA

The U.S.'s efforts to dismiss the real dangers that forced Haitians to flee the island supported an "illegal and irresponsible refugee policy" that gave Haitians little opportunity to make political asylum claims. A September 1993 report entitled *No Port in a Storm: The Misguided Use of In-Country Refugee Processing in Haiti* described U.S. policy, and its dire consequences for Haitian refugees.

⌐

When the September 30, 1991 military *coup d'état* exiled Haiti's democratically elected president and unleashed some of the most brutal repression in Haitian history, the U.S. government went to new extremes in curtailing the rights of Haitian asylum seekers. The damage done by this misguided and discriminatory refugee policy will persist long after a political settlement is achieved in Haiti.

For many years, the United States government has been interdicting Haitians on the high seas and returning them to Haiti with only minimal efforts at screening for refugee status. This policy, coupled with discriminatory treatment of Haitian asylum seekers in the U.S., has been the focus of longstanding criticism and a stream of legal challenges.

The Bush Administration's response to the September 1991 political crisis was feeble and to the refugee crisis, reprehensible. The United States joined other nations in the western hemisphere in condemning the coup, refusing to recognize the new military-backed government and imposing sanctions. However, after an initial hesitation, and in spite of widespread human rights violations and generalized violence, the interdiction policy continued. The exception was a short interlude when Haitians picked up at sea were taken to Guantánamo Bay to be screened for asylum seekers after a Florida federal district judge imposed a temporary restraining order halting forced repatriations. In February 1992, the Bush Administration established an in-country processing (ICP) program through the U.S. Embassy in Port-au-Prince. That same month, the Supreme Court lifted the ban on the involuntary return (*refoulement*) of Haitian refugees.

The parameters of debate shifted dramatically, however, when on May 24, 1992, then-President Bush ordered all Haitians to be interdicted on the high seas and summarily returned to Haiti, with no prior screening for refugees fearing persecution. ICP, which had historically been conceived as an additional avenue of protection for refugees in selected countries, became the only option for victims of Haiti's repressive military regime.

U.S. foreign policy and refugee policy have been historically inseparable and interdependent. The case of Haiti, and Haitians, is no exception. Newly elected President Clinton, who had made campaign promises to rectify the illegal and irresponsible refugee policy, opted instead to continue it. His administration justified this reversal by raising the spectre of a huge, uncontrollable invasion of economic refugees and by arguing that the policy saved lives.

The Clinton Administration has undeniably contributed to progress made thus far in the reinstatement of constitutional government. Nevertheless, the pre-inauguration announcement that the policy of forcibly returning refugees would continue, with the support of President Aristide, was inconsistent with the Administration's stated commitment to seeking justice in Haiti. Increased efforts on the political front became the excuse for forfeiting the rights of the refugees.

In January, the incoming and outgoing administrations agreed to blockade the island with U.S. Coast Guard cutters, Navy ships and helicopters in order to prevent refugee flight. Clinton's administration went so far as to defend the policy of forced return, successfully, before the Supreme Court, leaving the heretofore globally recognized principle of *non-refoulement* in a shambles. It further proposed to expand and improve ICP, thereby attaining what has since been touted as "complete coverage" for Haitian asylum seekers. Thus, in an ironic twist, non-refoulement is considered irrelevant to a major refugee crisis, and ICP, for the first time in history, is considered an appropriate sole remedy.

In March 1993, the Inter-American Commission on Human Rights of the Organization of American States issued an interim resolution, in response to a petition pending before it, challenging the U.S. government's Haitian interdiction program. The resolution found that the interdiction policy is in violation of international law and should be suspended immediately.

In spite of observable improvements made this year in the program, ICP in Haiti, while certainly able to help some people, cannot be considered an adequate sole remedy for asylum seekers. It is both a product and a victim of the flawed and politicized view of the Haitian refugee crisis held by the U.S. government, and as such, is isolated from and distrusted by international and local refugee experts and human rights organizations, not to mention the very people it is meant to assist.

The State Department runs the program and is responsible for every aspect of it. The Immigration and Naturalization Service (INS) handles the actual case adjudication, which is heavily influenced by the faulty premise behind the program and overly reliant on the State Department including information on country conditions and Haitian culture. Human rights analysis from the State Department is contradictory and at times appears tailored to fit the refugee policy. The fact that the U.S. government considers ICP an adequate response in the Haitian context is testimony to its biased perspective on human rights. . . .

THE HISTORY OF U.S. POLICY TOWARD HAITIAN REFUGEES

The U.S. government has long deplored the practice of totalitarian regimes of restricting the exit of their citizens. Nevertheless, it has lauded the Haitian government for measures it has taken since 1980 to restrict the exit of Haitian refugees. What's more, it has recently become the principal enforcer in denying Haitians the right to leave their country and particularly the right to seek asylum.

For years the U.S. has used a bilateral agreement with the Haitian government as the basis for the interdiction, screening and repatriation of Haitian asylum seekers. In 1981, the U.S.-Haitian interdiction program was launched based on an exchange of diplomatic letters between the two governments and an executive order from then-President Reagan.[1] Under that agreement, Haitian "flag vessels" found in international waters and bound for the U.S. would be interdicted and returned to Haiti. However, the agreement stipulated the U.S. obligation to screen Haitians for claims of persecution, thereby formally recognizing the application of the internationally recognized principle of non-refoulement.

During the next decade, the procedures used to screen boat people and determine refugee status were questioned and attacked by refugee advocates and human rights monitors. From 1981 until the September 1991 coup, 22,716 Haitians were repatriated, according to State Department figures. A total of twenty-eight were allowed to enter the U.S. to pursue asylum claims.[2] The harsh treatment afforded Haitians in the U.S., who have routinely suffered prolonged detention and asylum-approval rates of less than two percent, has also been a long-standing concern. However, at issue were the procedures, not the principle.

In the immediate aftermath of the coup, U.S. cutters initially continued to pick up Haitians on the high seas and screen them onboard for asylum seekers. When this practice was legally challenged as insufficient, screening at the U.S. Naval base at Guantánamo Bay, Cuba commenced. Then the discussion and the lawsuits focused on whether "screened-out" refugees could be forcibly repatriated and whether HIV-positive "screened-in" Haitians could be detained indefinitely at Guantánamo and denied due-process rights enjoyed by other screened-in asylum seekers.[3]

Ironically, it was not until the September, 1991 coup introduced some of the most brutal repression in Haitian history, that the U.S. decided to do away altogether with any pretense of screening fleeing refugees. On May 24, 1992, the parameters of debate shifted dramatically when then-President Bush issued the "Kennebunkport Order" under which all Haitian boats would be interdicted by the U.S. cutters and their passengers returned directly to Port-au-Prince with no prior screening for asylum seekers.[4] With the May 24 order, the Bush Administration abrogated the 1981 bilateral agreement with Haiti. The current policy is based on a unilateral action that lacks the formal consent of the Haitian government.

In this way, the Bush Administration solved the U.S. refugee "problem" through a policy of containment that has curtailed the flight, and the rights, of potential refugees. President Clinton inherited this policy, and, swallowing his pre-election aversions, fine-tuned it by blockading the island.

IN-COUNTRY PROCESSING IN HAITI

The United States set up an in-country processing program (ICP) in Port-au-Prince in February 1992 to afford Haitians the option of seeking asylum without first taking to the high seas. At this time refugee screening was still taking place at Guantánamo. Since the May 1992 U.S. presidential order, ICP has been the only recourse for Haitian asylum seekers and has become a palliative for critics of U.S. policy. When he announced the temporary continuation of the Bush interdiction policy, President Clinton added that ICP would be expanded and improved, thereby better justifying forced repatriation.

This novel application of ICP is a first worldwide. In-country processing is part of a broader set of procedures contained in the 1980 Refugee Act and was not intended as a sole means of protection.[5] Similar programs in Vietnam, Cuba and the former Soviet Union were designed to facilitate the processing of chosen groups of refugees the U.S. was already predisposed to accept based on a concept of "presumptive eligibility."[6] In Haiti, on the other hand, the program is designed to cut off a mass influx of people the U.S. is predisposed to reject. What's more, it is the first case where ICP has been imposed on asylum seekers as a substitute for the ability to escape and seek safe haven before articulating individual claims.[7] In the case of Vietnam, the U.S. played a forceful role in encouraging countries of first asylum to accept boat people temporarily until they could be resettled.[8]

Furthermore, in other countries where ICP became part of a U.S. strategy for resettling refugees, the period of acute political upheaval was over, human rights problems were chronic and predictable and government policies were solidified. In this context, agreements were reached with respective governments to facilitate the orderly processing of selected groups of people. In Haiti, political turmoil is at its height and more complicated yet, the U.S. does not even recognize the *de facto* government, much less enter into agreements with it. These factors effectively remove the safeguards which define the logic and efficiency of ICP in other countries. The driving force behind this plan seems to be the historically unshakable U.S. decision not to become a country of first asylum for Haitian refugees. . . .

THE CENTRAL ROLE AND BIASED VIEW OF THE STATE DEPARTMENT

The ICP program is based on the State Department's premise that the number of genuine asylum seekers is actually quite small. A State Department official involved in setting up the program voiced what seems to be the common belief that "most Haitians are economic migrants; it diminishes our program worldwide if we accept economic migrants."[9] Furthermore, as stated above, the reason that ICP became the antidote for the Haitian refugee problem in the first place was a desire to keep the numbers admitted to the U.S. to a minimum.

Ceiling determinations are limits on refugee admittance, made by the executive branch. They are often made independently of specific country conditions and do not lend themselves to responding to crises. The ceiling for Latin America for fiscal year 1993 was 3,500, of which 500 were allocated to Haiti. This decision was made in August 1992, in the midst of widespread human rights abuses and three months after the Kennebunkport Order made ICP the only option available for Haitians.[10]

Furthermore, refugees outside the United States in general have far fewer due-process rights than asylum seekers who have made it to U.S. shores, and admission is much more discretionary. Although U.S. refugee law, in contrast to international refugee law, does include the concept of a refugee still in his or her own country, there is an increased sense that any approvals are tantamount to altruism. In refugee processing the officer makes a final decision, there is no judicial or administrative review and the applicant bears a greater burden of proof.

U.S. Embassy personnel or IOM contract employees are the principal resources for IOM and INS interviewers.[11] The State Department official interviewed warned that one should not "take people's statements at face value. Past reports such as those put out by the American Immigration Lawyers Association, the Lawyers Committee for Human Rights, Amnesty International etc. contain lots of hearsay. We investigate the cases."[12] The fact that this view is being conveyed within the program certainly undermines the value of having non-governmental human rights material made available to ICP staff. For example, an asylum officer recently assigned to the quality assurance team told AW and NCHR in Haiti that at least some INS personnel consider reports from human rights NGOs and the United Nations/Organization of American States International Civilian Mission (UN/OAS Mission) totally unreliable.[13]

Furthermore, the State Department view of the human rights situation in Haiti seems to vary depending on who is asking. The most recent State Department report on country conditions in Haiti stated:

> Haitians suffered frequent human rights abuses throughout 1992 including extrajudicial killings by security forces, disappearances, beatings and other

mistreatment of detainees and prisoners, arbitrary arrest and detention, and executive interference with the judicial process...[14]

However, a May 7, 1993 State Department advisory opinion in the case of a Haitian popular-movement activist applying for asylum in the U.S. gave quite a different analysis of the situation:

> During 1992, the level of political violence has been considerably reduced...Despite Haiti's violent reputation, it is possible for many people to find safe residence in another part of the country...We do not believe the fact that an ordinary citizen is known to support or to have supported President Aristide by itself puts that person at particular risk of mistreatment or abuse.

Under the heading "False and Exaggerate Claims by Previous Returnees," the opinion goes on to say:

> . . . [I]nvestigations made by U.S. Embassy officers there indicate that many of the reports made by asylum applicants of arrests, killings and intimidation are exaggerated, unconfirmable or false . . .[15]

This view suggests a bias against Haitian asylum seekers by implying that if some have lied, then many probably lie.

In contrast, the June 3, 1993 report by the UN/OAS Mission stated as follows:

> The most serious and numerous human rights violations...involved arbitrary detentions, systematic beatings and torture perpetrated by members of the armed forces or persons operating at their instigation or with their tolerance. The Mission has also been informed of cases of arbitrary executions and deaths following torture inflicted while in detention.

As indicated below, these violations of the right to life and integrity and security of person are intended primarily to restrict or prohibit the exercise of the freedoms of opinion and expression, assembly and peaceful association. Unfortunately, the report provides only a partial picture of the extent to which human rights violations in Haiti are widespread and systematic.[16]

More recently, in an August 11, 1993 press release, the UN/OAS Mission:

> expresses its grave preoccupation at the numerous violations of human rights in Haiti. In particular, the Mission condemns the arbitrary executions and suspicious deaths which have reached alarming levels in the area of Port-au-Prince, where 36 cases have been identified since July 1st.

The targets of these grave human rights violations are members of popular organizations and neighborhood associations, but also simple citizens who had the misfortune to find themselves in the path of the killers.

...Attacks on freedom of association and expression continue, as well as violations against personal security and physical integrity.[17]

The U.S. Embassy's political officer in charge of human rights was reluctant to talk on the record to AW and NCHR about human rights issues. However, she painted a picture of random, undirected violence and general lawlessness merely tolerated from above, as opposed to the targeted, patterned and strategic repression, which includes a sense of chaos and lawlessness, that is reported by both local and international human rights groups. . . .

NO SAFE HAVEN

The most obvious weakness of the ICP program is that there is no safe haven component for asylum seekers. This means that they do not enjoy even the temporary protections and security to which asylum seekers are entitled under international law.[18] The State Department official interviewed told the authors, "We don't provide safe haven...So far it hasn't been an issue because people can call, send letters, access a church group."[19] Nevertheless, ICP applicants have been persecuted while awaiting final resolution of their cases. The Refugee Coordinator stated, "No cases tie in harassment, beatings or killings to the refugee program."[20] However, that distinction is quickly blurred, since applicants with genuine claims apply to the program precisely because they are at risk.

The authors were able to document several cases of persecution during early June 1993, invoking ICP applicants.[21]

One case reported confidentially occurred some time during the first two weeks of June. It involved a young man who had filled out a preliminary questionnaire to apply for asylum, but never made it back to his interview. When he left the ICP locale he was arrested and taken back to a Port-au-Prince police station. He was kicked and beaten. Someone who knew him helped him get released after at least one day and night in prison.[22]

NOTES

1. Executive Order 12324, September 29, 1981. See Bill Frelick, "Haitian Boat Interdiction and Return: Frist Asylum and First Principles of Refugee Protection," U.S. Committee for Refugees, February 20, 1993, p. 6.

2. L. Guttentag and L. Daugaard, "United States Treatment of Haitian Refugees: The Domestic Response and International Law," American Civil Liberties Union, *International Civil Liberties Report*, vol. 1, no. 2, June 1993, p. 10.

3. Refugees were "screened-in" based on a "credible fear" standard in order to pursue their asylum claims in the U.S. under the higher standard of a "well founded fear of persecution on account of race, religion, nationality, membership in a particular social group or political opinion." "Screened-out" refugees were then returned to Haiti. For a 1992 chronology of U.S. program, policy, and legislative decisions affecting refugees and asylum seekers, see "Refugee Reports," U.S. Committee for Refugees, vol. XIV, no. 1, January 29, 1993, p. 6.

4. Executive Order 12,807, Fed. Reg. 23,133, May 24, 1992.

5. As noted in the *amicus curie* brief filed in *Sales v. Haitian Centers Council* [in which the Supreme Court found that neither domestic nor international law prohibited the U.S. returning Haitian refugees picked up on the high seas], Joshua R. Florum (Attorney of Record) on behalf of Senator Edward Kennedy and former Representative Elizabeth Holtzman and other Members of Congress (hereinafter Members of Congress Amicus), "The language, structure and legislative history of the Act, as well as years of executive application of the Act, demonstrate that Congress intended that the Act's three separate but concurrent forms of refugee protection comprise a comprehensive scheme." (p. 5)

6. For example, Inzunza writes, "Although the statutory definition of refugee changed in 1980, until August 1988, all Soviet and some Indochinese refugee resettlement applications . . . were being found eligible for refugee status under what amounted to a presumption of eligibility . . . " (Inunza, "The Refugee Act of 1980 Ten Years After—Still the Way to Go," *International Journal of Refugee Law*, vol. 2, no. 3, 1990, p. 418.)

7. See, for example, Members of Congress Amicus, p. 10: "The government's conduct in forcing Haitians back to Haiti and funnelling them through section 207 overseas refugee processing violates the purpose of the Act to make these protections comprehensive and to reaffirm the principle of *non-refoulement.*"

8. "[A] similar in-country procedure for processing refugees was created at the height of the Vietnamese boat exodus. However, those who decided to flee by boat were never turned back because such a program existed. And the United States was vigilant in seeing that other governments would not summarily push back the boat people, demanding that they be given temporary asylum in the region. Bill Frelick, "Clinton's Haitian Policy: Same Old Story," *St. Louis Post-Dispatch*, January 19, 1993.

9. Interview with Ken Foster, Refugee Program, State Department, Washington, D.C., June 9, 1993.

10. There is no ceiling for asylum seekers in the U.S. The ceiling for overseas refugee admissions from Haiti for fiscal year 1993 was 500. Although that number has been surpassed and 1,000 unallocated slots were assigned to Haiti, the fact remains that a ceiling is in place affecting the number of Haitians who will eventually be admitted.

11. A review of asylum claims in the U.S. by Harvard University's National Asylum Study Project shows a heavy reliance by INS officers on State Department resources, according to the study coordinator.

12. Interview with Ken Foster.

13. The officer, T.J. Mills, was later suspended from the program.

14. Department of State, *Country Reports* (for 1992), p. 421.

15. According to the Harvard National Asylum Study Project, this kind of opinion is typical of Haitian cases.

16. As of May 1993, the UN/OAS Mission had 141 international staff members of which eighty-six were deployed in regional teams around the country and twenty were in training.

17. As translated by the Washington Office on Latin America.

18. For example, the UN High Commission on Refugees states that in cases of mass influx, temporary refuge should always be provided. See "Conclusions of the International Protection of Refugees" adopted by the Executive Committee of the UNHCR Programme, Office of the UNHCR (Geneva: 1980), p. 49.

19. Interview with Ken Foster.

20. Interviw with Louis Moreno, Port-au-Prince, June 14, 1993.

21. Real names were not used in the following testimonies except where stipulated. All interviews were carried out in Port-au-Prince during the week of June 13-20, 1993.

22. Interview with a Haitian source close to the ICP program on the condition of confidentiality, Port-au-Prince, June 17, 1993.

GUANTÁNAMO BAY:
WHEN WILL THE SUFFERING END?

Michael Ratner/Center for
Constitutional Rights

A continuing source of controversy and disgrace in U.S. policy toward Haitian refugees is the camp at the U.S. Naval Base in Guantánamo Bay, Cuba, where hundreds of Haitian asylum seekers who tested HIV-positive have been held by the U.S. military and I.N.S. In the fall of 1992, Michael Ratner of the Center for Constitutional Rights reported on his visit to the "first HIV detention camp in history."

˥

The barbed wire wasn't the worst thing. Nor was the stench at the military camp, nor the fear in the faces of the ragged group of prisoners. The worst thing wasn't even the children, scared and coughing. The worst thing was the singing.

When we heard the refugees sing, we were on a U.S. military base at Guantánamo Bay, Cuba for three days as part of a legal team interviewing nearly three hundred Haitians. The refugees were "screened-in," which means they had been determined by the United States Immigration and Naturalization Service (I.N.S.) to be legitimate candidates for political asylum. These men, women, and children are not criminals, but the U.S. Government continues to hold them incommunicado, indefinitely, in a squalid cluster of wooden barracks. Because they allegedly tested positive for the HIV virus, they have become inmates in the first HIV detention camp in history.

For three weeks we'd been hearing their stories of fear and flight, of families torn apart, hellish camp conditions and failing health. Then it came time for us to leave. Knowing it would be difficult, we all gathered in an old airplane hangar for our goodbyes. The government would let us stay no longer and we didn't know if we would ever return. The refugees did not know, as they still do not know today, whether their prison camp will be their permanent residence.

The group expressed their gratitude for our efforts, but felt abandoned. The entire group of prisoners, their children in their arms, began singing songs of thanks and songs of liberty. Their voices broke and singing turned to sobs and shrieks that lasted for twenty minutes as we all cried, and then turned to leave.

Tears are an understandable response for anyone who learns that she or he may have HIV. But these Haitian refugees are also furious, bewildered, terrified, and some even suicidal because of their imprisonment and treatment by U.S. military and I.N.S. officials at the U.S. Naval Base at Guantánamo Bay, Cuba.

These refugees fled Haiti in the violent aftermath of the September 1991 military-led coup against President Jean-Bertrand Aristide. The U.S. does not have a policy to HIV-test many other refugees, Cubans for example. Yet, in February of 1992, the I.N.S. decided to test all Haitians, denying entry into the U.S. to those who tested HIV-positive.

Interdicted at sea, the Haitians were brought to Guantánamo, where after initial I.N.S. screening had determined those eligible for political asylum, they were tested for HIV. Last spring, a group of refugee families who had passed I.N.S. interviews were gathered in an old airplane hangar, to await final processing that would allow them to leave the camp. Military officials, over a loudspeaker, announced that all the assembled people had the virus which causes AIDS and that they would not be going to America. In fact, they would not be going anywhere.

And so, the families have lived in limbo, some of them for as long as a year. A legal team, including members from the Lowenstein International Human Rights Clinic at Yale University, the Center for Consitutional Rights, the American Civil Liberties Union (ACLU), Simpson Thatcher & Bartlett, and the San Francisco Lawyers' Committee for Human Rights, have been representing the prisoners, with support from a broad coalition of Haitian community groups, AIDS activists and human rights groups.

In March 1992, the collective groups filed a suit (Haitian Centers Council v. McNary) challenging the policy of detaining refugees, incommunicado at Guantánamo. The suit, filed in Federal District Court in New York, was heard by Judge Sterling Johnson, Jr., who issued a temporary restraining order on March 17, and then a preliminary injunction on April 6, preventing the repatriation of screened-in Haitians to Haiti before they were able to speak to lawyers.

Judge Johnson, who called the government's conduct in the matter "unconscionable," wrote, ". . . the screened-in plaintiffs are isolated from the world and treated in a manner worse than the treatment that would be afforded to a criminal defendant. Their access to the outside world, whether by telephone, mail, or otherwise has been completely restricted. They are confined in a camp surrounded by razor wire and are not free to leave, even if they have the financial capability to do so, to any country but Haiti, from which they flee for fear of political persecution, torture, and even death."

The government failed in four attempts to stay Judge Johnson's order. But on April 22, the Supreme Court stayed the preliminary injunction pending an appeal. As a result, eighty-nine of the HIV-positive refugees were forcibly returned to Haiti, where they were pushed off a Coast Guard cutter with firehoses.

On June 10, the Second Circuit affirmed the injunction granting Haitians at Guantánamo the right to counsel. Rather than allow lawyers to travel to counsel the clients, however, the government stopped processing the refugees, essentially leaving them to languish on Guantánamo. Yes, the government conceded, the Haitians had the right to seek counsel if they were facing deportation, but no, the U.S. would not initiate deportation hearings against the HIV-positive detainees. The razor wire remains in place.

Meanwhile, the camp conditions, deplorable under any circumstances, but especially dangerous for anyone fighting off illness, continue to deteriorate. Members of the legal team have made two trips to Guantánamo, and have returned appalled by the suffering these families are enduring. Refugees sleep on canvas cots in crowded wooden buildings with rain pouring in; snakes, scorpions, insects and rats abound.

In March of 1992, Dr. Paul Effler of the Centers for Disease Control (CDC), warned of the "threat of an infections outbreak" if toilet and sanitary facilities at Guantánamo were not improved. The camp still lacks flushable toilets, and pools of stagnant water surround the sinks and showers. The refugees continue to be the victims of random brutality by the military police and peaceful demonstrations have been violently repressed.

The present medical staff does not include even one Creole-speaking doctor or counselor. Many of the refugees harbor doubts about their HIV status. Because of the careless, mass nature of the testing, the refugees are suspicious of the medicines they're given, and unable to ask for what they do need. Dr. Effler, who wrote that "concentrating people known to have an infection that causes immunosupression in a tent city is a potential public health disaster," has urged policymakers to change the rules, noting that the CDC does not support a policy of quarantine for people who are HIV positive.

The only way to get out of the camp is to get sick or pregnant. We have persuaded the government that it does not have the facilities on Guantánamo to deliver babies of HIV pregnant women. They are brought to the U.S. mainland a month prior to delivery. A few others who got eye infections that could cause blindness were brought in for treatment. But even in the U.S. these so-called "lucky" Haitians are kept in custody. Sometimes it's jail and sometimes less rigorous custodial conditions, but always under supervision. They are confined for only one reason; they are HIV positive.

The refugees have been treated like prisoners of war, for the "crime" of being HIV infected. Untreated, poorly fed, and denied the minimal dignity due any refugee, some of the Haitians have attempted suicide. Others live in terror that they, or their family members, will be repatriated forcibly. The I.N.S. itself recognized that all 274 screened-in refugees at Guantánamo have credible claims of political persecution in Haiti, the basis of the legal standard used to grant asylum. These people can be "paroled in" tomorrow to the United States, before more of them, desperate and abused, commit suicide or die from neglect.

Beyond the immediate step he must take to save the refugees now on Guantánamo, President-elect Bill Clinton can act to make simple humanity and medical common sense the norm for all U.S. immigration policy. The HIV exclusion itself has been denounced as scientifically groundless by the American Medical Association, the National Commission on AIDS, and virtually every other public health authority in this country.

In January 1991, the Department of Health and Human Services Secretary Louis Sullivan proposed removing HIV infection from the list of excludable diseases. Prior to his election, President Clinton promised that, if elected President, he would do so. The time is long overdue for this cruel and senseless policy to end.

The detention camp for HIV-positive people at Guantánamo is a symbol of shame for our nation. It should never have happened, and the refugees should not be there now. "We want our freedom," the refugees sang, "*Libert.*"

PART 4
CHRONOLOGY

Kay kule twompe solèy, men li pa twompe lapli.
(The leaky house can fool the sun,
but it can't fool the rain.)

—Haitian proverb

CHRONOLOGY

EVENTS IN HAITI, OCTOBER 15, 1990– MAY 11, 1994
Haitian Information Bureau

Since 1991, the Haitian Information Bureau, an independent, alternative news service based in Port-au-Prince, has documented and analyzed the course of events in Haiti. Its bi-weekly publication, *Haiti Info*, has often been the first—and sometimes the only— source of published information in English about what is going on inside post-coup Haiti. The bureau compiled the following chronology, which covers over three and a half years.

¬

October 15, 1990   In a surprise move three days before the candidate registers close, Father Jean-Bertrand Aristide announces he will run for president. Hundreds of thousands rush to register to vote. After Aristide announces his candidacy, U.S. Ambassador Alvin P. Adams says, ominously, "*Apre bal, tanbou lou*" ("After the dance, the drums are heavy"). Many interpret this as a warning. Aristide continues his campaign, responding, "*Men ampil, chay pa lou*" ("With many hands, the burden is not heavy"). (Since his arrival as ambassador, when he declared, in reference to the electoral process, "*Bourik chaje, pa kanpe*" ["A loaded donkey cannot stop"], Adams has been popularly referred to as "*Bourik Chaje*," or "Loaded Donkey.")

One of the most brutal incidents during the campaign was the bombing attack on a meeting of young pro-Aristide people in Pétionville on December 5, leaving five dead and fourteen maimed.

On the eve of elections, former U.S. Ambassador to the UN Andrew Young, reportedly with the backing of former President Jimmy Carter, visits Aristide and asks him to sign a letter accepting Marc L. Bazin, the U.S.-backed and funded candidate, as president should Bazin win. Young reportedly says there is fear that if Aristide does not win, people will take to the streets and reject the results. The letter and the incident are widely seen as yet another attempt by the U.S. government to influence internal politics in Haiti.

December 16, 1990   Elections are held. Aristide is swept into office with over 67 percent of the vote after a campaign wrought with terror and intimidation. Millions dance in the streets across the country.

January 6 and 7, 1991   Roger Lafontant, the former head of the VSN (Volontaires de la Securite Nationale), or Tonton Macoute corps, attempts a coup d'état against presidential incumbent Aristide. Angry crowds take to the streets, amassing in front of the palace and the headquarters of Lafontant's Duvalierist party, which was involved in the attempted coup. When people inside the party headquarters shoot at the crowds, the crowds retaliate, attacking the building and killing several party members. Crowds also attack and kill ex-Tonton Macoutes. A total of about 65 die.

February 7, 1991   Jean-Bertrand Aristide, the first democratically elected president in the history of the Republic of Haiti, is inaugurated. In his inaugural speech, Aristide proposes "a marriage between the army and the people"—a reshaping of the Haitian military to bring it under civilian control. Soon after, he obtains the resignations of six of the military's top seven commanders, and promotes then-Colonel Raoul Cédras to the position of chief of staff. Before long, Aristide will also embark on efforts to dismantle the system of "section chiefs" that wields power throughout the Haitian countryside, and to raise the minimum wage.

June 14, 1991   Joaquín Balaguer, president of the Dominican Republic, announces he will expel all Haitians over the age of 60 and under the age of 16. The Dominican military rounds up thousands of Haitians, some of whom are Dominican citizens, robs them, and force them across the border. About 20,000 are expelled in the next three months.

August 13, 1991   Thousands of people gather in front of the parliament with signs bearing slogans like "Down with Macoutes in parliament" to protest the Senate and Chamber of Deputies, which are threatening to demand that Aristide's prime minister, René Préval, step down. In press releases and on radio and television programs, many individuals and organizations of the democratic movement denounce the parliament's two houses for voting on only three of over 100 laws they have been asked to consider since Aristide's inauguration. Several parliamentarians, including Deputy Robert Mondé, are denounced as former members of the Tonton Macoute.

August 20, 1991   In the aftermath of unrest and instability in the parliament, the head of the executive committee of the Chamber of Deputies, a member of FNCD (the coalition party of Aristide, with a majority in parliament), steps aside to Duly Brutus of PANPRA, a member of the ANDP coalition (the party favored by the U.S. in the 1990 elections). Within a week, the Senate's executive committee has also resigned amidst reports of corruption, and Déjean Belizaire, also of ANDP, has become president of the committee, the most powerful seat in the Haitian parliament. Belizaire's election is made possible in part by the defection of FNCD Senator Thomas Eddy Dupiton, who had for some time been quietly agitating against President Aristide. All three men will become key "negotiators" after the coup.

September 27, 1991   President Aristide returns from a trip to New York City, where he addresses the United Nations General Assembly, criticizing the Dominican Republic for the expulsion of over 20,000 Haitians. Amidst rumors of an impending coup d'état, he makes a speech in front of the palace, urging the bourgeoisie to "come down from the hills" to join the people and take part in the country's development by respecting the laws, ending corruption, etc. This is perceived by many members of the upper class as a targeted threat.

September 29 and 30, 1991   Signs of an imminent military takeover grow as the night progresses. Crowds form around President Aristide's home.

The same night, Lafontant, recently convicted for the aborted 1990 coup attempt, is killed in his jail cell. Sylvio Claude, the president of the PDCH (Parti Démocrate Chrétien Haitien), is killed by unknown assailants after attending a meeting in Cayes with local people and army representatives. (Both murders will later be blamed on the president. But both victims were troublesome for the military, as they both felt entitled to the presidency. Lafontant had also recently threatened to reveal his military allies in the January coup attempt).

In the morning, Aristide makes his way to the palace. Most members of the presidential guard have vanished. The military, under the leadership of Lt. General Raoul Cédras, takes control. With the intervention of the French ambassador, Cédras agrees to allow Aristide to leave the country. He boards a plane for Venezuela.

At least 1,000 people are killed during the next few weeks, according to a report released on October 21 by the Platform of Haitian Human Rights Organizations. People report seeing mass graves, hundreds of bodies at the Port-au-Prince state hospital, and dogs devouring bodies on the highway outside the capital. At least 1,000 people are also injured in the attacks and hundreds of others—including singer Manno Charlemagne, pro-Aristide businessman Antoine Izmery, and numerous journalists—are beaten and arrested. Soldiers who refuse to cooperate with the coup are locked in the national penitentiary.

Soldiers also search and pillage the homes of various Aristide cabinet officials, offices of popular organizations like the Papaye Peasant Movement, and government offices. Soldiers attack and shut down a number of radio stations in the capital and in other cities. A popular radio announcer and director of Radio Caraïbes is arrested and murdered, and his mutilated body, missing a tongue and an ear, is found two days later. The army takes over the national radio and television, and from this date forward the national media are used to broadcast pro-coup propaganda, disinformation, lists of people to be attacked, and other "information" deemed necessary to help institutionalize the coup.

Over the following months, numerous human rights violations will be documented daily by local, national, and international organizations throughout the country. (Only some landmark attacks will be listed here.)

October 3, 1991   Port-au-Prince residents begin to flee the capital for the countryside, having endured what one human rights report calls "five days and five nights of continuous massacre" in poor neighborhoods like Cité Soleil, where the popular movement and Aristide have had wide support. Eventually about 200,000 will leave the capital. Over time, 25,000 will head across the border into the Dominican Republic.

October 5, 1991   Following an emergency session of the Organization of American States in Washington, D.C., an OAS delegation comes to Haiti for two days of meetings. Soldiers rough up some members of the delegation and those receiving them, including Port-au-Prince Mayor Evans Paul.

October 7, 1991   After the OAS mission visits Haiti, the OAS officially condemns the coup and votes for an embargo on Haiti to punish the military regime. In the following days, various international organizations working in Haiti close down their offices. Almost immediately, human rights monitors and others report a brisk and steady flow of merchandise across the Dominican border.

October 9, 1991   Outspoken enemy of Aristide and Duvalierist Jean-Jacques Honorat, director of CHADEL (Centre Haitian de Défence des Libertés Publiques), a human rights organization which in the past received numerous grants from the Ford Foundation, the National Endowment for Democracy, and others, is sworn in as prime minister of the illegal regime. The aging Judge Joseph Nerette is installed as "provisional president." Various Duvalierists and other right-wing people are installed in cabinet positions. The installations occur as the parliament is surrounded by gun-toting soldiers.

October 11, 1991   The UN General Assembly condemns the coup and announces that it does not recognize the illegal regime, further isolating the coup leaders diplomatically.

November 5, 1991   U.S. President George Bush signs a commercial embargo against Haiti on all products and commercial traffic except for humanitarian aid.

November 9, 1991   About 200 people, driving BMWs and other expensive cars, hold an "anti-embargo, anti-return" demonstration at the airport with military "protection." The group chants obscenities directed at the OAS, President Aristide, and the French ambassador to Haiti.

The same day, about 2,000 people demonstrate in the Bel Air neighborhood, where Aristide has wide support. The crowd is broken up by soldiers who shoot at them, killing one person. The demonstration is only one example of the resistance carried out by people and organizations, who continue to circulate petitions and clandestine newspapers and call for the return of the president during masses, at considerable risk to their lives.

A second OAS mission, headed by Colombian diplomat Augusto Ramirez Ocampo, visits Haiti, holding meetings with many representatives of the political parties and "particles" (insignificant parties with very few, if any, members), and also with members of the army and the business sector. In a November 8 letter, Prime Minister René Préval asks the mission to meet with broader and more representative members of "civil society."

November 10, 1991   Dominican soldiers dressed in civilian clothing visit Radio Enriquillo, a radio station in the Dominican Republic which has been broadcasting news in Creole across the border into Haiti. It has been practically the only independent source of information since the coup, when many radio stations were attacked and ransacked.

November 11, 1991   Over 15 non-governmental organizations write an open letter to U.S. Ambassador Alvin P. Adams calling him a "pro-consul" and protesting the ambiguity between his statements and the U.S.'s position. Adams has called for the president to be returned in six months, and for the resignation of Aristide's prime minister and choice of a new one—points which contrast with the supposed official U.S. government position calling for the immediate return of President Aristide.

November 12, 1991   Eight journalists are arrested while covering a press conference given by the student organization FENEH (Fédération Nationale des Etudiants Haitiens). Their tape recorders and other equipment are destroyed. About 250 students are also arrested.

November 13, 1991   A Haitian security guard at the U.S. Embassy is killed by soldiers. The embassy does not protest or call for any investigations. Some feel the assassination is connected to a document, apparently leaked from the embassy a few weeks earlier, which outlines potential strategies to assure Aristide never returns.

November 15, 1991   The U.S. Coast Guard repatriates 538 fleeing refugees, the first boatload since the coup. The refugees are fingerprinted by the army and given about U.S.$5. Over the next two years, the U.S. will repatriate more than 30,000 refugees.

November 22, 1991   A parliamentary delegation made up almost exclusively of coup supporters leaves Haiti for Cartagena, Colombia, for negotiations with President Aristide. Despite his declarations that no foreign representatives will accompany the group, U.S. Ambassador Adams slips onto the airplane at the last minute. When Aristide refuses to sign the agreement offered by the parliamentarians—which proposes lifting the embargo, but poses no date for the return of the president—he is accused of "intransigence."

November 28, 1991   In a strategic delivery to a regime quickly losing support, a Liberian tanker delivers 2.5 million gallons of diesel and 1.5 million of gasoline at the Shell port near the capital. Gas has also been received in drums hidden inside containers and from small tankers at regional ports.
 The same day, over 60 organizations and socio-professional organizations write an open letter to President Bush, protesting the U.S. Ambassador's activities.

December 5, 1991   Fifty deputies and senators write to President Aristide urging him not to succumb to what they say are national and international pressures to chose "a prime minister from the right or the extreme right."
 Soon after, the OAS announces its proposed strategy for the return to constitutionality to Haiti: the *de facto* regime steps down, the president names a new prime minister, the prime minister installs a government, and an OAS mission of 500 to 600 people ("OEA-DEMOC") arrives to prepare the terrain before the president returns.

December 10, 1991   Felix Lamy, director of Radio Galaxie, is kidnapped a few hours after having announced on the air that Police Chief Colonel Michel François had refused to follow army orders that he be transferred to another post or even to a foreign embassy. Lamy is never found, and his family has said they assume he is dead. One of François' assistants, Captain Jackson Joanis, calls and threatens Radio Tropic FM after it broadcasts the same information.

December 14, 1991   Ocampo returns to Haiti with another OAS mission.

December 15, 1991   The Haiti Commission of Inquiry into the September 30 Coup d'état arrives to investigate the coup and the repression that has followed it. The delegation is headed by ex-U.S. Attorney General Ramsey

Clark and contains union activists, lawyers, and others. At a press conference before they leave on December 18, the group declares "Haiti is a prison and the Haitian people are terrorized."

December 16, 1991   On the first anniversary of Aristide's election, soldiers, attachés, former members of the Tonton Macoutes, and others terrorize the population throughout the country. Macoutes broadcast on the radio a list of about 60 people and 200 organizations to be targeted, citing businessman Antoine Izmery as the "chief trouble-maker." One parliamentarian is shot and killed. Another's home is destroyed by fire, along with about 60 neighorhood houses. A third's neighborhood is terrorized by soldiers who shoot and kill at least two people and beat or arrest many others. Nevertheless, resistance is strong. Walls are covered with pro-Aristide graffitti, people hold demonstrations shouting slogans like "Long live Aristide" and "Up with the embargo," and 80 Port-au-Prince priests write a letter demanding the return of the president and an end to the U.S. repatriation of refugees.

The same night, two U.S. Air Force airplanes arrive and leave Port-au-Prince for an unknown reason. (This is only one example of the numerous nocturnal flights reported in the clandestine newspapers circulating inside Haiti and in the international solidarity community. When asked, a U.S. Embassy official says the flights are "routine.")

December 17, 1991   A Florida federal district court judge issues a temporary restraining order halting the forced repatriation of refugees. For a time, Haitians picked up at sea will be taken to the U.S. base at Guantánamo Bay, Cuba, for asylum "screenings."

December 21, 1991   Ocampo meets with the Haitian parliament. Despite the fact that President Aristide's first choice, Victor Benoit, the leader of the CONACOM political party, appears to have the support of the majority of the parliament, the session breaks down when his name comes up for discussion. Pro-coup parliamentarians (one of whom has a hand grenade) threaten to kill anyone who votes to ratify Benoit as prime minister. As a result of this disturbance and others, members of the parliament implore Ocampo to assure their security so that they can vote in safety.

The meeting is suspended and rescheduled for December 23, but Senate President Déjean Belizaire announces that Monday's agenda will consider the purchase of new cars before taking up the subject of prime minister again. Later in the week he says "the true partisans of 'the return' should encourage the choice of [Marc L.] Bazin."

December 22, 1991   Ocampo leaves Haiti, unilaterally announcing it will be impossible to ratify Benoit and suggesting René Théodore, the president of the PUCH (Parti Unifié des Communistes Haitiens), as the next best candidate. Théodore is rumored to be one of the choices of the U.S. Embassy, and Ocampo's announcement is hailed as a positive step by the U.S. State Department.

Théodore's candidacy is rejected by a number of Aristide supporters, including Bishop Willy Romelus, who says the Haitian people will never accept him. (In the 1990 presidential elections, Théodore obtained 1.83 percent of the national vote. Although his party is called "communist," he has repeatedly said he opposes any "socialist solution" for Haiti and has advocated a neoliberal economic agenda. His party is not considered to be "radical," nor even "left of center." Théodore supported the brutal regime of General Prosper Avril and was also one of the most vocal opponents of Aristide in the presidential elections.)

December 23, 1991   In a radio address, President Aristide reiterates that Benoit is his first choice. He says that if Benoit is not ratified, he will "accept to consider the case of René Théodore."

December 26, 1991   In a radio interview, Benoit says he believes he has a majority of the votes necessary for his ratification in both houses. But he says, "There are certain local and international sectors, very powerful, who oppose my candidacy."

January 1, 1992   A tanker delivers 22,000 tons of diesel to Shell.

January 6, 1992   Without a vote, the pro-coup presidents of both houses of parliament announce they are extending the term of the "provisional government" beyond its original termination, January 8. Two delegations—one pro-coup and the other favoring democracy—leave Haiti to travel to Venezuela to meet with the president.

January 8, 1992   President Aristide, the OAS, and the presidents of both houses approve the plan accepting Théodore as prime minister.

January 9, 1992   Fresh from Venezuela, pro-coup Senator Thomas Eddy Dupiton says it does not make sense to bring back the president because "there is already a government in place." The same day, U.S. Ambassador Adams visits parliament, for the second time in a week, to, in his own words, "greet . . . the presidents of the two chambers." He announces the U.S. is "ready to collaborate with René Théodore if he is ratified."

January 10, 1992   Another tanker arrives with diesel and other petroleum products.

January 13, 1992   Parliament opens. Belizaire denounces the OAS embargo and calls for the parliament to vote to impose Article 149 of the constitution, which would declare the government "empty" and enable new elections to take place. *De facto* Prime Minister Honorat declares that in the past 100 days his government "has not persecuted anyone, nor arrested anyone, for their political opinions." That same day, the Organisation Mondiale Contre la Torture (OMCT), an international human rights organization, kicks out CHADEL because of its "evolution," which betrays the ideals of human rights. (The American Bar Association, on the other hand, would not consider revoking a human rights award given to Honorat a few months before the coup.)

Théodore writes to Aristide to say he will accept the position of prime minister if the embargo is lifted as soon as he is ratified and if all international aid is resumed. Belizaire and Brutus say they will ratify Théodore if all of the *de facto* acts of the past three months are accepted by Aristide, and if Théodore is allowed to formulate the conditions of the president's return. The next day, Théodore calls for a "government of national consensus."

January 15, 1992   FNCD Deputy Alex Medard is elected president of the Chamber of Deputies. Baena Suarez, general secretary of the OAS, invites Senators Belizaire and Dupiton, along with Théodore, to Washington to discuss the prime minister question. All three will later refuse. The same day, the *de facto* government announces that the Vatican has a new nuncio for Haiti.

January 18, 1992   Over 90 human rights, popular, development, and other organizations write the international community an open letter entitled: "Haiti: A Case of Conscience? A Case of Unconsciousness? Or a Case of Lack of Conscience?"

January 24, 1992   The Senate creates a "Commission for Conciliation" to continue negotiations under the guidance of the OAS

January 25, 1992   Théodore's bodyguard is shot dead during a meeting of political leaders at the PUCH office by a police commando, dressed in civilian clothing, from the notorious police "anti-gang" headquarters. The parties had notified anti-gang of the meeting and had asked for protection. Bazin and his party are inexplicably absent from the meeting.

January 29, 1992   The U.S. recalls Ambassador Adams. Threats continue against Radio Enriquillo. Two men are caught photographing inside the studio at night. In a publication the same day, human rights organizations announce that the repression is changing form, to a less "visible" type of harrassment. In the capital, soldiers and attachés are a constant presence in popular neighborhoods. In the countryside, repression is now carried out by the section chiefs, who were declared unconstitutional in the 1987 constitution and were finally "retired" during Aristide's term. (One of Honorat's first acts as *de facto* prime minister was to "reinstate" them.) The repression is physical and also financial, with the section chiefs and their assistants demanding inordinate amounts of money for the release of those they "arrest."

February 3, 1992   The U.S. Supreme Court annuls the lower court's decision blocking the forced repatriation of refugees.

The same day, flaming barricades are spotted in at least 25 neighborhoods of the capital to demand the return of the president.

February 4, 1992   The U.S. announces it is "fine-tuning" the embargo to permit the assembly industries operating in Haiti (the majority of which are U.S.-owned or ship to the U.S.) to import and export so that they can resume work.

February 14, 1992   Radio Enriquillo is told it will no longer be allowed to broadcast news in Creole across the Dominican-Haitian border. The station begins to "sing" the news instead.

February 18, 1992   The first of many delegations of U.S. parliamentarians comes to Haiti.

February 19, 1992   The OAS announces it will send civilian observers to Haiti.

February 21, 1992   Three delegations go to Washington to continue the negotiations. Two days later they sign the "Protocole d'Accord à Washington" with President Aristide. The accord calls for amnesty for the army and other authors of the coup and preserves parliamentary legislation ratified after the coup. It does not include a fixed date for the president's return and it has to be approved by the Haitian parliament.

February 24, 1992   On ABC's "Nightline," President Aristide clarifies that the "amnesty" outlined in the new accord is for "political" and not "common law" criminals. He included Cédras in the latter category.

February 25, 1992   U.S. Ambassador Adams returns to Haiti. According to the State Department, Adams will work with all parties to help form a government of consensus. Concerning the army, Adams declares, "I am totally confident that everyone with good will who has in their hearts the best interests of the country will think about the future of their country and look for, together, hand in hand, '*tet ansanm*,' a sustainable solution."

February 26, 1992   In a radio interview in Haiti, Théodore repeats that it is not possible to fix a return date for the president because "society is torn . . . there are arrangements to be made, guarantees to be given to the sectors implicated in the crisis."

February 27, 1992   President Aristide addresses the UN Human Rights Commission in Geneva, denouncing the repression which has claimed over 1,500 victims in Haiti.

February 28, 1992   The Haitian Chamber of Commerce issues a statement supporting the Washington accord. In an interview with a Canadian newspaper, Aristide reiterates that Cédras cannot benefit from a full amnesty "because he has committed a crime against humanity."

February 29, 1992   The U.S. orders that those Haitians picked up at sea and delivered to the Guantánamo base who test positive for the HIV virus be interrogated at the base rather than in Florida. To date, over 16,000 refugees have been picked up at sea, about 6,000 are being considered for political asylum, and close to 300 are said to be HIV-positive and are being detained at Guantánamo.

March 7, 1992   In a speech to the nation, *de facto* President Nerette warns parliamentarians not to approve the Washington Accord or the presence of the OAS civilian mission, invoking "national sovereignty" and weeping as he finishes.

March 10, 1992   The Association of Haitian Industries (ADIH) announces it favors the Washington Accord and calls for the parliamentarians to vote for it. After a long debate, the Senate approves the Accord with 11 votes for, 10 against, and two abstentions. The accord is now scheduled to be voted on at a National Assembly—where both the Senate and Chamber of Deputies meet together—scheduled for March 18.

March 15, 1992   Three more tankers arrive in Port-au-Prince. One contains what the press calls "toxic gas" because of its nauseating odor. Greenpeace later will announce that it contains extremely high levels of lead, cadmium, and other chemicals.

March 17, 1992   Three lawyers, led by pro-coup lawyer Mireille Durocher Bertin, sign a document declaring the Washington Accord unconstitutional.

March 18, 1992   The National Assembly scheduled for consideration of the Washington Accord is disrupted by a few armed parliamentarians. At a certain signal, many pro-coup parliamentarians leave. The result: no quorum.

March 27, 1992   The Haitian Supreme Court, led by 81-year-old Judge Emile Jonassaint (who was brought out of retirement and installed after the coup), decrees that the Washington Accord is "unconstitutional and inoperative." Numerous political parties denounce the decree and say the court has no business ruling on the accord.

April 9, 1992   Cédras, in a televised declaration, rejects the Washington Accord.

April 10, 1992   The U.S. government announces it will take away U.S. visas for partisans of the coup.
    The same day, hundreds of university and high school students throughout Port-au-Prince protest the regime by banging on pots and other metal objects.

April 13, 1992   The *de facto* government calls for a "national conference." Both houses later reject the suggestion.

April 15, 1992   During the inauguration of his new cabinet, *de facto* Prime Minister Honorat declares, "We will not negotiate with *blancs!*" (whites, i.e. foreigners). Local newspapers remind Honorat that all of the funding for CHADEL comes from "*blancs.*"

April 20, 1992   The U.S. Embassy in Haiti announces it will examine the cases of refugees seeking political asylum, beginning the "in-country processing" program.

April 27, 1992   The Senate votes against the Washington Accord and in favor of "tri-partite" negotiations between the army, the (*de facto*) executive and the parliament.

April 30, 1992   The new Apostolic Nuncio, Bishop Lorenzo Baldisseri, presents his credentials to the *de facto* government, making the Vatican the first and only government to recognize the illegal regime.

May 8, 1992   The army, the *de facto* executive, and the presidents of the Senate and the Chamber of Deputies sign the "Villa d'Accueil" agreement, which calls for a "government of consensus." The U.S. government announces it still favors the Washington Accord, and the *de facto* government replies by protesting the Embassy's statements and declaring, "Haiti, love it or leave it." This slogan will soon appear on bumper stickers and t-shirts donned by partisans of the coup. The same day, the *de facto* minister of information declares that the press is no longer allowed to use the term "*de facto.*"

May 10, 1992   A number of religious and civilian leaders from the demo-cratic movement sign a document rejecting the Villa d'Accueil agreement. In the days that follow, numerous politicians and other leaders will declare the agreement "unconstitutional" and "*civilo-militaire*."

May 18, 1992   An airplane drops leaflets bearing the Haitian flag and Aristide's picture over cities and towns across Haiti in celebration of Flag Day. Many are arrested and/or beaten as they attempt to gather up and distribute the leaflets. The same day, 29 student, labor, and popular organizations sign a declaration protesting the illegal regime and calling a strike for May 21.

May 20, 1992   The Chamber of Deputies approves the Villa d'Accueil agree-ment.

May 21, 1992   Many Haitians join in the general strike.

May 26, 1992   George Izmery, brother of the well-known Aristide supporter Antoine Izmery, is gunned down in the street in front of his downtown store. Police take him to the morgue before he is actually dead, and he dies at the morgue. He is only the most well-known of the increasing numbers of recent victims who are members of student organizations, peasant groups, and other groups struggling for democracy.

May 24, 1992   President George Bush signs the "Kennebunkport Order," under which all Haitian refugee boats will be interdicted and their passengers returned to Port-au-Prince with no prior screening for asylum-seekers.

May 27, 1992   Candidate for president Bill Clinton promises that if elected, he will change the Bush Administration's policy on Haitian refugees and "give them temporary asylum until we restored the elected government of Haiti."

May 29, 1992   President Aristide meets with UN General Secretary Boutros Boutros-Ghali and asks the UN to support the OAS efforts to restore democ-racy to Haiti.

June 4, 1992   Marc L. Bazin (president of the MIDH party and the ANDP coalition, the U.S.-supported candidate for president in 1990, where he came in second to Aristide with about 13 percent of the vote) is ratified as "Villa d'Accueil" prime minister by the Senate. The same day, two deputies report their houses were surrounded by soldiers and then searched. A third deputy resigns. Numerous organizations issue statements deploring the selection of Bazin. The Chamber of Deputies ratifies Bazin on June 10.

June 14, 1992 La Fanmi Selavi, the home for street children founded in 1986 by Aristide, is attacked by arsonists. Over the next 22 months it will be continually targeted by soldiers and armed attachés who will beat and threaten the boys living there.

June 19, 1992 Bazin is invested in ceremonies at the palace.

On the same day, 250 students and four teachers holding a demonstration at the State Teachers' College to protest Bazin are held hostage for a day and a night by police and armed civilians, who surround the building and break all of its windows. On July 1 and 2, students at other colleges also protest the Bazin regime.

July 14, 1992 Aristide names a ten-member "Presidential Commission" to represent his government inside Haiti.

The same day, the director of the Dominican telecommunications board arrives at Radio Enriquillo with two truckloads of armed soldiers to force the radio to stop all broadcasts—spoken or sung—in Creole.

July 17, 1992 At least thirty would-be refugees drown or are shot when soldiers attack them as they attempt to get from shore to a waiting sailboat about 15 miles north of the capital.

July 21, 1992 A group of U.S. business people, led by the Caribbean/Latin American Action lobbying organization, meet with the U.S. ambassador and the Presidential Commission.

August 17, 1992 Three men, members of a new, pro-Aristide political party, are shot dead as they put up Aristide posters the night before the arrival of an OAS delegation.

August 25, 1992 A U.S. court declares that international and national law do not allow for the interception of Haitian refugees on the high seas.

September 14, 1992 Bazin signs an agreement with "Rice Corporation of Haiti," an American/Haitian venture aimed at supplying Haiti with U.S.-grown rice. The deal is loudly criticized by leaders and organizations of the democratic movement.

September 16, 1992 Eighteen members of the OAS civilian mission arrive in Haiti. One is immediately expelled by the *de facto* regime, almost certainly because of his previous work with the Washington Office on Haiti. The team will be largely confined to the Montana Hotel for the next few months.

September 18, 1992   A huge, unexplained midday explosion at the Vallieres pharmacy in downtown Port-au-Prince kills over a dozen and injures at least 150 people. The pharmacy is owned by Dr. Reginald Boulos, a major recipient of "humanitarian" supplies.

September 24, 1992   Bishop Willy Romelus, an outspoken supporter of democracy and of President Aristide, is nearly kidnapped by soldiers and armed civilians near Jeremie.

October 17, 1992   An airplane drops resistance leaflets over a number of cities, towns, and villages.

October 23, 1992   The *de facto* regime illegally forms an election board to prepare for Senate elections.

November 12, 1992   High school and university students protest the regime, the presence of soldiers in the classrooms, and the general conditions at the schools and colleges. Students and others at one of the colleges are held hostage by soldiers and armed civilians, who surround the building for several hours. Two journalists and four students are arrested.

November 22, 1992   Two well-known members of the CONACOM party are kidnapped. The body of one is found later. A third member, an engineer, will be kidnapped from outside his son's school on December 2 and his body will be discovered in his car near Port-au-Prince.

The murders are indicative of the rapid increase in terror and repression throughout the country. For instance, a peasant group in St. Michel de l'Attalaye in the Artibonite Valley reported that over 200 farmers were arrested, beaten, and forced to pay U.S.$40 each in early November.

November 24, 1992   The UN Security Council passes a resolution reaffirming its support of Aristide.

November 25 and 27, 1992   The *de facto* government fails to convoke a National Assembly because of a lack of quorum. The same day, the Creole weekly *Libète* begins publication after a 13-month hiatus. Throughout November, popular organizations and others have also been quietly distributing audio and video recordings of an address from President Aristide called "Koze Lakay," the equivalent of Franklin Roosevelt's "Fireside Chats."

December 1, 1992   Soldiers attack students at the agronomy college, beating and injuring over 60 and taking away at least a dozen. The attack comes after students protest the regime's arbitrary dissolution of the student-elected management councils of the state university's colleges.

December 6, 1992   High school student Jean Sony Philogène is murdered by soldiers. Philogène had been taken with five other youths to be assassinated at the Titanyen burial grounds (frequently used for this purpose by the army), but had managed to crawl to the highway, badly injured, when the soldiers left him for dead. Later that night, soldiers hear he is in a city hospital and finish the job, shooting him in the head and heart in front of his grandmother.

December 16, 1992   A group of U.S. citizens—visitors as well as residents, including many from religious orders—holds a sit-in in front of the U.S. Embassy to protest U.S. policies, the weak embargo, and the continued flow of gasoline, and demanding that the U.S. freeze the assets of the coup leaders. It is the second such demonstration, and will be repeated at least a half-dozen times again in the coming year-and-a-half of the crisis.

December 23, 1992   In a Christmas message, *de facto* Prime Minister Bazin calls for Aristide to meet with him to find a "negotiated solution to the crisis." Father Antoine Adrien, head of Aristide's Presidential Commission, later says Bazin's calls for negotiations are "pure farce."

December 29, 1992   Canadian Prime Minister Brian Mulroney calls for a naval blockade against the *de facto* government of Haiti.

January 14, 1993   In a move totally contradictory to his campaign promises, U.S. President Bill Clinton announces he will continue the Bush policy of repatriating Haitian refugees. Amnesty International and 34 other organizations criticize the decision. Despite the U.S. government's action, Aristide acquiesces to Clinton's request and broadcasts a message to the Haitian people asking them not to "*pran kanntè,*" or take to the sea in boats for Miami. The U.S. deploys "Operation Able Manner," encircling the island with Coast Guard boats.

January 18, 1993   Bazin's *de facto* government oversees "elections" (dubbed "selections" by the press and others), which the U.S., the UN, and dozens of local organizations denounce as illegal. Very few people (about one percent of those eligible) vote, and some of the balloting places are attacked with rocks or small fires. The 14 senators and deputies who will later claim to have been elected will become a major block to resolving the crisis.

January 23, 1993   During a visit to Leogane, Jesse Jackson is detained by four armed soldiers who threaten him with hand grenades and guns. On the same day, businessman Antoine Izmery is arrested at the airport. He will be held at the national prison for three days.

February 1, 1993   Argentine diplomat Dante Caputo, the UN special envoy who replaced OAS envoy Ocampo, arrives and is met by anti-UN demonstrators, who also detain and abuse journalists at the airport and later at a hotel. One journalist disappears for a week. On February 7, after a week of non-stop pleas from his parents broadcast on his radio station, he will be dumped, half-naked, at the station, and will tell of being brutally beaten, interrogated, and shown photo books of those working for democracy.

February 16, 1993   The Neptune ferry boat sinks, killing at least 1,743 people and many livestock en route from Jeremie to Port-au-Prince. The boat was extremely overloaded, in part because the *de facto* government never repaired the state highway between the two cities (as Aristide's government had planned), and because of a total lack of state controls and an entrenched extortion structure at the ports.

February 25, 1993   Bishop Willy Romelus and others are brutally beaten by military attachés, as police watch, after a large memorial service for the Neptune victims. The attachés also hold the cathedral in Port-au-Prince hostage for several hours and arrest and beat a journalist. Members of the civilian mission (now a UN as well as an OAS project), help people leave in groups of five and ten in diplomatic vehicles.

March 2, 1993   Soldiers and police invade parliament and expel 13 legal pro-democracy senators in an attempt to consolidate the position of the pro-coup senators and those who claim they were elected in January.

March 4, 1993   Students and professors at the state university call a general strike in response to the *de facto* regime's illegal measures there. The *de facto* Rector Gérard Bissainthe (former *de facto* minister of information) closes down the teachers' college, and will later close other colleges as well.

March 7, 1993   The UN/OAS Civilian Mission begins to deploy members throughout the country. Over the next few months they will establish at least one office in each of the country's nine departments, where about 240 "observers" will monitor abuses and write reports, mostly for authorities in Washington and New York. After a few weeks, local press and grassroots organizations will begin to criticize the mission for its "neutrality," which often translates into meting out the same treatment to both the repressive military apparatus and its civilian victims.

March 16, 1993   Presidents Aristide and Clinton meet at the White House for what appears to be little more than a "photo opportunity."

April 12, 1993   U.S. media reveal that the U.S., UN, OAS, and Aristide have reached agreement on the broad outlines of a plan to resolve the crisis.

April 21, 1993   The Haitian army protests accusations in the *New York Times* that it is involved in drug-running. The topic will become an increasingly important one as the crisis proceeds.

April 26, 1993   A national strike called by a number of labor, mass, and neighborhood groups to protest the regime is between 75 and 100 percent successful in cities across the country. However, in the course of publicizing the strike, three labor leaders from the country's most outspoken union are arrested and severely beaten, one almost to death. The three are later released—one not until a month later—after intense international condemnation.

May 1, 1993   Dozens of people demonstrate in Gonaïves in favor of the return of the president and are attacked by soldiers, who beat and arrest demonstrators.

May 6, 1993   In an interview with a Mexican newspaper, Cédras declares Aristide's return to power would be unconstitutional "because he violated the constitution more than 100 times while in power." Cédras' rhetoric mimics an offensive launched by the pro-coup lawyer Mireille Durocher Bertin the previous month with a series of demonstrations in front of parliament and letters demanding that the president be judged for his alleged violations of the constitution.

May 18, 1993   Soccer fans in Cap-Haitien demonstrate, shouting "Aristide or death!" Police beat dozens and arrest seven. A week earlier, students in Gonaïves demonstrated for several days in a row and were viciously attacked by soldiers, despite the presence of members of the civilian mission.

May 24, 1993   Caputo and U.S. Special Envoy Lawrence Pezzullo leave Haiti after Caputo's sixth mission here, still with no solution in hand.

May 31, 1993   The Haitian gourde passes the "200 percent" mark, meaning its value has fallen from about 14 cents (under Aristide) to 10 cents, a psychological landmark in the currency's continuing devaluation. It will bottom out at about seven cents.

June 1, 1993   The U.S.-based National Labor Committee Education Fund in

Support of Worker and Human Rights in Central America releases a report that shows that over the past ten years, U.S. AID spent more than hundreds of millions of dollars in 1990 and 1991 alone "promoting underdevelopment" in Haiti. Among other things, the report documents how U.S.AID fought a minimum wage increase and other changes advocated by Aristide's government while it was in office. The report also outlines the activities of Haiti's wealthy "monopolist" families; the Mevs family—accused in the report of supporting the coup—will later threaten to sue the National Labor Committee.

June 4, 1993   The U.S. government announces sanctions against 83 people or institutions that supported the coup and the current regime.

June 8, 1993   Bazin resigns.

June 12, 1993   Cédras announces that he will attend negotiations in New York only if the embargo is lifted and he is permitted to address the UN General Assembly.

June 14, 1993   Fourteen popular and labor organizations call for mobilization of the population to demand the departure of the military regime.

June 16, 1993   The UN Security Council votes to impose a worldwide fuel and arms embargo on Haiti if the military continues to refuse to cooperate with negotiations for the return of democracy. The same day, Dupiton threatens that the pro-coup parliamentarians will vote for the application of Article 149 of the constitution, calling for presidential elections within 90 days. That night bombs go off in the capital and in Pétionville.

June 23, 1993   The sanctions go into effect.

June 26, 1993   Cédras and a delegation leave Haiti for negotiations in New York.

June 27, 1993   Negotiations between the Aristide and Cédras delegations, overseen by Dante Caputo and other UN and U.S. diplomats, begin on Governors Island, in New York City's harbor. The negotiations are held on the island to avoid massive demonstrations of Haitians and Haitian-Americans at the UN.

The same day, a mass in the capital turns into a pro-Aristide rally and, as television cameras broadcast the images across the country, armed soldiers dressed in riot gear burst in and beat parishioners. The next day residents of Cité Soleil fill the streets of the poor neighborhood to demand the

People in other cities and towns also demonstrate and are beaten and arrested in the same manner.

July 3, 1993   Cédras agrees to the "Governor's Island" accord at noon, and goes back to Haiti where cheering coup supporters celebrate his return. "Not a single canon shot was heard during my absence," Cédras proclaims. At about midnight, under extreme and consistent pressure from U.S. and UN diplomats, President Aristide also signs.

The ten-point accord calls for the naming of a new prime minister by Aristide, a series of parliamentary reforms of the police and army under UN supervision, a blanket amnesty for those involved in the coup, and the voluntary retirement of Cédras at some point prior to Aristide's return, which is set for October 30. Members of Aristide's government and many leaders and organizations in the popular movement immediately warn of the accord's dangers, including the lifting of the embargo before the president's return.

July 12, 1993   In a message to the nation, Aristide calls for peace and reconciliation to ensure justice and security for all citizens.

July 17, 1993   Many politicians representing the political parties in parliament approve the agreements signed in New York, but about half of the pro-democracy camp refuses, noting the pact's ambiguities concerning the January 18 parliamentarians, and the fact that it has been "forced" on the participants.

July 22, 1993   Aristide and Clinton meet again at the White House. Clinton reaffirms his determination to see Aristide restored to power. The same day, over 70 representatives of the Haitian private sector, as well as representatives of international governmental and non-governmental organizations, meet in Miami with Aristide's government, including his designated prime minister, U.S.-leaning businessman and publisher Robert Malval.

July 28, 1993   Caputo presents the UN with a letter from Aristide requesting an international presence of 600 police officers to be stationed throughout Haiti, along with another 50 to 60 trainers and 500 engineers and military experts.

August 10, 1993   In accordance with the agreements signed in New York, the parliament is "normalized," the January 18 group leaves, and new executive committees are elected for both houses. The new committees are a compromise, with the pro-coup forces retaining considerable control.

August 11, 1993   The civilian mission reports an upsurge in repression, with 36 suspicious deaths and arbitrary executions since July 1.

August 17, 1993   A number of members of the group directed by business-man Antoine Izmery, KOMEVEB (which stands for "Committee Working Together to Spread the Truth"), are arrested in Pétionville as they put up photos of Aristide. The campaign ("Operation Put Up Photos") is part of a nationwide activity organized by KOMEVEB to test the regime's commitment to the return of democracy.

August 26, 1993   The civilian mission issues another report noting the alarming increase in murders and also in disappearances—ten in recent weeks. Most victims are members of popular and democractic organizations. Those released after being held and beaten report being systematically interrogated in a secret headquarters by people with sophisticated equipment and photo books of leaders of the democratic movement.

August 27, 1993   The UN Security Council suspends the embargo after the parliament ratifies Prime Minister Robert Malval and his new cabinet.

September 2, 1993   Malval inaugurates his cabinet members, calling for "reconciliation." Outside the palace, attachés violently break up a peaceful demonstration in favor of the return of democracy and of Aristide.

September 6, 1993   Cédras announces that he does not think Malval's government reflects the broad "concorde" mentioned in the New York pact.

September 7, 1993   Malval's justice minister, Guy Malary, informs the head of the Supreme Court, retired Judge Emile Jonassaint (appointed illegally by the *de facto* regime), that he has to step down.

September 8, 1993   Attachés as well as soldiers attack a crowd gathered in front of the Port-au-Prince city hall to welcome Mayor Evans Paul, return-ing to his office for the first time since the coup. At least five people are killed and many more are wounded. Paul will not return to his office again for many months.

September 11, 1993   Antoine Izmery is brutally assassinated after being dragged out of a memorial service for the victims of the St. John Bosco massa-cre. (St. John Bosco was Aristide's parish. At least 13 people were killed and 72 injured in the 1988 massacre.) Another man, witness to the well-planned and executed murder, is also shot and killed. The civilian mission will later determine the execution was planned at a high level and carried out by the military and its attachés. Anti-Aristide and anti-democracy propaganda in-creases, with threats to radio stations, leaflets, and virulent radio broadcasts.

September 12, 1993 Aristide and many others call for the resignation of the heads of the army and police. The same day, Cédras announces that the army is fulfilling its part of the Governor's Island accord and that the president's declarations run contrary "to the spirit and the letter of the accord" and constitute "obstacles to the climate of appeasement." Caputo tells the international press that Police Chief Col. Michel François "is responsible for the wave of political assassinations . . . including that of Haitian businessman Antoine Izmery."

September 15, 1993 Parliament fails to obtain a quorum for a National Assembly to consider the law for separating the police and the army, because some pro-coup members boycott, claiming they want to vote for an amnesty law first. Aristide declares the army has commited a "second coup" by controlling the country and its institutions, like the state television and radio, through terror.

September 17, 1993 Gun-toting members of a new organization calling itself FRAPH (Front pour l'Avancement et Progrès Haitien) burst into the installation of Malval's foreign minister and demand that Caputo and all other foreign advisors be replaced with U.S. citizens.

September 20, 1993 A delegation of U.S. government officials, including Pezzullo and a general, arrives.

September 22, 1993 Duvalierists, neo-Duvalierists, and the capital's deputy mayor announce the formation of a new political party at a rally on the anniversary of François Duvalier's inauguration. In a related ceremony, men claiming to direct FRAPH organize a march of gun-carrying supporters who hand out photos of the Duvaliers, wave a large U.S. flag, and release doves in the park. FRAPH calls for "reconciliation," while the new party proclaims, "We are demanding power," and expounds on how Duvalier "protected the rural and urban masses." FRAPH is soon recognized as a front group for the army, made up of a number of ex-Tonton Macoutes and other thugs, many of them associated with previous repressive regimes.

September 28, 1993 In New York, Malval tells journalists about a "secret memo" signed at Governor's Island which says members of the army's high command will be sent overseas to diplomatic posts. Cédras announces he knows of no such agreement.

October 4, 1993 In open defiance of the constitutional government, "Judge" Jonassaint presides over an illegal ceremony to open the Supreme Court's session. Cédras and a number of others attend. The same day, armed attachés prevent the opening of the government accounting office, where the *de facto* head has also refused to leave.

In *Newsweek*, published the same day, Malval says he would have no problem if Jean-Claude Duvalier returned to Haiti, and that the Duvalierists could "build up a political party . . . It could be a good thing for this country. I would encourage it."

October 5, 1993 FRAPH demands that Malval "open" his government. The same day, FRAPH members, police, and attachés attack and arrest former Senator Wesner Emmanuel, a known Aristide supporter, seize his documents, and ransack the parliament-executive liaison office where Emmanuel works. They also make an attempt on Mayor Paul's life.

October 7, 1993 FRAPH enforces an armed strike in the capital, wounding about a dozen people who venture out. Malval's defense minister writes a letter to Cédras, criticizing his attendance at the Supreme Court earlier in the week.

October 8, 1993 FRAPH and other right-wing people demonstrate to demand the departure of Caputo and the "broadening" of Malval's cabinet.

October 10, 1993 On the eve of the arrival of U.S. military trainers in Haiti, U.S. Defense Secretary Les Aspin tries to fend off critics who fear "another Somalia" by saying the soldiers will be carrying M-16s. Within hours, Cédras tells the press here that he does not agree with Aspin's declaration.

October 11, 1993 The USS *Harlan County* arrives in Port-au-Prince carrying 200 Canadian and U.S. military instructors. FRAPH "supporters" demonstrate at the port, shoving and threatening reporters and diplomats. At a press conference, Caputo criticizes the Haitian army, while U.S. diplomats claim the boat did not unload for "bureaucratic" reasons. The U.S. then unilaterally orders the boat back to Guantánamo. Caputo discovers the move only when he sees the boat leave from a hotel room window. Cédras declares the FRAPH people are "patriots."

October 12, 1993 FRAPH demonstrates again as citizens stay home. A visiting U.S. general says he still believes the Haitian army is "on board" and that he trusts them. Clinton declares that Aristide has fulfilled his obligations according to the accord and that Cédras and François should resign.

October 13, 1993 The UN votes to reimpose the embargo if Cédras does not resign by October 15. François announces he has been given the choice of exile or assassination by "a great power." The new U.S. ambassador to Haiti, William Lacy Swing, presents his credentials to Aristide in Washington.

October 14, 1993   Guy Malary, the minister of justice, is gunned down with two others as he leaves his office. Canada pulls out its 50 police trainers. FRAPH bursts into parliament, demanding "reconciliation" between Cédras and the president and threatening to kill all FNCD members.

October 15, 1993   The embargo is reimposed. The civilian mission pulls out all of its 270 observers. Five U.S. warships arrive in Haitian waters to patrol against boats attempting to break the embargo. Eventually, over a dozen ships from a number of different countries will join the exercise.

October 20, 1993   The U.S. announces it has blocked the funds of 41 Haitians, including Cédras and the FRAPH leaders. Malval announces he will resign if Aristide does not return on October 30 as planned. Swing announces a $250,000 job program to clean up Cité Soleil, which will employ 800 people for eight months (at an approximate wage of $4.70 per day). The same day, Swing asks Malval to broaden his government to include two pro-military ministers.

October 22, 1993   The CIA holds a special briefing for U.S. lawmakers on Capitol Hill on Aristide's so-called "mental instability." The briefing is only one episode in a lengthy and organized disinformation campaign.

October 24, 1993   In Miami, pro-democracy Haitian journalist Dona St. Plite is assassinated. Reporters and radio stations in Haiti are also being harrassed more frequently.

October 28, 1993   Aristide addresses the UN, calling for a total blockade and labelling the military repression as "genocide." The same day, in a radio broadcast, Cédras demands amnesty for the entire army and "all of civil society."

October 29, 1993   The U.S. press reveals that the CIA report on Aristide's supposed mental health is based on invented doctors at hospitals the president never visited.

October 30, 1993   The country is held hostage by a wave of repression on the days surrounding the president's planned return. Deputy Samuel Madistin's parents and brothers are terrorized and flee into the hills. Many others are arrested, beaten, and killed.

November 5, 1993   The army boycotts a three-way meeting (army-executive-international community) called by Caputo.

November 9, 1993 *The New York Times* publishes a front page story, supposedly based on a Harvard University study, claiming the economic embargo is causing 1,000 extra child-deaths in Haiti each month. *Times* reporter Howard French has based his story on a summary of the study he received before all other newspapers, and even before many of the participants. Three days later, doctors from Harvard write to the *Times* to say their study was misquoted, and that the increase in deaths is due to the overall political crisis, including the repression, and not to the embargo alone. On November 23, 1993, Physicians for Human Rights, which also participated in the study, will hold a press conference at the UN to denounce the study's methods and to stress that "human rights abuses, mismanagement and the blatant corruption of the current and previous Haitian regimes—not UN sanctions—are the fundamental causes of the continued deterioration of health in Haiti."

November 14, 1993 *The New York Times* reveals that from 1986 on, the CIA maintained a number of high-ranking army officers, includir.g Lt. General Raoul Cédras, on its payrolls "until the ouster of Father Aristide in 1991." The article also says that the CIA set up and funded (at the rate of $500,000 to $1 million per year) the Service d'Intelligence National—which was supposed to fight the drug trade, but in fact carried out political repression. Many U.S. lawmakers begin to openly criticize the CIA and sectors of the State Department for carrying out "their own foreign policy."

November 16, 1993 In an interview with *Le Figaro*, Cédras calls for a "true government of *concorde*" with representatives from the right and the left. After repeated threats from the regime, two of the three international fuel companies decide to distribute the fuel in their tanks. The third soon follows suit.

On the same day, FRAPH threatens to storm parliament and to "tie up" lawmakers if they do not dissolve the two houses.

November 24, 1993 The U.S. embassy announces it supports Malval's recent spate of meetings with representatives of different sectors, including Cédras and other coup supporters. "Washington will be ready to support an eventual enlargement of the government," it says. Meanwhile, Malval comes under increasing criticism from the democratic camp.

November 26, 1993 The civilian mission issues a report on the Izmery murder directly blaming the army and "political groups opposed to the return of President Aristide" and naming some of the assailants. (In the December issue of the French *Jeune Afrique* magazine, a former mission team member will write that the assassination was planned the night before at the home of coup-supporter and former Senator Eddy Dupiton, but the civilian mission in Haiti will refuse to confirm this.)

The same day, U.S. Congressman Joseph Kennedy and 73 of his colleagues sign a letter to President Clinton asking the U.S. government to enforce sanctions against the coup supporters.

November 29, 1993   The constitutional government and U.S.AID sign a $32 million agreement authorizing the aid agency to organize garbage collection in the capital.

December 6, 1993   During a visit to Washington, and 11 days before his scheduled resignation, Malval proposes a "national reconciliation conference" between the pro-democracy camp and the coup supporters. The suggestion is immediately criticized by members of the constitutional government and others as yet one more concession to the anti-democratic camp, which has been calling for such a "conference" for over a year.

December 10, 1993   During a visit to the Vatican, Malval affirms his support for a conference. Malval's visit is criticized by many, including Aristide's ambassador to the U.S., in part because the Vatican is the only government in the world which has recognized the coup regime.

December 13, 1993   Nine out of Malval's ten ministers reject the conference idea in a letter later released to the press.

December 14, 1993   After a visit to Haiti, U.S. Assistant Secretary of State for Human Rights John Shattuck declares U.S. policy toward Haitian refugees should be "reviewed." The next day his superiors refute his statement, saying Shattuck was misquoted.

That same day, diplomats from the "four friends" (Canada, France, the U.S., and Venezuela) meet and declare that if the army does not take steps toward resuming the Governor's Island process by January 15, 1994, they will strengthen sanctions.

December 15, 1993   Malval returns to Haiti, announces there will be no conference, and resigns.

December 21, 1993   Accompanied by heavily armed soldiers, the *de facto* head of the accounting office retakes his office, which he had ceded to the constitutional head earlier in the fall.

December 23, 1993   As an alternative to the "national reconciliation conference," President Aristide announces a conference on the refugee issue for January 14–16, 1994, in Miami.

December 27, 1993   Over 1,000 homes in Cité Soleil are burned to the ground in a fire set after the discovery of the body of a FRAPH treasurer. The final toll: 37 dead, 26 disappeared, and 10 injured. Witnesses report FRAPH members helped set the fire and prevented the fire engines from approaching the neighborhood, a stronghold for Aristide and the democratic movement.

Reports from journalists and from Centres de Développement et de Santé (CDS)—a large non-governmental organization which receives over $2 million in U.S.AID funding for its Cité Soleil programs—put the number of houses destroyed at only 200 or 300, and imply the fire was a reprisal for the supposed "necklacing" of the FRAPH treasurer. U.S. AID immediately announces CDS and a conservative priest will be the sole distributors of post-fire aid. (CDS is the only health provider in the slum, which is home to 200,000, and also has a number of "training" projects. CDS is run by Dr. Reginald Boulos, an open and key supporter of Marc L. Bazin, the U.S.-backed presidential candidate in 1990 and the illegal prime minister in 1992 and 1993.)

January 1, 1994   In a speech from abroad to the nation on the 180th anniversary of Haitian independence, President Aristide adopts a more militant pose, saying *"fè koupe fè,"* or "steel cuts steel," indicating a potential shift from the passive acceptance of violence from the pro-coup camp and its supporters. Aristide also calls for more mobilization and for people to stand up for their rights and to work together for democracy.

January 10, 1994   Senator Jean-Louis opens the 1994 parliamentary session. Almost immediately, the hall is invaded by the people claiming to have been elected on January 18, 1993, and pro-democratic senators leave. Illegal senators briefly manhandle one democratically elected senator, and armed attachés hold the building hostage for about an hour.

January 13, 1994   A tanker of "humanitarian gas" arrives in Port-au-Prince, to be distributed to non-governmental agencies, hospitals, and others. Right-wing groups who had threatened to block the tanker if the gas was not delivered to gas stations do not intervene. Later reports will say about one-quarter of the gas went to the military.

In a session boycotted by many pro-democracy deputies, former Tonton Macoute and FRAPH member Deputy Robert Mondé is elected president of the Chamber of Deputies.

January 16, 1994   The three-day conference in Miami concludes. The conference was originally called to discuss refugee issues, but was broadened after the U.S. reportedly applied pressure because it feared the event would be a three-day attack on its policy. The meetings were attended by over 500 people from the U.S. and foreign governments, Haitian organizations, and many U.S. human rights, development, and solidarity groups. The Haitian army and private business sector did not attend. The resolutions harshly criticize U.S. Haitian refugee policy, call for a "truth commission" to investigate crimes committed during and since the coup, and make a number of other recommendations. U.S. lawmakers and others in attendance attacked the U.S. government, causing a State Department representative to get up and walk out twice.

January 17, 1994 A report from Commission Justice et Paix, the human rights group associated with the Catholic church, calls for an investigation into the causes of the Cité Soleil fire, the reports of bodies being carried off and dumped in mass graves, and the constant presence of FRAPH members around CDS offices, where victims are supposed to receive aid. Justice et Paix also says the FRAPH member killed on December 26 was not "necklaced," that there was evidence he was killed in an inter-FRAPH dispute over money, and that the international media unfairly blamed Aristide supporters for his death.

January 20, 1994 The Conference of the Haitian People for National Rescue, convened by a group of businessmen from the north of Haiti and attended by coup supporters such as former *de facto* Prime Minister Honorat, General Phillipe Biamby, and others, ends with resolutions calling for the dissolution of parliament, the cancellation of the 1987 constitution, and new elections. The following week, some participants will demonstrate in front of parliament, threatening the lawmakers and throwing rocks at the building.

January 22, 1994 A professor at the state university's school of public administration kidnapped at gunpoint the day before is released. The attack is part of a continuing battle for control of this crucial institution, where almost all public administration employees receive their training.

January 24, 1994 The "four friends" meet, supposedly to plan the tightening of sanctions. In Haiti, the price of gas continues to rise, peaking at U.S.$10 per gallon, as the effects of the embargo finally begin to be felt. Many businesses reduce hours or close during January, despite an increasing flow of gas across the Dominican-Haitian border.

January 25, 1994 The Chamber of Deputies votes to give President Aristide a 48-hour ultimatum to name a new prime minister or they will invoke Article 149 of the constitution, declaring the government "empty" and calling for new presidential elections. The deadline passes quietly.

January 26, 1994 Yvon Desanges, 28, kidnapped by soldiers and armed civilians from his Port-au-Prince home a few days earlier, is found dead and profoundly disfigured. He was a refugee who was picked up at sea by the U.S. Coast Guard and then repatriated from Guantánamo in 1992, and he had been hunted, along with his siblings, ever since. He was a member of a neighborhood pro-democracy group.

January 27, 1994   The U.S. visas of 500 Haitian army officers are cancelled. The same day, Canada announces it is willing to help train a Haitian police force, some of whose members might be selected from the Haitian community in Canada. The press release is part of an ongoing struggle between Canada, France, and the U.S. for full control of the training of the hypothetical new police force, which is supposed to replace the army in most of its functions. Also that day, a dozen members of the civilian mission return to Haiti.

January 28, 1994   Fifteen business groups, led by the Centre pour la Libre Entreprise et la Démocratie (CLED), a group founded with help from the Washington-based Center for Democracy (CFD), begin a 12-day "strike" aimed at getting the embargo lifted. Most factories and many businesses close, but supermarkets and smaller shops remain quietly open, with reduced hours.

February 2, 1994   At least a dozen young men, all originally from Cité Soleil and most members of pro-democracy neighborhood groups, are murdered in a house where they are hiding a few miles from the capital. Witnesses report the attackers were both soldiers and heavily armed civilians. One of the house's residents, who decided not to sleep there that night, later says the young men had fled because FRAPH was telling all Cité Soleil residents to either join FRAPH, leave, "or you will be dead." Repression is rising throughout the country, with well-known peasant leaders and others selectively targeted.

February 4, 1994   About 1,000 people—some of them bussed in from the provinces—led by FRAPH and Hubert de Ronceray, a vehement coup supporter, demonstrate in front of parliament and the U.S. and French Embassies, demanding the installation of Judge Joseph Nerette, installed as *de facto* president in 1991. That same day, Senator Bernard Sansaricq, backed by a few pro-coup senators and the people who claim they were elected on January 18, 1993, declares that he heads a new executive committee of the Senate, and that the other committee (headed by Senator Jean-Louis and supported by the legal majority of the Senate) is "dissolved." The same day, the national television and radio stations, controlled by coup supporters, function briefly.

February 7, 1994   The day marks the third anniversary of President Aristide's inauguration and eighth anniversary of Jean-Claude Duvalier's departure. A delegation of parliamentarians, including Senate President Jean-Louis (FNCD) and Robert Mondé, president of the Chamber of Deputies, leaves for Washington after being invited by the Center for Democracy (CFD), a semi-government-funded organization.

February 8, 1994   President Aristide, horrified by the recent drowning deaths of four refugees a few yards off a Miami beach, says the U.S. has imposed a "floating Berlin Wall" on Haiti and hints he may suspend the 1981 agreement which allows the U.S. to repatriate "boat people." U.S. State Department officials say the president's remarks are "mystifying" and "peculiar."

February 9, 1994   After their 12-day "strike," the business groups issue an arrogant and hypocritical resolution calling for, among other things, the lifting of the embargo, the resignation of Lt. General Raoul Cédras and "the return of democracy." Carnival begins, but will be only moderately attended. Racine or roots music bands do not play, and several bands associated with the military and the coup play lewd songs later criticized by religious leaders. National television broadcasts Carnival live, despite the fact that it was officially closed down by the information minister in September, 1993.

February 10, 1994   Three more bodies are found in Cité Soleil.

February 11, 1994   Armed gunmen kidnap Judge Laraque Exantus and his brother. Exantus had been in the news the previous week when he refused to give Sansaricq the keys to Jean-Louis' office. The two men will never be seen again.

February 12, 1994   A fire burns in downtown Port-au-Prince for ten hours, destroying about a dozen buildings on one of the main streets where the thriving black market in Dominican gasoline is carried out.

February 15, 1994   In a new offensive, the U.S. government pushes President Aristide to accept a plan, supposedly drawn up by the parliamentarians visiting Washington, which calls for the selection of a prime minister to form a broad "coalition" government, a vote on amnesty and other laws, the retirement of Cédras and "transfer" of Police Chief Col. Michel François, and the lifting of the embargo, but gives no date for the president's return. The U.S. State Department's Michael McCurry says the U.S. will support a "comprehensive embargo" (referring to the "strengthening" which was supposed to have taken place on January 15), but only if the president supports the so-called parliamentary plan. Despite the pressure, the president rejects the plan, calling instead for the resignation of the military strongmen and a full embargo. Aristide's spokesman says appointing a prime minister under current conditions would be sending him "to the butchershop."

February 19, 1994   Many politicians and leaders from the democratic sector—including Senator Jean-Louis, who bowed out of the Washington meetings—as well as over 15 organizations in Haiti, reject the parliamentary plan and the U.S. State Department's pressure on the president. Victor Benoit, Minister of Education and President of the CONACOM party (which is a member of the FNCD), throws his support in with the plan. (Benoit is well-known for his quest for the offices of president or prime minister; he was originally the FNCD candidate for president in the 1990 elections and stepped down when Aristide entered the race.)

February 22, 1994   Caputo announces he supports the parliamentary plan. The same day, President Aristide presents an eight-step alternative to the plan which would reactivate the Governor's Island accord. The first step is the departure of the army's high command and the police chief.

The same day, the UN/OAS civilian mission issues a press release saying it is preoccupied by the rising number of "disappearances."

February 26, 1994   The Gonaïves branch of Justice et Paix announces its delegation witnessed 40 trucks arriving in Ouanaminthe (on the Dominican-Haitian border) and leaving loaded with gas—importing a total of about 66,000 gallons in only one day.

March 2, 1994   The Chamber of Deputies votes its approval of the parliamentary plan and immediately both the U.S. Embassy and business group CLED issue congratulatory notes.

March 4, 1994   Deputy Madistin and other deputies hold a press conference in which they denounce the Center for Democracy (CFD) as an organization "whose function . . . is to destabilize democratic movements in Latin America," and say that the parliamentary plan affair was planned by the U.S. State Department in order to put pressure on the constitutional government. Mondé denies that the plan was written with or by the U.S. government. The deputies also release a contract illegally signed by Malval's minister of commerce renting part of the historically important Môle St. Nicolas to a tourism company, causing the President and others to publicly criticize the Minister. The deputies are immediately targeted for repression and are forced to sleep away from home for several days.

March 5, 1994   After meeting with UN General Secretary Boutros Boutros-Ghali, President Aristide denounces the "ambiguity" and cynicism of certain big powers. He also rejects a proposed Security Council resolution which gives Boutros-Ghali the power to lift the embargo if he feels the president is not taking steps toward the return of democracy. The resolution is never voted on.

March 8, 1994   At a hearing on Capitol Hill, Pezzullo admits the parliamentary plan originated as a State Department document, that he and U.S. Ambassador Swing hand-picked the delegation, and also that U.S. AID, through the CFD, paid for the trip and the delegation's three-week stay in Washington. Other lawmakers attack the U.S. for its refugee policy and its duplicitous behavior regarding President Aristide's return.

March 10, 1994   Nine popular organizations issue a press release attacking the so-called parliamentary plan, as well as Benoit, other supposedly "democratic" politicians, and the U.S. government for blocking the return of President Aristide.

March 11, 1994   Cité Soleil residents find the body of Daddy Pierre, a well-known Aristide supporter, with his face hacked off.

The same day, the head of the UN Security Council says he does not think naming a prime minister would be helpful to the resolution of the crisis. The U.S. Embassy calls for the January 18 people to evacuate the Senate so the elected senators can consider the parliamentary plan.

March 15, 1994   An amnesty law, which includes "fiscal amnesty," goes to the Justice Committee in the Chamber of Deputies. The bill was written together with a leading member of CLED, businessman Bernard Craan.

March 17, 1994   Three more bodies are found in Cité Soleil. Dozens of popular and human rights organizations denounce the wave of violence sweeping the neighborhood, the capital, and the entire country.

March 21, 1994   The Civilian Mission issues a press release denouncing FRAPH and the army for being involved in an increasing number of politically motivated rapes. The mission also says it is investigating 71 murders committed between February 1 and March 15.

March 23, 1994   Members of the Civilian Mission are attacked by FRAPH members in Hinche and threatened with guns.

The same day, at a large press conference attended by a number of Hollywood stars from "Artists for Democracy," the Congressional Black Caucus announces a bill calling for the president to tighten the sanctions on Haiti, cease repatriation of refugees, and other steps aimed at insuring President Aristide's return. The National Coalition for Haitian Refugees (NCHR) issues a press release suggesting the U.S. government reopen Guantánamo as a temporary "safe haven" for refugees.

March 25, 1994   President Aristide meets with Vice President Al Gore, who presents him with what is supposed to be a new plan in which the military, and not the constitutional government, will be forced to make concessions. In reality, the plan is the parliamentary plan, but with some of the steps occurring "simultaneously." Although Aristide immediately expresses his reservations, the news is "leaked" to the *New York Times* the next day, causing a flurry of news stories about a "new plan" and placing more pressure on the president to avoid appearing "intransigent."

March 26, 1994   FRAPH, Senator Sansaricq, and their allies demonstrate at the Port-au-Prince port and succeed in preventing the unloading of a ship carrying 300,000 tons of food aid from France. The demonstrators threaten to use "the arms you know about," and directly threaten French diplomats. After a few days, the boat turns around and leaves, without any public denunciation from either the French or the U.S. Embassies.

March 28, 1994   President Aristide formally rejects Gore's plan.

March 31, 1994   The German Embassy in Port-au-Prince closes due to lack of security for its employees and "an absence of public order."

April 4, 1994   President Aristide sends a letter to the U.S. administration announcing he is suspending the 1981 repatriation treaty, which means that in six months it will be illegal for the U.S. government to pick up refugees at sea to repatriate them.

The same day the U.S. embassy issues a press release openly criticizing the Haitian army for "deliberately eliminating their political enemies" with "total impunity." Other organizations, including the Civilian Mission, go further, accusing FRAPH of being responsible for the steadily rising and violent repression. Many Haitian organizations accuse the U.S. government of complicity and worse, noting that the rise in violence accompanied the recent and well-planned parliamentary plan offensive against President Aristide.

April 6, 1994   An ultimatum that FRAPH, some businessmen from the north, and coup-supporter Hubert de Ronceray gave to the Chamber of Deputies to enact Article 149 passes quietly.

April 8, 1994   Deputy Mondé and the legal executive committee of the Senate meet to discuss how to get the parliament working normally. The pro-democracy senators and their staffs have been prevented from going to work for over a month because the illegal committee has repeatedly threatened them with arms.

April 8 and 9, 1994   In a well-planned attack on the small northern city of Le Borgne (or what some suggest is a clash with armed resisters in the area), the army masses over 250 soldiers to carry out a series of arrests, beatings, and rapes of the local population. Soldiers also burn down over 100 homes and arrest the magistrate. Rumors circulate saying over 200 well-armed guerrillas are hiding in nearby mountains.

April 10, 1994   The illegal Senate executive committee and its followers vote for Article 149 of the constitution and declare that Judge Jonassaint is now president of Haiti. The same day, NCHR and Human Rights Watch/Americas release a 52-page report entitled *Terror Prevails in Haiti*, which harshly criticizes the Clinton administration and calls for the replacement of Pezzullo, opposes any broad amnesty for the coup leaders, and calls for an investigation into CIA activities in Haiti. The report takes a somewhat accommodating position vis-a-vis the refugees, and calls for the "establishment of safe havens," implying they would accept refugee camps rather than pushing for the U.S. to take in all refugees.

April 11, 1994   The "Children of FRAPH" sing, "Down with the embargo! Down with Aristide!" in front of the parliament.

In the U.S., the National Labor Committee issues a report announcing that the U.S. government buys some of the millions of baseballs and softballs made in Haiti by employees earning about U.S.$1.00 per day under a special loophole in the OAS embargo.

April 13, 1994   In a speech "to the nation," Deputy Mondé announces he will undertake a series of meetings with different sectors to investigate how to "fill the vacancy at the executive level." He is accussed by many of paving the way for the enactment of Article 149.

April 21, 1994   A number of senators, led by Senate President Jean-Louis, unveil a proposed amnesty law giving full amnesty for all crimes committed beginning with the coup and ending when the law is approved by both houses. The "Women of FRAPH" attempt to demonstrate against the embargo and in favor of Article 149, but end up squabbling amongst themselves when FRAPH does not deliver the usual free food and drink given to its "members" at demonstrations.

The same day, a former Colombian drug trafficker who is serving a federal prison sentence in the U.S. testifies before a U.S. Senate subcommittee, accusing Police Chief François and General Prosper Avril of being involved in drug deals with Colombian dealers.

April 22, 1994   In an alarming press release, the civilian mission announces it is investigating 16 "disappearances" in the capital alone which took place in April. The total number of disappearances reported to the civilian mission since January 31 is 53. Sixteen people have been returned alive, 26 are still missing, and the bodies of 11 have been found.

The same day, in Gonaïves, soldiers and members of FRAPH carry out an assault on the poor neighborhood of Raboteau, killing what human rights monitors and journalists will later estimate is at least 27 residents as they run away from their assailants or try to escape on the sea in small boats. The army later releases a press release saying the people were killed in a fight with "armed subversives." Local human rights groups, leaders of neighborhood groups, the civilian mission, and even the U.S. State Department denounce this version as a lie, saying the people killed were unarmed civilians.

April 24, 1994   Ninety-four Haitian refugees are repatriated from the Bahamas with the assistance of the UN High Commission on Refugees (UNHCR). A delegation of lawyers and journalists reports that the U.S. government (through the UNHCR) and U.S. soldiers are assisting in the construction and enlargement of the camp there.

April 25 and 26, 1994   Soldiers attack the hamlet of Bassin Caiman, near Le Borgne, burning hundreds of houses, destroying hectares of crops, killing animals and also perhaps peasants. Because the area continues to be occupied by between 250 and 500 soldiers who will not permit access to anyone, including the civilian mission or journalists, the final death toll and amount of property destroyed remains unknown.

April 26, 1994   U.S. Special Envoy Lawrence Pezzullo submits a letter of resignation.

The same day, Mondé announces he will undertake a series of meetings with different sectors in order to figure out how to fill the "political void" at the executive level. Also, the army issues a press release blaming the violence in Cité Soleil, in Gonaïves, and in the north, as well as the "murders and disappearances of soldiers and peaceful citizens," on the constitutional government.

April 28, 1994   The civilian mission announces 44 executions or "suspicious deaths" during the month of April.

May 1, 1994   The CONACOM party declares it opposes a full embargo.

May 6, 1994   The UN Security Council votes unanimously on a resolution calling for the resignation or retirement of three high-ranking members of the

Haitian army, imposing immediate sanctions on the army, the coup's support-ers, and their families, and threatening a tightened embargo in 15 days.

May 7, 1994   A U.S. official leaks an 11-page cable from the U.S. embassy in Port-au-Prince which says that "the Haitian left manipulates and fabricates human rights abuses as a propaganda tool," and that the civilian mission and others have been duped into reporting on violence. Human rights officials and others are outraged at the cynical and arrogant language in the cable.

May 8, 1994   The U.S. government announces a change in its Haitian refugee policy, saying that all refugees picked up at sea will be given a chance to apply for political asylum at sea or "in a third country"—but implying that no more than 10 percent will be accepted. A U.S. government spokesperson in Haiti declares, "The majority of refugees are economic refugees."

May 9, 1994   Because of the split in the parliament, the two houses are not able to meet together in a National Assembly to close the winter parliamen-tary session, as called for in the constitution. Leaders of the FNCD announce that CONACOM is no longer a member of its political front.

May 11, 1994   The U.S. State Department says it is considering endorsing a UN Peace-Keeping Mission for Haiti.
     The same day, in a ceremony attended by the entire army high command and many coup supporters, and led by Senator Sansaricq and his supporters, Judge Jonassaint is installed as "provisional president" of Haiti.

SOURCES

Grateful acknowledgement is made to the following individuals and publishers for permission to reprint work in *The Haiti Files*:

"The Tragedy of Haiti" from *Year 501: The Conquest Continues* by Noam Chomsky (Boston: South End Press, 1993), © 1993 by Noam Chomsky. Reprinted by permission of the author and South End Press.

"President for Life" from *Papa Doc: Haiti and Its Dictator* by Bernard Diederich and Al Burt (Princeton, N.J.: Markus Wiener Publishing, 1969, reissued 1991), © 1991 by Bernard Diederich. Reprinted by permission of the authors.

"Haiti in the Eyes of the World" from *Haiti: Family Business* by Rod Prince (London: Latin America Bureau, 1985), © 1985 by the Latin America Bureau. Reprinted by permission of the Latin America Bureau.

"Haiti's Family Affairs" by James Ridgeway, based on articles that appeared in *The Village Voice*, October 26, 1993 and May 17, 1994, © 1993/1994 by *The Village Voice*. Reprinted by permission of the author and *The Village Voice*.

"As Brown Fiddled, Haiti Burned" by Juan Gonzalez, from *The New York Daily News*, February 9, 1994, © New York Daily News, L.P. Used with permission of the New York Daily News.

"Paper Laws, Steel Bayonets" from *Paper Laws, Steel Bayonets: Breakdown of the Rule of Law in Haiti* by the Lawyers Committee for Human Rights (New York, November 1990), © 1990 by the Lawyers Committee for Human Rights. Reprinted by permission of the Lawyers Committee for Human Rights.

"The Tonton Macoute" from *The Military and Society in Haiti* by Michel S. Laguerre (Knoxville: University of Tennessee Press, 1993), © 1993 by Michel S. Laguerre. Reprinted by permission of the author and University of Tennessee Press.

"The Evolution of FRAPH" by the Haitian Information Bureau, from *Haiti Info*, v. 2, #3 (October 3, 1993) and v. 2, #4 (October 17, 1993), © 1993 by the Haitian Information Bureau. Reprinted by permission of the Haitian Information Bureau.

"The Tenth Department" by Jean Jean-Pierre, from *NACLA Report on the Americas*, v. XXVII, no. 4 (January/February 1994), © 1994 by Jean Jean-Pierre. Reprinted by permission of the author and the North American Congress on Latin America.